good
comfort

For Guy and Stewart
Thanks for being there, and here

Hugh Fearnley-Whittingstall

RIVER COTTAGE

good comfort

best loved favourites,
made better for you

Photography by Simon Wheeler

Illustrations by Lucinda Rogers

BLOOMSBURY PUBLISHING

LONDON · OXFORD · NEW YORK · NEW DELHI · SYDNEY

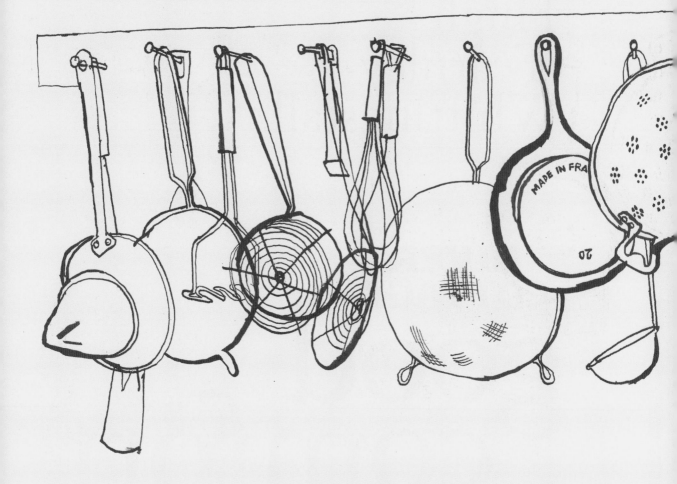

Introduction

Bangers and mash, macaroni cheese, roast chicken dinner, hot buttered crumpets, steamed sponge with custard... I'm betting that some of these (perhaps all of them) make your tummy rumble and your mouth water. But perhaps they also make your heart sink a bit, as you contemplate the 'not so good for you' reputation of such lavish and comforting food. There's a general perception that the food we crave and love is one thing, while the food that's actually good for us is another, and never the twain shall meet. I promise you, it doesn't have to be that way.

I have produced my fair share of rib-sticking comfort recipes down the years. More recently I have been giving a lot of attention to the foods, and combinations of ingredients, that help to keep us well. And far from thinking that these approaches run on parallel tracks, I'm convinced they can, and should, happily come together.

And so I'm setting out to show you how our most beloved dishes – including those I've just mentioned – can be gently tweaked to be not only wholeheartedly delicious, but also wonderfully nutritious. I've taken the classics of the comfort canon – the pies and crumbles, stews and curries, puds and cakes – and reworked them for you, sometimes just a little, sometimes quite a lot. So next time you're craving a plate of spag bol or a chunk of very chocolatey brownie, you've got a brand new go-to version that will absolutely hit the treaty spot – but in a better, healthier way.

Of course, comfort food means different things to each of us – the point of our very favourite dishes is that they are *our* favourites, and not necessarily everyone else's. But here are a few comforting qualities I bet most of us can sign up to: the tender texture of a much-loved cake, contrasted with a fruity jammy filling; the crisply browned ridged topping of a mash-covered pie (with the filling bubbling up at the edges); the rich sweet-savoury sauciness of a favourite stew or curry; the contrasting layers of well-seasoned burger and tangy salsa, trapped within a yielding bap. We might each rank these lovely qualities slightly differently, but surely most of us can get pretty enthusiastic about them!

Perhaps one thing we can all agree on is how comfort food makes us *feel*. Comfort*ed,* obviously! But it's also about the *anticipation* of that feeling: a meal that you can look forward to knowing that, if nothing else, everything in life will seem just a little bit better once you tuck into it. For that to be true, the dish has to be delicious,

of course, but also generous in the deepest sense – heart-warming if not actively stomach-warming (though often that too).

It shouldn't be overly complicated or 'fancy' either, but full of textures and flavours that are soothingly familiar, often recalling our childhoods, or those formative experiences that make us who we are. If we can add to these wonderful, resonant feelings the notion that the foods we love the most will not only make us feel good, but do our bodies good too, doesn't that make them even more comforting?

What food doesn't need to be to comfort us is heavy, cloying, too rich or too sweet. You should feel good after you've eaten it, not comatose. And that is so often to do with balance. In reworking these recipes for you, I've focussed on the key principles of a good diet that I outlined in my last book, *Eat Better Forever*. Underpinning it all is my exhortation to 'Go Whole'. The more whole, unrefined ingredients we can get on our plates, the better.

I'm not just talking about the grains and pulses we typically associate with the term 'wholefoods' (great as they are, and they feature generously here). I'm talking about all foods that are whole, or very close to it, when we take them into our kitchens. Primary among them are vegetables and fruits; but meat, fish and milk are also whole; as are nuts and seeds, and those much-vaunted grains and pulses.

Alongside them, I am very comfortable using the minimally processed 'first tier' products derived from the whole food repertoire: wholegrain flours and ground nuts; dried and ground spices; dried fruits and some tinned vegetables (especially beans and pulses, which are very successfully tinned with a minimum of processing or additives – usually just water and a little salt).

The skimming, churning or fermenting of milk gives us a wonderfully versatile spectrum of dairy products: cream and butter, crème fraîche, yoghurt and kefir, and many, many delicious cheeses. Now, of course, there is also an ever-increasing range of plant-based dairy alternatives. Some are wholer than others, but there's no doubt they can be helpful in making some of our favourite comfort dishes vegan.

When you look at it like this, it no longer seems remotely surprising that 'whole foods' can and should be the building blocks of our favourite comfort dishes. And you might describe the ways in which

I have tweaked and honed the comfort classics that follow as a general strategy of 'wholing up'. So you will find lots more veg and fruit in many of my recipes than you would in conventional versions of them. That includes (in ways I'm confident will surprise and delight you) many of the cakes and sweet treats. It's amazing how root vegetables and fresh and dried fruits can add natural sweetness and a welcome moist texture to teatime treats and puds. We often do this kind of recipe a favour by freeing it from the timewarp of tradition.

My savoury recipes, meanwhile, are often full of beans, as it were (lentils and chickpeas also get some good outings), but never *too* full. I'm confident I know just where to draw the line between these pulses' mild, tender creaminess, which contrasts so pleasingly with a well-flavoured sauce or liquor, and the danger zone of using them as 'padding'. My embracing of wholeness even extends to a preference for scrubbed but usually unpeeled potatoes and carrots – a choice that is up to you, but which all adds to the nutritious value of a dish.

You'll spot my preference for wholemeal flour, which has about three times as much fibre as more highly processed white, not to mention the minerals and vitamins that get left in too. Sometimes I've gone all out for the fine plain wholemeal flour that is now my default choice for most of the cakes and biscuits I make at home. At other times, where full-on wholemeal may take you a little far from textures you know and love (think scones and crumpets, pastry and pasta), I've gone 'half wholemeal'. It's a satisfying place to be.

You've probably realised that there is no such thing as 'wholemeal sugar'. And most researchers agree that the physical benefits of switching to 'alternative sugars' like agave syrup, coconut sugar, or even honey, are marginal at best (although unpasteurised honey often contains some micronutrients and enzymes that may bring us benefits).

However, it is certainly the case that our palates can quickly adapt to dishes that simply use less of this dangerously appealing ingredient. It may even turn out that we already prefer our cakes and biscuits a little less sugary – it's just that we are hardly ever given the choice. (At River Cottage we have systematically reduced the sugar in our cakes, treats and puds by around 20 per cent. The few guests who notice this change invariably comment positively: 'I really like that it isn't too sweet.')

9

Along with 'wholing up', the other mission I'm on is to bring you a much greater variety of good ingredients. Increasing the sheer number of different whole foods we eat each week ensures that a broad range of nutrients are reaching our systems. We know that a varied diet is associated with better gut health – and increasingly we are discovering what profound benefits that brings. So be ready to expect a little of the unexpected: a creamy mash on a fish pie that includes crushed butter beans as well as spuds; 'oven chips' made from three or more roots; cookies, cakes and crumbles with oats, nuts and seeds. And, wherever I see the chance, generous amounts of veg (with lots of options for seasonal and personal variations) added to those meaty saucy dishes, our much-loved stews, curries, casseroles, pies and ragus...

These additions are never gratuitous. They are thoughtful, and they are tried and tested – on my family, and the wide and varied taste buds of the families of my merry band of recipe testers. They've been signed off only when they've received an enthusiastic thumbs up all round.

So this definitely isn't a book about denial. It doesn't preach, and it's not focussed on calories or weight loss. You'll find butter, sugar and some white flour in these recipes, but in amounts calibrated to satisfy, not swamp, your senses. That idea of moderation and balance is one you can also apply to the portions and proportions in which you serve up these dishes and their accompaniments.

I predict you'll find many of my recipes satisfying in modest portions. My fruit loaf and carrot cake – made with far less refined sugar and far more fruit, veg and fibre than is typical – punch above their weight: you'll get more pleasure, and more comfort, from less of them. Likewise, when you're dishing up my tagine, bolognese or stew, already generously laden with veg and/or pulses, I think you will find that a good spoonful of brown rice, wholegrain pasta, or skin-on mash, rather than a whole plateful, does the job nicely.

I'm not saying that in moving to wholer versions of your best-loved comfort foods, 'you'll never notice the difference'. Rather, I'm betting that you'll *positively enjoy* the difference. Hotpots plump with pulses and sweet dried fruit, a creamy onion tart enlivened with garden greens, a fish finger sandwich spiked with kimchi rather than ketchup, millionaire's wholemeal shortbread built around a date 'caramel' – these are all a bit different from the norm. And I promise you they are all delicious. I've tried to make our favourite dishes healthier not by taking stuff out, but by putting more good and delicious things in – more nutty wholegrains, more sweet or sour, crisp or tender, colourful veg and fruit, more gut-friendly ingredients like live yoghurt and fermented veg. I want you to love eating them – perhaps in blissful solitude, at the end of a long day, or maybe in the company of the people you live with or others you have invited to enjoy your bounty and share your good comfort.

If there's anything more fulfilling than putting a dish of something delicious and nourishing in front of someone you care about, then I'm afraid it's passed me by. Maybe you'll sit down with friends to relish a hearty winter stew that is deeply beefy but also jam-packed with veg – right up to the dumplings on top. Or bake a pie for someone who needs it even more than you do, knowing that the filling is wholesome and the pastry is awesome. And I hope you'll enjoy putting teatime treats on the table, confident they will bring your family and friends, and kids in particular, unqualified goodness as well as unbridled happiness.

In the end, that's what comfort food is about: the two-fold pleasure of satisfying the senses and soothing the soul so that, for this moment at least, with good food in front of you and loved ones around you, all is well with the world.

11

Key to symbols

Vg

Suitable for Vegans

VgO

Suitable for vegans if the vegan options in the recipe are chosen

Using the recipes

· All spoon measures are level unless otherwise stated:
  1 tsp = 5ml spoon; 1 tbsp = 15ml spoon.

· All herbs are fresh unless otherwise suggested.

· Use freshly ground black pepper unless otherwise listed.

· All fruit and vegetables should be washed before
  you start cooking. Use organic fruit and veg if you can.

· If using the zest of citrus fruit, choose unwaxed fruit.

· Onions, garlic and ginger are peeled unless otherwise suggested.

· Please use free-range eggs, preferably organic.

· Oven timings are provided for both conventional and fan-assisted ovens.
  As ovens vary, these are intended as guidelines, with a description of the
  desired final colour or texture of the dish as a further guide.

Breakfast
and
Brunch

A mug of hot tea clasped in grateful hands, the kitchen-filling smell of bread in the toaster or pancakes in the pan, the gentle clatter of plates and cups and spoons, and the burble of the radio... The start of our day, whether that's at the crack of dawn or halfway through a lazy weekend morning (or even past noon!), is often warmly domestic and comfortingly familiar. Breakfast should be a source of reassurance, as well as of the fuel that enables us to tackle the hours ahead. It's the perfect opportunity to give ourselves and our families the very best boost we can.

So, it's a shame that so many brazenly marketed breakfast foods – certain sugar-laden cereals, over-sweetened yoghurts, white breads and too-sweet spreads – can let us down. They might give a short-term rush of energy, but because they are full of refined carbohydrates, that energy quickly subsides to leave us with a growling stomach and bottomed-out blood sugar.

We can do much better. Whole grains, nuts and seeds, fresh fruit (and lightly poached compotes too), natural dairy products, eggs, even fish – these are the ingredients that can truly nourish and sustain us at the start of our day. And it need not be time-consuming or complicated to rustle them up into truly delicious breakfasts.

Granted, they may be a bit less instant than popping open a packet and upending it into a bowl. But there are recipes here that don't take much longer than that, and some that can be prepared ahead so they are standing by each morning, ready for duty. Others are well suited to days working at home, or unhurried weekends, when a late (and thoughtful) breakfast elides into an early (and nurturing) lunch. At which point, long live brunch!

You'll find my key touchstones of better eating here – wholeness and variety matched by zestiness and flavour. I've replaced the jam and ketchup in a couple of classic breakfast sarnies with fresh fruit, for example, and 'wholed up' my recipes for porridge, pancakes and breakfast flapjacks, so that they contain more grains and seeds, and often come with a side order of tangy fruit too. And I've taken ingredients we absolutely know are good for us, but don't always get enough of – like oily fish and fermented veg – and folded them into some breakfast and brunch classics, with a twist.

I am confident that all of my breakfasts and brunches will help you feel nourished and cared-for. And that will set the tone for the rest of the day... just as it should.

Multigrainola

Granola can make such a great breakfast, but ready-made versions are often glued together with a lot of syrup or honey. This gorgeous recipe, which is full of different grains and seeds, is more restrained on the sweet stuff and has a delicately crunchy texture. If you haven't any rye or quinoa flakes, just replace with extra porridge oats. Similarly with the flax, hemp and chia seeds; if any are missing, add more of the others, or extra sunflower or pumpkin seeds.

8–10 SERVINGS

250g porridge oats (not jumbo), or more (see above)

50g rye flakes (optional)

50g quinoa flakes (optional)

25g whole or ground flaxseed (optional)

25g whole or hulled hempseed (optional)

25g chia seeds (optional)

100g mixed pumpkin and sunflower seeds

100g walnuts (or hazelnuts), roughly chopped

A generous pinch of salt

50g soft light brown sugar or honey

50ml vegetable oil or melted coconut oil

150ml apple or orange juice (freshly pressed, or natural)

2 tsp vanilla extract

1 egg white (optional)

OPTIONAL ADDITIONS

100g raisins, sultanas, diced prunes and/or dried apricots

Preheat the oven to 170°C/150°C Fan/Gas 3. Have ready a large baking tray.

In a large bowl, thoroughly combine the oats, rye and quinoa flakes if using, all the seeds, the nuts and salt.

Put the brown sugar or honey, oil, fruit juice and vanilla extract into a pan and melt together, stirring gently – it doesn't need to get too hot, just warm. Whisk in the egg white, if using. Trickle this liquor over the dry mix and stir it in thoroughly to get a damp, slightly sticky mixture.

Take handfuls of the mix and squish them in your hands, then break up these big lumps into smaller lumps, dropping them onto the baking tray in a fairly even layer of different-sized clumps and looser flakes. (Or tip the whole lot onto the tray and then do the squishing, as you prefer.)

Bake in the oven for 35–40 minutes until golden brown, giving the granola a couple of gentle stirs after about 20 and 30 minutes. Leave to cool and crisp up completely.

You can stir in some dried fruit at this point (or simply add when you serve up the granola). It will keep in a jar or other airtight container for a couple of weeks.

Note: The egg white aids 'clumping' – but it can be left out for a vegan version.

SERVING OPTIONS

Serve with natural yoghurt (dairy or plant-based) and dried fruit, like raisins, dried cherries or chopped dried apricots, or fresh fruit, such as sliced banana or berries, or a fruit compote (like the plum compote on page 21).

Porridge plus

Classic oat porridge is a sustaining breakfast and very good for you: oats are a source of soluble fibre that's great for gut health and can lower cholesterol. And you can add a few more nutritious grains to your porridge pot, such as nutty rye flakes and fine milled flaxseed. If you're not using these grains, just replace with extra porridge oats. Mix up a tub of this porridge base (it takes moments) and breakfast can be ready at the drop of a hat. It's also an excellent base for a muesli, or overnight oats (see below).

10−12 SERVINGS

400g porridge oats (not jumbo), or more (see above)

200g rye flakes (optional)

50g ground flaxseed (optional)

Milk (and/or water), to cook

A pinch of salt (optional)

TO SERVE

Any (or all) of the following:

Milk (dairy or plant-based) or cream

Seeds, such as pumpkin or sunflower

Fruit: fresh, roasted, compote or dried, such as dried apricots (pre-soaked if preferred) or try the apricot filling for the cake on page 313

A little honey, brown sugar or maple syrup

Combine the porridge oats with the rye flakes and ground flaxseed if using, in a large airtight container and seal.

When you are ready to cook, for each person weigh out 60g of the dry mix, tip into a pan and add 125ml milk and 125ml water (or you can use all milk or all water if you prefer). Add a pinch of salt if you like – to enhance the grains' natural flavours.

Place over a medium-low heat and let the porridge come gradually to a simmer, stirring often with a wooden spoon; this will take a couple of minutes. Let it puff and floop gently for another minute or two, stirring often, until thickened. If it's thicker than you like to eat it, add a dash of water – hot from the kettle if that's handy. If you think it looks a touch on the loose side, don't panic. It will start to thicken up a bit as soon as you put it into a bowl.

Ladle the porridge into a bowl and the rest is up to you. A dash of cold milk or even a trickle of cream is nice to cool it down a touch. Seeds add texture, and fruit brings flavour. For sweetness (and you'd have to be very austere to enjoy your porridge completely unsweetened), I like a trickle of honey, but you might prefer brown sugar or maple syrup.

VARIATION

Overnight oats plus: For 2 servings, in a bowl, combine a mugful (about 125g) of the above dry porridge mix with a small handful of mixed seeds (such as pumpkin and sunflower), 1 grated eating apple (include the skin) and 300ml apple or orange juice. Cover and leave in the fridge overnight. Take it out a little ahead of time so the mix can return to room temperature, then serve with yoghurt and more fruit.

Eggy bread with fruit

Whether you call it French toast, *pain perdu* or plain old eggy bread, this is a great way to turn a slice of bread into something more filling and balanced. It's usually made with white bread, but most wholemeal breads work well (a very open-textured sourdough is not ideal). Add a tangy fruit compote with minimal sugar and a blob of yoghurt, and you're well on the way to brunch.

I like to serve this with the plum compote below, while roast rhubarb is another great accompaniment. But sometimes fresh berries are all that's required.

SERVES 2

2 medium eggs

1 tbsp milk

1 tsp soft brown sugar or honey

2 fairly thick slices of wholemeal bread

A small knob of butter

2 tsp vegetable oil

TO SERVE

A little honey or maple syrup (optional)

Fresh berries, plum compote (see below) or roast rhubarb (page 270)

Natural yoghurt (optional)

In a bowl, beat the eggs thoroughly with the milk and sugar then pour into a shallow dish. Add the slices of wholemeal bread and leave to soak for at least 10 minutes (or up to 30 minutes on a leisurely brunch day), turning them over now and again so they absorb as much egg as possible.

Heat a frying pan over a medium heat and add the butter and oil, swirling them around in the pan. When hot, add the egg-soaked bread slices, pouring any remaining egg onto them once they are in the pan. Fry for a couple of minutes, until golden brown underneath, then flip the slices over and fry for a couple of minutes more. Transfer to warmed plates.

Trickle a little honey or maple syrup over the bread if you like. Add a generous helping of berries, plum compote or roast rhubarb and serve, with a spoonful of yoghurt if you like.

SERVING OPTION

Plum compote: Put 500g roughly chopped plums into a pan with 1 tbsp sugar, a few gratings of lemon zest, a squeeze of lemon juice and 2 tbsp water. Heat gently, stirring, until the juices start to flow. Bring to a gentle simmer, then cook for just a few minutes until all the fruit is completely tender but still chunky. Leave to cool completely.

Wholemeal pancakes with lemon and honey

A freshly flipped pancake is one of the simplest comfort foods. These wholemeal pancakes are slightly more robust than the classic all-white crêpe, and all the tastier for it. But you can start with half-wholemeal if you like, until you get the hang of them! We make these at least once a week at home, and my family just love them.

You can serve the pancakes with jam or fruit, of course, but I like them best of all with a squeeze of lemon juice and either a trickle of honey or a sprinkle of brown sugar.

MAKES 10–12

200g fine plain wholemeal flour (or 100g fine plain wholemeal and 100g plain white flour)

A pinch of salt

3 medium eggs

About 400ml milk (dairy or plant-based)

Vegetable oil, for frying

TO SERVE

Lemon wedges

Honey or brown sugar

Put the flour and salt into a large bowl. Make a well in the centre and break in the eggs, then pour in about 50ml milk. Use your whisk to start whisking the eggs and milk together in the middle of the bowl, gradually drawing in the flour as you do so. Keep going, pouring in more milk, until you have a smooth, thin batter with a consistency like single cream. Leave to rest for 30 minutes.

Stir the batter, check the consistency again and whisk in a little more milk or water if it has thickened up at all. Err on the side of liquid – you definitely don't want a too-thick batter.

Place a non-stick frying pan or crêpe pan, about 20cm in diameter, over a fairly high heat. When hot, add a small splash of oil, swirl it around to coat the surface of the pan and then pour out any excess. Pour a small ladleful (about 50ml) of batter into the pan and swirl it around quickly to spread it out. Cook for a minute or so, until golden on the base (you might need to loosen it at the edge with a palette knife, or give it a shake in the pan), then flip it over and cook the other side for another minute.

The first pancake out of the pan is likely to be imperfect. Don't worry, it will still taste good and the next one will be better. (If it sticks, it's probably because the pan wasn't hot enough.) Do lightly re-oil the pan every couple of pancakes to stop them sticking.

Transfer each pancake to a warm plate and cover with a tea towel – or deliver straight to the table if you favour the first-come-first-served approach. Repeat with the remaining batter. If you have any left over, keep it in the fridge for the next day.

Spritz your pancakes with lemon juice and trickle with a little honey or sprinkle with sugar before eating. You can roll them up or fold into quarters, whichever you prefer.

22

Wholemeal drop scones

If you think making drop scones (aka Scotch pancakes) with wholemeal flour is putting virtue before taste, give these a try and think again. These puffy pancakes go so well with so many things – and they can be real waste-busters too, as they're a great way to use up odds and ends of flour, handfuls of seeds or ripe bananas. The simple main recipe here is a winner every time but see my suggestions overleaf for variations.

MAKES 12–15

250g fine plain wholemeal flour

2 tsp baking powder

1 tsp bicarbonate of soda

A pinch of salt

15g golden caster sugar

2 medium eggs

Up to 200ml milk

50g butter, melted

Vegetable oil, for frying

TO SERVE

Any of the following:

A little butter or natural yoghurt

Fresh berries, sliced banana, fried apple slices or fruit compote

A little honey or lower-sugar jam

Put the flour into a large bowl with the baking powder, bicarbonate of soda, salt and sugar and whisk together well. Make a well in the centre and break in the eggs, then pour in about 150ml of the milk. Start whisking the eggs and milk together in the middle of the bowl, gradually drawing in the flour as you do so.

When you have a thick paste, whisk in the melted butter, then keep whisking, gradually adding dashes of milk, until you have a batter with a consistency a little thicker than double cream, but thinner than a cake batter.

If you want to keep the drop scones warm once cooked, set the oven to a low heat (around 80°C or as low as your gas will go). Alternatively, just hand them out as soon as they are ready.

You will need to cook the batter in 3 or 4 batches. Put a large, heavy-based frying pan or griddle over a medium heat. When hot, add a scant teaspoonful of oil and brush it over the bottom of the pan.

Spoon a generous tablespoonful of batter into the pan and let it spread out, then repeat with a few more tablespoonfuls, as many as you can fit comfortably into the pan. After about a minute, little bubbles will start to appear on the surface of the scones. As soon as they cover the surface, flip the scones over with a spatula.

Cook the drop scones for a minute or so until golden brown on the other side and firm to the touch. If they are looking bit pale, give them a bit longer on each side. Then transfer to a dish and put into the low oven, if you like.

If your first drop scones are spreading too much, whisk a little extra shake of flour into the batter. If they are a bit fat and cakey, add a dash more milk.

Continued overleaf →

25

Cook the remaining batter in the same way, adjusting the temperature as necessary if the pan starts to get too hot and the drop scones are browning too fast, and adding a drop more oil now and again between batches.

Serve the drop scones hot, as soon as they are all cooked, with a little butter or natural yoghurt and fresh berries, sliced banana, fried apple slices or fruit compote, or a little honey or jam.

VARIATIONS

Seeds: Add 50–100g mixed seeds, such as sunflower, sesame, poppy and/or flaxseed, to the flour mix before beating in the eggs and milk.

Flours: Keep at least 50 per cent fine plain wholemeal flour, but use wholegrain rye, spelt, buckwheat, khorasan (kamut) or emmer flour to replace some or all of the rest. You can also replace 20g of the flour(s) with ground flaxseed or hempseed, or ground almonds. All these additions subtly change the taste, and they are all delicious.

Raisins: Stir 75g raisins and ½ tsp ground cinnamon into the flour mixture before adding the eggs and milk.

Apple: Peel an eating apple and coarsely grate the flesh into the flour mix. A pinch of ground cinnamon in the batter is nice here too.

Vg

Banana: For this lovely vegan version, leave out the eggs. Thoroughly mash 2 very ripe, medium-sized bananas, to give about 200g. Stir in 50ml vegetable oil. Combine 200g fine plain wholemeal flour with 1 tbsp baking powder, 15g caster sugar and the salt. Mix with the banana, then whisk in about 150ml plant-based milk. Cook as above.

Eggs on toast with kimchi and greens

This is a modern twist on the brunch classics, Eggs Benedict and Eggs Florentine – and I prefer it to either. The kimchi gives a lovely tang and the creaminess comes from a chive-y yoghurt/mayo mix rather than buttery hollandaise. For a quicker version, fry rather than poach the eggs. You can also leave out the greens if you prefer.

SERVES 2

2 tbsp natural yoghurt

2 tsp mayonnaise

1 tbsp snipped chives or
2 spring onions, sliced

2 tbsp 'live' kimchi (i.e. unpasteurised or homemade), or spicy sauerkraut (at room temperature)

300g spinach, or 150g cavolo nero, any tough stalks removed, roughly shredded

A small knob of butter

2–4 medium eggs

2 slices of wholemeal bread

1 tbsp extra virgin olive, rapeseed or hemp oil

Sea salt and black pepper

First, prepare the yoghurt/mayo mix: in a bowl, combine the yoghurt and mayonnaise, stir in most of the chives or spring onions and season with pepper to taste; set aside. Make sure your kimchi or kraut is out of the fridge by now too (so it also loses its chill).

Heat a saucepan over a medium heat then add the shredded spinach or cavolo nero, with the water still clinging to the leaves from washing (cavolo may need an extra splash). Add a little salt and pepper and gently stir until the greens are wilted and tender – a minute or two for spinach, around 5 minutes for cavolo nero.

Take the pan off the heat and drain off any liquid (a quick press with the back of the spoon will help). Toss the greens with a knob of butter, put the lid on the pan and keep warm.

Pour a 3–4cm depth of boiling water into a lidded medium-large saucepan (wide enough for all the eggs you're poaching) and add a pinch of salt. Return to the boil then turn the heat right down – the water should be barely simmering.

Break each egg into a ramekin or small cup. Carefully slip the eggs into the hot water, put the lid on the pan and immediately start timing 2 minutes. Meanwhile, toast the bread.

Transfer the toast to warmed plates and trickle a little extra virgin oil over each. Spoon the kimchi or kraut on top.

Once the cooking time is up, carefully scoop up a poached egg using a slotted spoon. Check that the white is set and not at all jelly-ish (if necessary, return the egg to the water briefly). Allow as much water as possible to drain off the egg through the spoon and dab away any excess water with a clean cloth.

Place the poached egg on top of the kimchi and repeat with the other egg(s). Season generously with pepper. Heap the wilted greens beside the toast and spoon some (or all) of the yoghurt/mayo mix over the eggs and greens to serve.

28

Dippy eggs with green veg

Everybody loves a dippy egg. (Well *almost* everybody... there's still one member of my family who insists on hard-boiled.) I like to make a brunch-time occasion of dippy eggs with two per person and some lovely greenery, according to the season, to dip alongside brown toast soldiers. Sprouting broccoli, asparagus and green beans are ideal for their dipability...

PER PERSON

2 medium eggs in their shells (at room temperature)

About 4–5 slender sprouting broccoli stems, 6 asparagus spears or 12 French beans

1 slice of wholemeal bread

A small knob of butter

A few drops of lemon juice or cider vinegar (optional)

Sea salt and black pepper

Fill a pan with enough water to completely cover the number of eggs you are cooking and bring to a rolling boil. Gently lower the eggs into the pan on a spoon and immediately start timing 4–5 minutes (4 minutes if you like a real 'runny egg', 5 minutes if you prefer the white well set with the yolk just beginning to set at the edges). Keep the water at a simmer rather than a full boil.

If you have a perforated steamer (and you're organised), you can steam the broccoli/asparagus/beans over the eggs – they'll take about 5 minutes. If they are still a bit crunchy when you've fished the eggs out you can pop the steamer back over the simmering water for a minute or two. Alternatively, simmer the veg in a separate saucepan of lightly salted boiling water, allowing about 4 minutes.

Toast the bread too while the eggs are boiling – we are multi-tasking here! Spread with a little butter and cut into soldiers.

Serve the hot eggs, veg and soldiers straight away. Bash the top of each egg and scoop off with a teaspoon. Sprinkle a pinch of salt and a little pepper inside, and add a small knob of butter.

Dip in your chosen veg, alternating with the toast soldiers. I also like a few drops of lemon juice or cider vinegar stirred into the runny yolk with the butter – it makes a kind of instant hollandaise. Add a little more butter, seasoning and vinegar/lemon juice as you get to the bottom of the yolk if you like.

31

Mushrooms and greens on toast

Toast is great, but it's what goes on it that makes all the difference! The idea here is to load up your toast so it becomes a vehicle for a heap of delicious juicy veg. Mushrooms on toast is a classic, and this version includes some lovely greens. We are in bruschetta territory here and some of the variations opposite reflect that crossover.

PER PERSON

About 100g spinach or chard

1 tbsp olive or vegetable oil

200g mushrooms, thickly sliced

1 large slice of robust wholemeal bread (ideally sourdough)

1 large garlic clove

Extra virgin olive oil, to trickle

A squeeze of lemon juice

Sea salt and black pepper

Cheddar or Parmesan, or similar hard cheese, shaved or grated, to finish (optional)

If you're using chard, separate the stalks from the leaves and finely slice the stalks. Roughly shred the leaves.

Heat the oil in a large frying pan over a medium-high heat. Add the chard stalks, if using, and the thickly sliced mushrooms, along with some salt and pepper. Fry for 4–5 minutes, tossing and stirring regularly, until the liquid released by the mushrooms has evaporated and the mushrooms are starting to colour (this may take longer than 5 minutes, depending on your pan, and the mushrooms).

Meanwhile, toast the bread, making sure you get it nice and crisp and brown (so it will stand up to all the juices). Slice the garlic clove in half and rub one cut half over the hot toast. Keep the toast warm.

Chop the garlic clove and add it to the pan with the mushrooms. Cook for a minute or two to take the rawness out of the garlic, then add the spinach leaves or shredded chard leaves. Cook for a few more minutes, stirring or tossing regularly, so that the leaves wilt. If the mix is looking a bit wet, keep cooking until most of the juices have evaporated – just enough juice to tickle the toast is what you are after.

Trickle the garlicky toast generously with extra virgin olive oil. Heap the mushroom and spinach/chard mixture on top. Add a squeeze of lemon juice and a little more salt and pepper. Finish, if you like, with some shaved or grated hard cheese.

32

VARIATIONS

Tomato bruschetta: Use either the cherry tomato salsa on page 36 or the fresh tomato sauce on page 108. Spoon onto your garlicky toast and add a little torn mozzarella or shaved Parmesan.

Beetroot and fennel bruschetta: Toss 2cm beetroot cubes with olive oil, salt and pepper and roast for 30 minutes. Add some chopped fennel and continue roasting for about 15 minutes until both veg are soft and caramelised. Pile onto garlicky toast and sprinkle with Dukka (page 43).

Vg

Beany mash bruschetta: Drain and rinse a 400g tin white beans. Toss with a little finely diced red onion or spring onion, a dash of olive oil, a squeeze of lemon and some salt and pepper. Leave for 15 minutes, then crush the beans to a rough mash. Spread some vegan pesto or my pestomega (page 93) on your hot garlicky toast, add the beany mash and finish with a trickle more olive oil and torn basil or chopped parsley.

Vg

Sardines on tomato toast

Wholemeal toast, antioxidant-rich tomatoes, sardines bursting with essential omega oils – what a deliciously good-for-you mash-up this is! Inspired by the Catalan *pa amb tomàquet* (tomato toast), I can imagine eating it on a sun-drenched balcony in Barcelona, gazing out over the Mediterranean. (I can only imagine because I've never been to Barcelona – it's on the bucket list!) Luckily it will taste just as good on a sunny Saturday morning at my kitchen table... or indeed in front of the TV on a rainy Tuesday evening. Look for sustainably caught or MSC-certified sardines – my favourite brand is Fish 4 Ever.

SERVES 2

120g tin sardines or mackerel, ideally in olive oil (see note)

A squeeze of lemon juice

2 fairly thick slices of wholemeal sourdough bread

1 garlic clove, halved

2 medium or 1 large ripe, juicy tomato(es)

Sea salt and black pepper

A few snipped chives, or a sliced spring onion, to finish (optional)

Fork the sardines out of the tin into a bowl and add about half of the oil remaining in the tin, reserving the rest. Add a generous grinding of black pepper and a squeeze of lemon to the bowl and mash the fish roughly.

Toast the bread well – you want it nice and brown and crunchy so it can take all the toppings – then rub the cut surface of the garlic clove over its hot, rough surface. Trickle over the remaining oil from the tin.

Now cut the tomato(es) in half and rub the cut surfaces firmly onto the toast, crushing the toms as you do so, to encourage all their juices to soak into the toast. The idea is to get pretty much everything but the skin into or onto the toast. Don't worry if it's a bit messy, just pile the tomato pulp onto the toast.

Spoon the mashed sardines over the tomato toast. Add a pinch of salt if you like and finish with snipped chives or a finely sliced spring onion if you have either. Eat straight away.

Note: There are quite a few fancy 'recipe' versions of tinned sardines these days, so if you can't find sustainably caught sardines or mackerel in plain olive or sunflower oil, then a little lemon or chilli, or a few herbs, definitely won't hurt.

35

Hot mackerel bap with cheaty tartare sauce

A hot fish fillet in a yielding bun, with a dollop of mayonnaise or tartare sauce, is a great comforting treat. Mackerel is my favourite fish for this treatment, but pretty much any fresh fish fillet will do. My cheaty tartare sauce has all the creaminess and bite you need. The fresh herbs in it are optional, but lovely if you have them. The tomato salsa (see below) is an excellent alternative. And I must admit I have made a HMB with both – and it was awesome! This isn't a neat and tidy snack – but that's part of the fun. Embrace the mess...

SERVES 2

2 large, soft wholemeal baps

A little butter, softened

A handful of lettuce or other salad leaves

2 medium or 1 large mackerel, filleted

1 tbsp vegetable oil

1 bay leaf (optional)

1 garlic clove, peeled (optional)

A squeeze of lemon juice and/ or a dash of Tabasco

Sea salt and black pepper

CHEATY TARTARE SAUCE

2 generous tbsp natural yoghurt

1 tbsp mayonnaise

4–6 small gherkins, chopped

1 hard-boiled egg, chopped

A small bunch of chives or 2 spring onions, chopped (optional)

1 tbsp chopped parsley (optional)

1 tsp capers, chopped

A dab of English mustard

First, stir together all the ingredients for the cheaty tartare sauce, season with pepper to taste and set aside.

Split and lightly butter the baps, add the salad leaves, and have them standing by too.

Check the mackerel fillets for pin-bones, removing any you find with tweezers. Season the mackerel all over with salt and pepper.

Heat the oil in a non-stick frying pan over a medium heat. Add the bay leaf and garlic clove, if using, and fry until they start to change colour.

Add the fish fillets to the pan, skin side down, and fry for about 3 minutes, until the skin is crisp and the fish is nearly cooked through, then carefully flip the fillets over and cook for a minute or so more on the other side.

Put the hot mackerel fillets straight into the baps (cutting them in half first if you have 2 large fillets from 1 big fish) and give them a squeeze of lemon juice and/or a couple of drops of Tabasco. Spoon on the tartare sauce, close the baps and eat straight away.

SERVING OPTION

Cherry tomato salsa: You can serve this instead of, or in addition to, the tartare sauce. Cut about 10 cherry tomatoes into eighths and combine with ½ small red onion, finely sliced; a small handful of parsley, basil or chives, roughly chopped; a trickle of olive oil; and a couple of drops of cider vinegar or lemon juice. Season with a pinch of salt and a little pepper, then taste and add more seasoning or vinegar if needed.

Smoked mackerel pâté with pickled beetroot

Food doesn't have to be hot to be comforting: try this smoky, creamy, rough-textured fish pâté spread thickly over oatcakes or wholegrain toast, and topped with a little tangy beetroot pickle – and I think you'll agree. As well as a snacky brunch/lunch, this is a great canapé, as you can see from the picture!

The key here is to make it all about the fish – I like the pâté to be nearly all mackerel. Then you can really go to town on the black pepper, lemon juice and pickled beetroot that cut through the richness. For the creamy element, you can make labneh following the simple method on page 316; unstrained thick yoghurt works really well too, as does half-fat crème fraîche.

SERVES 4–6

250g smoked mackerel fillets, skinned

1–2 tbsp labneh or natural yoghurt, or half-fat crème fraîche

2 tsp freshly grated horseradish root and/or 1 tsp English mustard

A good squeeze of lemon juice, plus a little extra to finish

Sea salt and black pepper

QUICK-PICKLED BEETROOT

2 small raw beetroot (about 200g)

1 tbsp cider vinegar

A tiny pinch of sugar (about ¼ tsp)

1 tsp chopped dill (or chives or parsley), plus extra to finish

TO SERVE

Coarse oatcakes or wholemeal toast

Start with the beetroot pickle. Peel the beetroot and cut it into thin slices, 2–3mm thick (use a mandoline if you like). Lay these flat, slice into little matchsticks and put into a bowl. Add the cider vinegar, sugar, chopped dill or other herb and some salt and pepper. Stir well and set aside.

Skin the smoked mackerel, flake it into chunks (removing any stray pin-bones you find) and place in a large bowl. Add 1 tbsp labneh, yoghurt or crème fraîche, the horseradish or mustard (or both, for a bit more of a kick) and a generous squeeze of lemon juice. Season liberally with black pepper (no salt yet).

Use a fork to mash everything together into a rough, coarse pâté. Add a little more labneh/yoghurt/crème fraîche if you feel it needs it, but no more than 2 tbsp overall. Taste and add more lemon juice, horseradish/mustard, salt and/or pepper if needed.

Generously pile the smoked mackerel pâté on the oatcakes or toast and top with some beetroot pickle. Finish with little chopped dill (or chives or parsley) and a squeeze of lemon juice.

> **VARIATION**
>
> **Cooked beetroot pickle:** Large beetroot can be a bit coarse and tannic served raw, even if pickled. If big beetroot are all you can get, halve or quarter then simmer in lightly salted water for about 30 minutes, until tender. When cool, peel and cut into slightly chunkier 'batons' (5mm–1cm) rather than matchsticks, and pickle as above.

Fruity bacon roll

This is a quirky take on a bacon roll – the busy person's favourite working breakfast. It's also a fine brunch. Instead of tangy HP sauce or ketchup I'm giving you tangy fresh fruit. Believe me, it works!

SERVES 2

2 ripe plums or 1 ripe nectarine (about 75g in total)

A few drops of cider vinegar or lemon juice

A tiny trickle of honey or a pinch of brown sugar

1 tsp vegetable oil

4 rashers of organic back bacon (smoked or unsmoked)

2 soft wholemeal baps

½ ripe, medium avocado, stoned (optional)

A small pinch of dried chilli flakes (optional)

A handful of salad leaves, such as rocket, lettuce or chicory

A smidgeon of mustard (optional)

Sea salt and black pepper

Halve and stone the plums or nectarine and cut into slim wedges. Place these in a small bowl and sprinkle on a few drops of cider vinegar or lemon juice. Add a tiny trickle of honey or a pinch of brown sugar and leave to macerate while you cook the bacon.

Heat the oil in a frying pan over a medium heat. When hot, add the bacon rashers and fry for 3–5 minutes, turning regularly, until done to your liking. (You can cook the bacon on a baking tray in the oven if you prefer.) Keep warm.

Split the baps and lightly toast them if you like (if they are lovely and fresh they may not need toasting).

If using avocado, scoop out the flesh from the skin with a teaspoon and press or mash it onto the bottom halves of the baps, using a fork. Season with salt and pepper and sprinkle on a few chilli flakes if you like.

Add the hot bacon rashers, then the sliced fruit. Season with a touch more salt and pepper, then top with the salad leaves.

Take the top halves of the baps and rub their cut surface around the frying pan to absorb any bacon fat and juices. Smear a little mustard on them if you like, then place the bap lids on top of the leaves to sandwich the baps together. Tuck in!

40

Dukka

This is such a brilliant sprinkle to have on hand. Scatter it over salads, bruschetta – such as the beetroot and fennel bruschetta on page 33 – and soups, like the spicy squash and lentil on page 63 or 'cream of' roasted mushroom on page 57. Indeed, breakfast seems an unusual place to find dukka. But I really like it in the morning, as a dry dip for good bread and oil.

MAKES A JARFUL, OR 10–12 GOOD SPRINKLES

30g whole, skin-on almonds or hazelnuts, roughly chopped or bashed

30g cashew nuts or peanuts, roughly chopped or bashed

30g pumpkin seeds or sunflower seeds or a mix

2 tsp cumin or caraway seeds

2 tsp coriander seeds

A good pinch of flaky salt

A few twists of black pepper

A small pinch of dried chilli flakes

A sprig of mint, leaves picked and finely chopped, to finish (optional)

TO SERVE

Good wholemeal bread

Extra virgin olive or rapeseed oil

Put a small, heavy-based frying pan over a medium-high heat. Add the nuts and pumpkin/sunflower seeds to the pan and toast them for 2–3 minutes, shaking the pan regularly so they take on some even colour.

While the seeds and nuts are toasting, lightly crush all the spice seeds using a pestle and mortar – breaking rather than grinding the spices; leaving a few whole seeds is fine. Add these to the pan of nuts and seeds, along with the salt, pepper and chilli flakes.

Continue to heat for 2–3 minutes, moving or turning the mix now and then, to toast the nuts and spices until well coloured (keeping a close eye on them because they can burn quite easily). When done, tip out onto a plate and set aside to cool.

You can use the dukka immediately or store in it an airtight container for a week or so. Adding some finely chopped fresh mint when you serve up the dukka is a lovely touch. Just stir it through the dukka before sprinkling.

To serve as a 'dry dip', simply put a bowl of dukka on the table with torn bread and good oil. Dip the bread first in the oil, then press into the dukka to gather it up. Eat and repeat. Best shared with intimate members of your household as double-dipping is practically unavoidable!

43

PBF sandwich

I've always been a bit conflicted by the peanut butter and jelly/jam sandwich. I get that the nut/jam/bread combo delivers a punchy hit of complementary flavours and textures. But the white bread/refined peanut butter/average jam experience always left me feeling a bit queasy. A wholemeal version, with nutty brown bread, crunchy nut butter and plenty of fresh fruit is not only more virtuous, but also genuinely more delicious. I give you the PBF sandwich.

PER PERSON

A handful of strawberries or raspberries (as many as you can squeeze into your sandwich)

A trickle of honey (or a scant tsp brown sugar)

A squeeze of lemon or lime juice

2 slices of wholemeal bread

A little butter, softened (optional)

2 knife-scoops of no-sugar-added crunchy peanut butter (or another nut butter of your choice)

If you're using strawberries, hull and slice them thickly. Raspberries don't need any prep. Trickle the fruit with honey (or sprinkle with a little sugar) and a squeeze of lemon or lime juice, toss together and set aside.

Lightly toast the slices of bread and butter the toast sparingly if you like. Spread one scoop of the nut butter over one slice. Spoon the prepared strawberries or raspberries thickly and evenly over the nut butter.

Spread the remaining nut butter on the other slice of bread and finish your sandwich by squishing it on top.

44

Fruity, nutty, seedy flapjacks

Classic flapjacks get their chewy-crispy character from a hefty dose of sugar and syrup, which can make them quite sickly after just a couple of bites. These alternative oaty bakes have a softer texture and use little refined sugar, with most of the sweetness (and plenty of fibre) coming from dates and other dried fruit. The addition of lemon juice and zest gives a nice tang to this fruity sweetness, and seeds and nut butter add to the goodness. They are ideal for a quick breakfast on-the-go, or a leisurely elevenses treat. You can make a vegan version, using coconut oil instead of butter.

MAKES 16

100g butter, softened, or 80g coconut oil

75g soft brown sugar (light or dark) or golden syrup

150g pitted dates, roughly chopped

150g no-sugar almond butter or peanut butter

Finely grated zest and juice of 1 lemon

200g porridge oats (not jumbo)

100g dried cranberries, raisins or chopped dried apricots (or a mix)

75g sunflower or pumpkin seeds, or a mix

Preheat the oven to 170°C/150°C Fan/Gas 3. Line a baking tin, about 16 x 24cm, with baking paper.

Put the butter or coconut oil, brown sugar or golden syrup, dates, nut butter and the lemon zest and juice into a pan and melt gently together over a low heat.

Combine the oats, dried fruit and seeds in a large bowl. Pour in the melted mixture and mix well with a wooden spoon.

Tip the mixture into the prepared tin and press down firmly with your hands to pack it into the tin evenly. Bake in the oven for 25–30 minutes, until golden brown.

Leave the flapjack to cool completely in the tin before slicing into bars. They will keep for 4–5 days in a tin or airtight container.

47

Hot chocolate

The thought of a steaming mug of hot chocolate is certainly a promise of comfort. Too often though, sugar overpowers chocolate and even if the first sip feels like a treat, it quickly cloys. This version is based on raw cacao, which is the unrefined starting point of all chocolate, and a rich source of flavonoids (natural antioxidants), as well as minerals such as copper, iron, zinc and magnesium. It has a slightly bitter edge and is deeply chocolatey with warm fruity notes, and it makes a rich and rewarding hot chocolate that you can relish right down to the empty mug. If you can't get cacao, a good cocoa powder also works well.

PER PERSON

300ml oat milk or whole cow's milk

1 tbsp raw cacao powder, or cocoa powder

1 tsp soft brown sugar (light or dark)

2 cardamom pods, bashed (optional)

Put all the ingredients into a small saucepan over a medium heat and bring to the boil, whisking often. When it just reaches boiling point, take the pan off the heat. Keep whisking for a minute to cool a little and get a nice froth on top.

Pour the hot chocolate into a mug and enjoy, stirring a couple of times as you drink it to keep it well blended.

Try pairing this up with a fruity seedy flapjack (page 47) for an elevenses and a half (a half past elevenses?).

48

Soups

I love making soups, whether I'm visiting old favourites or seeking out new combinations – or indeed conjuring up experimental hybrids of the tried-and-trusted and the slightly far out! And I must say the hit rate is high (he said modestly...).

There aren't many quicker routes to comfort than a steaming bowl of soup. And most good soups are already essentially good for you too, while also delivering both satisfaction and substance. Nevertheless, I have taken steps to make sure the soups here represent even better-for-you comfort than they already might. Mostly, I've boosted them with extra fresh veg and often some pulses too. So my Smoky fish chowder (on page 69) has onions, sweetcorn and greens to offset the salty smoky fish, while my tribute to the Portuguese classic *caldo verde*, Cabbage and chorizo soup (on page 73), is topped up with roots and creamy white beans too.

The key to making sure these additions are gratefully received and not merely gratuitous, is balance. That means adding variety and goodness, without distracting from, or diluting the stars of the soup. I think this is a valid approach whatever soup you are making – there's no reason not to veg-up favourite recipes with added greens or pulses or roots – just not so much of anything that it overwhelms.

A handful of frozen peas and shredded greens popped into a chicken noodle broth can only enhance. And if it's a too-tired-to-cook evening, you can even add veg to ready-made soup from a carton or tin. Some wilted spinach and half a tin of chickpeas added to your cream of tomato turns a sip of soup into a warm hug of a supper.

I've also pared back the saturated fats that sometimes get built into a bowl of soup. There's a dash of dairy here and there – a spoonful or two of half-fat crème fraîche or a scattering of cheese – but not much, because you don't need much. I've tipped the scales towards plants, without overbalancing the soupy see-saw, whereby every spoonful is both unique and representative. So, the ham in my hearty and homely Pea and ham soup (on page 67) is a treat rather than a portion, and my richly flavoured 'Cream of' roasted mushroom soup (on page 57) gets its lovely velvety texture from creamy cashew nuts, not creamy cream.

In all cases, the 'whole' idea is that you can hunker down (on the sofa if you like) and enjoy every warming slurp and spoonful, secure in the knowledge that you are nourishing both body and soul.

Cream of roasted tomato soup

There's something so soothing about a bowlful of deep orange-red, savoury tomato soup. Built around the flavour of roasted fresh tomatoes, this one is tangy and sweet, yet rich and velvety. Any leftovers can double-up as a pasta sauce. You can also make it with tinned tomatoes – and it's still better than soup from a tin!

SERVES 6

1.2–1.5kg ripe, flavoursome tomatoes (any size or kind, or a mix)

1 medium onion, finely sliced

1–2 tender inner celery sticks, finely sliced

1 medium carrot, scrubbed or peeled and thinly sliced

3 garlic cloves, thickly sliced

A couple of bay leaves

A sprig of thyme (optional)

3 tbsp olive oil

4 tbsp soured cream or half-fat crème fraîche, plus extra (optional) to serve

200–500ml hot vegetable stock

Sea salt and black pepper

Chopped parsley or chives, to finish (optional)

Preheat the oven to 190°C/170°C Fan/Gas 5. Halve the tomatoes (little cherry ones can stay whole) and put them into your largest roasting tray with all the other prepared veg, garlic and herbs. Season with salt and pepper and trickle over the olive oil. Toss well to coat everything in the oil and seasoning.

Roast in the oven, stirring the veg every 20 minutes or so, until the tomatoes are completely soft, pulpy and starting to colour, and the carrot feels tender when tested with the point of a knife (it doesn't need to be soft). If you have a huge oven tray and a very efficient oven, it might be done in 45 minutes; with a more compact tray and a less punchy oven, it may take an hour or longer.

Remove and discard the bay and thyme, if used, then transfer the contents of the tray to a jug blender. Blitz thoroughly to a smooth, velvety purée. A powerful blender should take care of the tomato skins and pips but if yours won't break them down completely, rub the purée through a big sieve to remove them.

Pour the soup into a pan. Add the soured cream or crème fraîche and just enough hot stock to get a thick but slurpable consistency. Taste to check the seasoning and reheat gently.

Serve in warmed bowls topped with a creamy swirl if you like, and a sprinkling of chopped parsley or chives if you have some.

VARIATIONS

Tinned tomato version: When tomatoes aren't in season, replace them with 3 x 400g tins plum tomatoes. Tip them, juice and all, into a large roasting tin. Add the carrot, celery, onion, garlic and herbs. Season, oil, roast and finish as above.

Vegan tomato soup: Add 75g plain cashew nuts to the roasting tray with the tomatoes for the last 30 minutes of the roasting time. Purée with the hot stock, as above, but no cream. Finish the soup with a few dots of extra virgin olive oil or a good plant-based yoghurt or cream.

Vg

'Cream of' roasted mushroom soup

Roasting intensifies the wonderful savoury flavour of mushrooms for this chuck-it-in-the-oven, honest-to-goodness soup, while cashew nuts break down in the blender to lend a lovely creamy tenderness. This recipe makes a good-sized batch; any you don't need straight away can be frozen for quick meals further down the line. Try serving this with a wedge of Porridge soda bread (page 259).

SERVES 6

750g mushrooms (ideally darker varieties, such as chestnut, portobello or open-cap)

1 onion, roughly chopped

2 celery sticks, sliced

1 medium carrot, scrubbed or peeled and roughly chopped

3 garlic cloves, thickly sliced

75g plain cashew nuts

A couple of bay leaves

A couple of sprigs of thyme (optional)

2 tbsp olive oil

100ml dry white wine

800ml hot vegetable stock

Sea salt and black pepper

Chopped parsley, to finish (optional)

Preheat the oven to 190°C/170°C Fan/Gas 5. Very roughly chop the mushrooms (stalks and all). Divide them and all the other veg between two large roasting trays. Add the garlic, cashews, bay leaves and thyme if using, distributing them evenly between the trays. Season with salt and pepper, trickle 1 tbsp olive oil over each tray, toss together and roast for 20 minutes.

Trickle the wine over the roasted veg, stir, then return the trays to the oven for 20 minutes or until the mushrooms are soft and the carrots are tender. Discard the bay leaves and thyme, if used.

Scrape all the veg and any juices into a jug blender. Add the hot stock and blitz to a smooth soup. If you only have a small blender, you might need to do this in batches – the total volume of soup is not far off 2 litres.

Taste and add more salt and pepper if needed, plus a splash of hot water if the soup is too thick. Reheat the soup gently in a saucepan, without boiling.

Serve the soup in warmed bowls, topped with a sprinkling of chopped parsley if you have some, and any of the toppings suggested below if you fancy.

TOPPING IDEAS

Wholegrain croûtons: Cut 1 or 2 thick slices of wholemeal bread into 2cm cubes and fry in a little olive oil until golden and crisp.

Toasted cashews (and other nuts): Roughly chop a good handful of cashews, walnuts or hazelnuts (or cooked chestnuts). Toast in the oven or a dry frying pan for a few minutes until lightly browned and fragrant.

Nettle soup (with a poached egg)

You may think that a soup made from stinging nettles struggles to stake a claim as a comfort dish. But for me it has become just that. I make big batches of it during the nettle season (typically February to April) and freeze half-litre tubfuls for a standby lunch or supper. Adding a poached egg makes it even more luxurious and nourishing.

Arm yourself with a stout glove (or two!) and locate nettles that are young, bright green, ideally no higher than your knee and, crucially, haven't yet got flower-heads. Pick the 'crown' (the top 6 leaves or so) from each nettle and put into a bag or basket to carry back to the kitchen. A generous half bag should give you around 400g.

SERVES 4

About 400g freshly picked nettle tops

1 tbsp olive or rapeseed oil, or butter

1 medium onion or leek, trimmed and sliced or chopped

1 large carrot, scrubbed or peeled and chopped

1 large or 2 slender celery sticks, finely sliced

1 medium potato (150–200g), scrubbed or peeled and cut into 2–3cm chunks

1 bay leaf

500ml hot vegetable stock or water

Sea salt and black pepper

OPTIONS TO FINISH

4 poached eggs (see page 28)

Natural yoghurt (dairy or plant-based) or crème fraîche

Extra virgin olive or rapeseed oil

Don stout rubber gloves and wash the nettles thoroughly, picking out any grass stems or other bits that are not nettle. Shake the excess water off as you go and pile the nettles into a large bowl.

Heat the oil or butter in a large saucepan over a medium heat. Add the onion or leek, carrot, celery, potato, bay leaf and some salt and pepper. Stir well and get the veg sizzling, then turn down the heat and sweat gently, stirring occasionally, for 5–6 minutes until the veg are becoming tender.

Pour in the hot stock or water and bring to a simmer. Cover and cook gently for 8–10 minutes, until the potato is completely tender.

Add the nettles – you may need to add them in a couple of batches, waiting for the first lot to wilt down a bit and make room for the next. Cover again and cook gently for around another 5 minutes. Take off the heat and remove the bay leaf.

Blitz the soup, using a stick blender in the pan, or a jug blender, until smooth. Most blenders should handle the soup with no trouble but, if you find any little fibres from the celery or nettles left in the soup, pass it through a sieve to remove them. If the soup seems overly thick, add a little more hot water or stock. Taste the soup and add more salt or pepper if needed.

Gently reheat the soup, without boiling. Serve in warmed bowls, with a poached egg slipped into each bowl if you fancy. Top with a swirl of yoghurt or crème fraîche and/or a trickle of extra virgin oil if you like. Finish with a grinding of pepper. A slice of wholemeal toast, lightly buttered or trickled with oil, is great for dunking into the soup and dipping into the egg.

GREEN VARIATIONS

If watercress (foraged or bought) is easier to come by, you can do a straight swap or go 50:50 watercress:nettles. And you can include varying amounts of spinach or flat-leaf parsley in the mix too. Any of these vivid green soups will be both delicious and virtuous, and that's a very comforting combination!

English onion soup

This is a very classy way to get a couple of your five a day: a lovely 'old-fashioned' onion soup. I wouldn't tag it as 'French', given that I've tweaked it quite a bit and made it a veggie recipe. You could revert to something more traditional by using beef stock, but I think you'll find the cunning deployment of soy, coffee and red wine does the job well here, giving the soup a rich and well-rounded umami flavour, and of course keeping the soup veggie. The long, slow cooking of the onions to sweet, melting tenderness is a labour of love, but it's well worth it.

SERVES 4

1kg onions

40g unsalted butter, or 3 tbsp olive or vegetable oil

3 garlic cloves, sliced

1 bay leaf

A sprig of thyme

100ml red wine

2 tbsp strong black coffee

1 tbsp tamari or soy sauce

800ml hot vegetable stock

Sea salt and black pepper

HERB CROÛTONS

2 thick slices of wholemeal bread, cut into chunks

A small bunch of sage, rosemary or thyme, leaves picked and roughly chopped

2 tbsp olive or vegetable oil

50g strong cheese, such as Gruyère, Cheddar or Parmesan, grated (optional)

Slice the onions very thinly (using a mandoline or food processor is the speediest way to do this).

Heat the butter or oil in a large saucepan or deep, wide frying pan, over a medium-low heat. Add the sliced onions with some salt and pepper. As soon as they are sizzling, turn down the heat, cover the pan and let them sweat for 45–60 minutes until soft, silky and significantly reduced in volume, lifting the lid to stir them fairly often.

Uncover the pan, add the garlic, turn up the heat a little and cook for another 15–30 minutes, stirring often, until the onions are very soft, wilted and golden. Don't let them catch or burn at any point.

Add the bay leaf and thyme, wine, coffee and tamari/soy and simmer until the liquid is reduced to almost nothing, around 3 minutes. Add the stock, bring to a simmer and cook gently for another 10 minutes. Season to taste with salt and pepper (you can add a dash more tamari/soy or coffee too – but be restrained as you don't want the soup to actually taste of either).

Meanwhile, for the herb croûtons, preheat the oven to 170°C/150°C Fan/Gas 3. Toss the cubes of bread with the chopped herbs and oil. Spread out in an oven dish and bake for about 10 minutes until crisp and golden. Set aside.

Ladle the soup into warmed bowls and top with the herb croûtons. Add a sprinkle of grated cheese to each bowl, if you like, and serve.

Spicy squash and lentil soup

This soup is a splicing of two comforting recipes: a hearty squash soup and a spicy lentil dhal and it can be served as either. Satisfying, thick and spicy with a touch of sweetness, it works both 'rough' and 'smooth' (i.e. completely blended); just try whichever appeals most to you. The raita's not essential, but it's a lovely complement.

SERVES 6

2 tbsp vegetable or coconut oil

2 tsp cumin seeds

2 tsp coriander seeds

1 bay leaf

1 large onion, chopped

1kg squash, such as Crown Prince, kabocha or butternut

3 garlic cloves, roughly chopped or coarsely grated

A knob of fresh ginger, finely grated

1 tsp ground turmeric or 1 tbsp finely grated fresh turmeric

½–1 red chilli, chopped (deseeded for less heat if you prefer), or ½ tsp dried chilli flakes

150g red lentils, well rinsed

800ml vegetable stock

Sea salt and black pepper

RAITA (OPTIONAL)

½ medium cucumber

100ml natural yoghurt (dairy or plant-based)

2 tbsp chopped mint or coriander (optional)

TO SERVE

Dukka (page 43, optional)

Olive or chilli oil (optional)

Heat the oil in a large pan over a medium heat and add the cumin and coriander seeds and the bay leaf. Fry for a few minutes until they start to sizzle, then add the onion. As soon as it is sizzling, reduce the heat and sweat for 10 minutes, stirring once or twice.

Meanwhile, peel and deseed the squash, then cut into large cubes (you need about 600g prepared weight).

Add the garlic, ginger, turmeric and chilli to the onion and continue to fry gently for 3–4 minutes, then add the chopped squash and toss with the onion over the heat for a minute or two.

Add the rinsed lentils to the pan, pour in the stock and bring to a simmer. Then cover the pan and let the soup cook gently for 15–20 minutes, lifting the lid to stir regularly, until the squash is tender and the lentils have broken down into a rough purée.

Meanwhile, make the raita: coarsely grate the cucumber, wrap it in a clean tea towel and squeeze to remove excess liquid, then tip into a bowl. Add the yoghurt, and herbs if using, mix well and season with a little salt and pepper. Set aside or keep in the fridge if you are making the raita more than an hour ahead of serving.

Remove the bay leaf from the soup. Either bash and crush the squash with a wooden spoon or potato masher to get a nice rough texture, or blitz the soup until smooth, using a stick blender in the pan, or a jug blender. Add some hot water if needed to loosen the texture a little – I like it thick but not so that you can actually stand a spoon up in it. Season to taste with salt and pepper.

Reheat the soup gently if necessary and ladle into warmed bowls. Dollop some raita on top. Finish, if you like, with a sprinkle of dukka and/or a trickle of olive oil, or chilli oil if you have some and fancy an extra kick of heat.

Spicy noodle soup

Two of my kids love spicy food and noodle soups, and they especially love a spicy noodle soup. I do too! I improvise many variations, depending on what veg I have to hand, and whether there might be some leftover fish or meat to bring to the party. But the underpinnings are pretty consistent: a well-flavoured stock, made hot, sour, savoury and aromatic with chilli, lemon or lime juice, soy, seaweed (sometimes), ginger and garlic (always). A few bashed makrut lime leaves will usually be part of the mix too, but that's by no means essential. My favourite proteinaceous additions are listed opposite.

200g fine wholegrain noodles, such as brown rice or buckwheat

1 tsp sesame or vegetable oil, for the noodles

1 litre vegetable stock (or homemade chicken or fish stock if you have some)

2 fat garlic cloves, cut into fine slivers

3cm piece of fresh ginger, grated or cut into very fine matchsticks

2 tsp flaked seaweed, such as dulse or wakame, or mixed seaweed flakes (optional)

½–1 red chilli (the heat is up to you!), finely sliced, or a good pinch of dried chilli flakes

1–2 makrut lime leaves, bruised, or 1 lemongrass stem, bashed, or lemongrass trimmings (optional)

1 medium carrot, scrubbed or peeled and cut into matchsticks or very thin slices

1 medium kohlrabi or ½ daikon, peeled and cut into matchsticks or very thin slices (optional)

3–4 spring onions, finely sliced

1 pak choi, sliced, or a good handful of spinach leaves, roughly chopped

Leftover meat or fish, tofu or a thin two-egg omelette (see right)

2 tbsp tamari or soy sauce, plus extra (optional) to finish

Juice of 1 lime or ½ lemon, plus extra (optional) to finish

A pinch of soft light brown sugar

Sea salt and black pepper

Cook the noodles according to the packet instructions, drain well, rinse thoroughly with cold water, and drain again. Toss with the 1 tsp oil and keep ready.

Put the stock, garlic, ginger, seaweed if using, and the chilli (fresh or dried) into a large pan. Add the lime leaves or lemongrass if you have either. Bring to a simmer, then add the carrot, and kohlrabi or daikon if using, and return to a simmer. Cook for a minute then add the spring onions, and sliced pak choi if using. Bring back to a simmer and cook for a minute to just soften the pak choi stems.

If using spinach, add the leaves at this point, to wilt. You can leave the soup as it is or stir in one of the extras below, prepped while the soup is cooking.

Give the extras a minute or so to heat through, then take off the heat. Stir in the tamari/soy, lime or lemon juice, sugar and some salt and pepper. Transfer a ladleful of the broth to a small bowl and taste – it should be hot, sour and aromatic. Add more chilli, tamari/soy, salt and/or lime or lemon juice to taste, as needed.

Divide the noodles between warmed soup bowls and ladle over the hot soup. Serve at once with chopsticks and/or spoons.

65

EXTRAS

Meat: Scraps of chicken, pork or beef can be dropped straight in, or crisped in a frying pan first – in which case seasoning them with a little chopped garlic and chilli, and a pinch of salt, will add to their impact.

Fish: Add flakes of cooked fish, or small slices of raw fish that will cook through in just a minute or two. You can use fish stock (as above) if you're going to add fish, but it's not vital.

Eggs: Make a simple thin two-egg omelette, seasoned with pepper or a pinch of dried chilli flakes and a dash of soy sauce. Cook until firm, leave to cool then cut into 1–2cm strips.

Tofu: Cut 100g tofu into small cubes and fry until golden and crisp. Finish with toasted sesame seeds and a trickle of toasted sesame oil.

VARIATION

Spicy coconut noodle soup: Just replace 400ml of the stock with a 400ml tin of coconut milk. Add any of the above extras and finish with extra lemon or lime juice to cut the richness.

Pea and ham soup

My mum used to make a traditional split pea and ham soup with leftover ham, and I've always loved it. This is a fresher, quicker version, made with fresh or frozen peas and fast-cooking red lentils instead of split peas, which need pre-soaking.

SERVES 4

2 tbsp olive or vegetable oil

1 onion, chopped

1 celery stick, chopped

1 garlic clove, chopped

150g red lentils, well rinsed

1 litre hot vegetable stock

200g frozen peas or petits pois

About 100g chopped ham, bacon or pancetta

Sea salt and black pepper

Chopped parsley, to finish (optional)

Heat 1 tbsp oil in a large saucepan over a medium heat. Add the onion and celery and get them sizzling, then turn the heat down and let the veg sweat gently for about 10 minutes. Add the garlic and cook for another minute or two.

Stir in the rinsed lentils, add the vegetable stock and bring to a simmer. Partially cover and cook over a low heat for about 15 minutes, stirring from time to time, until the lentils are soft. Don't worry if some froth forms on the surface – just stir it in. Add the peas, bring back to a simmer and cook for a further 5 minutes.

Meanwhile, heat the remaining 1 tbsp oil in a non-stick frying pan over a medium heat and add the ham, bacon or pancetta. Fry for a few minutes, turning now and again, until your chosen addition is golden and a little crispy. Set aside while you finish the soup.

Take the pan off the heat. Add about half of the fried ham, bacon or pancetta to the soup and use a stick blender or a jug blender to blitz the soup (I like to leave it quite chunky). It should be fairly thick but if it seems excessively so, add a little hot water to loosen it. Taste the soup and add salt and pepper if needed.

Gently reheat the soup if necessary and ladle into warmed bowls. Scatter over the rest of the ham, bacon or pancetta and finish with a sprinkle of chopped parsley if you like.

VARIATIONS

Traditional pea and ham soup: Use 150g split green or yellow peas in place of the red lentils and soak them in cold water for at least 4 hours (or overnight). Rinse the soaked peas well then add to the soup with the stock. They will take a fair bit longer than the lentils to soften – a good 45 minutes to an hour.

Pea soup with ginger and turmeric: Add 1 tbsp each of finely grated ginger and turmeric to the onion and celery at the start (or you can use 1 tsp ground turmeric). Leave out the ham or bacon.

Vg

67

Smoky fish chowder

A milky, smoky chowder is one of the most comforting of all soups, and you can easily build layers of extra goodness into it. I add plenty of vegetables – sweetcorn or peas at the least, and often greens and/or herbs too. And I sometimes boost the omega-3 content with a few freshly cooked mussels too (see variation overleaf).

SERVES 4

About 500g sustainably caught, undyed smoked haddock, cod or pollack

1 bay leaf

A few black peppercorns

300–400ml milk (dairy or plant-based)

1 tbsp rapeseed or olive oil

A knob of butter (or a little more oil)

1 large onion, finely sliced, or 1 large or 2 medium leeks, trimmed and sliced into 1cm rounds

250g waxy potatoes (1–2 medium), scrubbed or peeled

About 150g sweetcorn kernels (you should get this from 1 large cob, but frozen is also fine) or frozen peas

2 handfuls of roughly chopped spinach or finely shredded kale, cavolo nero or spring greens (optional)

Sea salt and black pepper

Chopped parsley and/or chives, to finish (optional)

Put the fish into a wide saucepan, cutting it to fit in a single layer, and add the bay leaf and peppercorns. Pour on enough milk to just cover the fish; add a splash of water too, if needed. Slowly bring to a gentle simmer, cover the pan, then turn off the heat and leave the fish to cook through in the residual heat for about 5 minutes – it might take a bit longer if it's a thick piece.

Lift the fish out of the pan and onto a plate. Set aside to cool. Retain the cooking liquid.

Heat the oil and/or butter in a large saucepan over a medium heat. Add the onion or leek and some salt and pepper. Once sizzling, reduce the heat, cover the pan and let the veg sweat gently for about 10 minutes until softened and tender.

Meanwhile, cut the potato(es) into quarters or 2–3cm chunks if large. Add to the pan and cook for another couple of minutes.

Strain the retained milk from the fish over the softened veg in the pan, discarding the bay leaf and peppercorns, then pour in 300ml hot water. Bring to a gentle simmer and cook for about 10 minutes until the potato is tender.

Meanwhile, flake the smoked fish off its skin. Don't worry if it is a little undercooked in places, it will finish cooking in the hot soup.

Add the sweetcorn or frozen peas to the soup, and the greens if using, and return to a gentle simmer for 3–4 minutes to cook the sweetcorn or peas. Add the flaked fish last of all and reheat gently, without simmering. Taste the soup and add more salt and pepper if needed.

Sprinkle the chowder generously with chopped parsley or chives, or both, if you have some.

Variations overleaf →

With mussels: For an extra special chowder, finish with a few handfuls of freshly steamed mussels. Thoroughly rinse about 500g fresh mussels, discarding any that are broken or won't close. Pour 100ml white wine into a wide pan with a tight-fitting lid and bring to the boil. Add the mussels, put the lid on and cook for 3 minutes, shaking the pan once or twice. Check the mussels – they should almost all be open; if not, re-cover and give them another minute. Discard any that are still unopened at this stage. Strain the cooking liquor into the hot soup, stir and ladle into warmed bowls. Remove some of the mussels from the shells, leave others in the shell or half-shell. Top each bowl with some whole and some shelled mussels, and the herbs.

With oysters: Allow 2 oysters per person. Either steam them open in a little wine, as for mussels (above), and add the oysters (without shells) along with the strained liquor from the pan; or shuck them and add the raw oysters, with the shell juices, to the chowder at the end.

With egg: Finish each bowl of chowder with a freshly poached egg (see page 28).

With curry: To give the chowder a spicy note, stir 1 tbsp curry paste or powder into the sweating onion and leeks. Finish with a scattering of roughly chopped coriander leaves if you like.

70

Cabbage and chorizo soup

This warming dish is my tribute to the classic Portuguese *caldo verde*, a simple soup of potatoes and cabbage with *chouriço* sausage. I've diverged a bit, adding other veg for variety, and creamy beans for extra body and goodness, but keeping that lovely smoky, spicy sausage. It's easily hearty enough to be supper, and just the thing for days when you're feeling a little chilly, mopey or under par.

SERVES 4

1 tbsp olive oil

100g chorizo (or Portuguese chouriço), cut into 5mm slices or chunky cubes

1 large onion, sliced

1 medium carrot, scrubbed or peeled and chunkily chopped

1 celery stick, chunkily chopped

2 garlic cloves, slivered

200g waxy or new potatoes, scrubbed or peeled and cut into quarters, or 2–3cm cubes if large

500ml vegetable stock

400g tin beans, such as cannellini, haricot or borlotti, drained and rinsed

½ green cabbage, halved again, core removed, shredded

Sea salt and black pepper

Extra virgin olive, hempseed or rapeseed oil, to finish

Heat the olive oil in a large saucepan over a medium heat. Toss in the chorizo and fry gently until it starts to release its red fat. Add the onion, carrot and celery and fry gently for 5 minutes, then add the garlic and fry for another couple of minutes.

Add the potatoes and cook for a couple of minutes then pour in the stock and 500ml water. Bring to a simmer and cook, uncovered, until the veg is just tender, about 10 minutes.

Add the beans, pile the cabbage into the soup and put on the lid. Cook for another 5–7 minutes, stirring once or twice, until the cabbage is wilted and tender.

Season the soup with salt and pepper to taste and serve, with a trickle of extra virgin oil on top.

73

VARIATIONS

With bacon: Swap the chorizo for pancetta or streaky bacon, adding a pinch of smoked paprika to the soup at the end, to get that smoky savour.

With other greens: The cabbage can be replaced with other brassica greens: spring greens or cavolo nero, or other types of kale. Or you can use spinach or chard, for a change.

Pasta and Rice

Why do we crave carbohydrate-rich food when we are weary, cold or feeling down – when we're in need of comfort? The simplest answer is that carbohydrate is our bodies' favourite fuel – an easily utilised source of energy, not just for our muscles but for our brains, which cannot function well without it.

Of course, there are carbs and there are carbs... On one end of the spectrum are highly processed, stripped-down forms – including sugar and white flour, and the many processed foods spun out of them – that give short-term spikes of energy. And on the other are the unprocessed alternatives – whole grains, wholemeal flours, and the foods prepared from them – that sustain us for much longer, and offer our bodies more good things besides mere calories (the all-important fibre among them).

You will notice that some of the recipes in this book walk a careful line between the two! Sugar is not banished, white flour is not demonised, but those ingredients are deployed in proportion, and in combination, with a cornucopia of others that bring in fibre, nutrients, proteins and healthy fats.

So here is a chapter that offers an all-out celebration of the wholewheat pasta and brown rice that have become my go-to choices. I rarely return to white pasta these days, and when I do I find it a bit too bland; likewise, white rice feels insubstantial to me now and never seems to fill me up.

This is evidence of the mutability of our palates. We are powerfully affected by our conditioning: if we have always eaten white pasta and white bread, they will seem 'normal' to us. But that's just a point of view, and one that we can easily change by stepping outside our white carb comfort zone and creating, guess what – a whole new one! It's so worth doing. Because if you can get your best gratification from food that is genuinely nourishing you, providing you with the nutrients you really need and feeding your all-important gut bacteria to boot, then you are winning on every level.

What you won't find here is any hair-shirt-ism. One vital element of comfort is pleasure. It's not enough to just eat a pile of plain brown pasta – it's got to be served in such a way that it tastes great. We need texture and flavour, and often generous amounts of sauce, to join forces with our satisfying carbs to deliver dishes that are not just pleasing, but truly memorable.

So, when only pasta or rice will hit the spot, I urge you to try one of these recipes. Based on whole grains, augmented with lots of veg, plenty of herbs and spices and, in some cases, well-chosen fish and meat, they're rammed with more-ish flavours, as well as nurturing goodness. When you get that balance right, as I believe I have here, these heart-warming meals invite you to come back for more. They will soon take their place in your canon of comfort classics.

Pasta with cooked tomato sauce

Pasta sauced with tomato is a mainstay of family tables far and wide. This recipe features wholewheat pasta, which is a great source of fibre, and good at 'grabbing' loose sauces like this because of its rougher texture. When it comes to a cooked tomato sauce, I do think simple is best – I don't even put onion in mine. Tinned whole plum tomatoes cost more than the chopped ones but they are richer and they do make a better sauce.

This is also a great sauce for a pizza base (see page 167), though you may want to cook it a little longer to reduce and thicken more.

SERVES 4

COOKED TOMATO SAUCE

3 tbsp olive oil

2 bay leaves

2–3 garlic cloves, thinly sliced or coarsely grated

2 x 400g tins plum tomatoes

A pinch of brown sugar (optional)

A pinch of dried chilli flakes (optional)

Sea salt and black pepper

TO SERVE

300g wholewheat pasta of your choice

A trickle of olive oil

Finely grated Parmesan or Cheddar (optional)

Crispy bacon bits (optional)

Heat the olive oil in a large, wide heavy-based frying pan over a medium heat. Add the bay leaves and garlic and let them sizzle and spit until the garlic is just starting to turn golden.

Add the tomatoes to the pan with their juice – they will spit as they hit the hot oil, but they soon calm down. Rinse out each tin out with a little water so you get all the tomato juice, and add this too. Add a pinch of salt and some pepper.

Bring the sauce to a simmer, using a potato masher or a fork to crush the tomatoes in the pan so they start to break down. Simmer the sauce, stirring fairly frequently, and crushing any larger chunks with your spoon, for 25–30 minutes, or until reduced by about one-third and tasting rich and intense. Any obvious bits of skin, or the whitish fibrous ends of the tomatoes that won't break down, can be removed with a fork.

The acidity will mellow and the sweetness increase as the sauce cooks, but you can add a pinch of sugar if you like. Taste to check the seasoning, adding more salt and pepper only if needed. If you'd like a little heat, add a pinch of chilli flakes. Remove the bay leaves. I like the sauce rough with a little tomato texture remaining, but you can blitz it until smooth with a stick blender or jug blender if you prefer it like that.

Bring a large pan of water to the boil, add salt and then the pasta. Cook until *al dente* (tender but firm to the bite), drain and return to the hot pan. Add the hot tomato sauce and stir well.

Serve the pasta in tomato sauce just as it is, with a trickle of olive oil and some freshly ground salt and pepper on top, or add a grating of cheese or a sprinkle of crisp bacon bits.

78

Spag bol

I've been adding extra veg and pulses to my spag bol for years, with no complaints from my family. The switch to wholewheat spaghetti was a little more controversial – at first. But now it slips down with as much relish as the white stuff ever did (I start with 50g dry spaghetti per person). You can make the bol more pulse-y, by adding a 400g tin of kidney or butter beans as well as the lentils and serve it 'spag-free', with some wilted kale or spinach or a leafy side salad.

SERVES 6–8

2 tbsp olive or vegetable oil, plus an extra trickle

1 large onion, chopped

1 medium leek, sliced

2 medium carrots, scrubbed or peeled and diced

2 celery sticks, thinly sliced

About 150g swede or kohlrabi, peeled and diced (optional)

2 garlic cloves, chopped

2 tbsp tomato purée

2 x 400g tins plum tomatoes, crushed, or 800ml passata

1 bay leaf

A sprig of thyme and/or some parsley stalks (optional)

100g unsmoked streaky bacon, chopped, or bacon lardons

500g minced beef (15% fat)

200ml red wine

250ml beef or vegetable stock

400g tin lentils, drained, or 300g cooked Puy lentils

Sea salt and black pepper

TO SERVE

Wholewheat spaghetti or extra pulses/veg (see above)

Finely grated Parmesan

Heat the 2 tbsp oil in a very large saucepan or a flameproof casserole over a medium heat. Add the onion, leek, carrots, celery, swede or kohlrabi if using, and garlic, with some salt and pepper. Cover and sauté for about 10 minutes, stirring often, until the veg are starting to soften. Add the tomato purée and tinned tomatoes (crushing or mashing them as they go in) or passata, then add the bay leaf and any other herbs. Bring this sauce up to a simmer.

You can start browning the meat while the veg is sautéing (or just do it after you've got the tomato sauce simmering away nicely, if that's easier). Heat the trickle of oil in a large frying pan over a fairly high heat. Add the bacon and cook for a few minutes, until crisp and golden. Scoop this into the pan of simmering veg and tomato sauce, leaving as much fat as possible in the frying pan.

Now add the beef to the frying pan (you can brown it in two batches if your frying pan isn't really large), along with some salt and pepper, and cook, stirring often, until the meat is nicely browned. This takes a good 10 minutes and is important because the browning creates lots of flavour. Initially, the beef will release some liquid: let this simmer away and then it will start to colour. Scoop the beef into the pan of simmering veg and tomato. Repeat with the rest of the beef, if browning in batches.

Tip the wine into the hot frying pan to deglaze it, scraping up any bits of caramelised meat as it bubbles. When the wine is reduced by about half, tip it into the pan of sauce. Add the stock now too. Cook, covered, stirring occasionally to make sure the sauce isn't catching on the bottom of the pan, for about 1 hour, until it is rich and thick. Add a dash more stock or water if it's getting too thick.

Add the lentils, simmer briefly to heat through then taste to check the seasoning. Serve your bolognese sauce with spaghetti, or extra veg (as suggested above), and a generous sprinkling of Parmesan.

Kedgeree

This classically comforting rice and fish dish – traditionally enjoyed for breakfast or brunch but also a lovely supper – has always been a big F-W family favourite. I've evolved the recipe over the years, replacing white rice with brown basmati, upping the spice a little, and incorporating peas (and sometimes lentils). This version is, I dare to claim, 'best ever' – both for taste and goodness. If you are wavering about the raisins I urge you to give them a try.

SERVES 4

175g brown basmati rice

1 tbsp olive or vegetable oil

1 large onion, finely sliced

4 medium eggs

500g sustainably caught smoked pollack or haddock fillet

150g frozen peas or petits pois

100g cavolo nero, stalks removed and leaves shredded (optional)

A knob of butter (about 15g)

1 tbsp mild curry powder or paste

½–1 small red chilli, finely chopped (deseeded for less heat if you prefer)

25g raisins (optional)

100g cooked brown, green or Puy lentils, or drained, tinned lentils (optional)

2 tbsp chopped coriander or parsley

1 tbsp chopped lovage (optional)

Sea salt and black pepper

Lemon wedges, to serve

Rinse the brown rice well and leave it to soak in cold water for at least 15 minutes, or up to 2 hours.

Drain the rice, rinse it again, then transfer to a large pan (it needs to be large because you'll be mixing all the other kedgeree ingredients into this before serving).

Cover the rice with plenty of cold water, bring to a simmer, cover and cook for the time suggested on the packet, minus 5 minutes (soaking reduces the cooking time).

While the rice is cooking, heat the oil in a large frying pan over a medium heat. Add the sliced onion with a pinch of salt and get everything sizzling, then put the lid on the pan and reduce the heat. Let the onion sweat gently for 12–15 minutes, until nicely soft and golden.

This is also a good time to cook the eggs: bring a small saucepan of water to the boil, carefully lower the eggs into the pan and simmer for 7–8 minutes.

Meanwhile, slice the smoked fish off its skin and then cut it into 2–3cm chunks; set aside.

Once cooked, lift the eggs out of the pan and run them under cold water to stop the cooking, then lightly crack and peel the shells (under a gently running cool tap).

Test the rice – it should be tender but still have a slight bite at this point. When it is, stir in the peas, and cavolo if using, bring to a simmer and cook for 4–5 minutes. Drain thoroughly and return the rice and green veg to the hot pan, drop in a knob of butter and stir lightly with a fork. Turn off the heat and cover the pan to keep the rice warm while you cook the fish with the onions.

Continued overleaf →

Stir the curry powder or paste into the softened onions, along with the fresh chilli, and the raisins if using, and cook for a minute or so longer.

Add the chunks of raw smoked fish to the spicy onions and cook for about 5 minutes, until just cooked through. Stir in the lentils, if using, and cook for a minute or two, to heat them through.

Add the spicy fish mixture to the pan of rice and green veg, along with half the chopped herbs, and toss through gently. Taste and add more salt or pepper if needed.

Halve or quarter the warm boiled eggs and place on top of the rice. Finish with the rest of the chopped herbs and a grinding of black pepper then serve, with lemon wedges.

VARIATIONS

Vg

Aubergine vegeree: You can swap in roasted aubergine to replace the raw smoked fish, and if you leave out the eggs and swap the butter for oil, the vegeree will be vegan. Cut a fairly large aubergine or 2 medium-small ones (around 500g in total) into 2–3cm chunks. Put these into a large roasting tin, trickle over 2 tbsp vegetable oil and season with salt and pepper. Roast at 190°C/170°C Fan/Gas 5 for about 40 minutes, stirring halfway through, until tender and golden. While the aubergine is cooking, proceed with the recipe above, adding the aubergine just after the chilli, curry powder or paste and raisins.

Leftovers kedgeree: The recipe is also easily adapted to use leftover cooked fish in place of raw smoked fish. Flake the cooked fish and add to the kedgeree with the lentils, just to heat through. You're unlikely to have 500g leftover fish, I'm guessing, but this might be an option for when you only have two to feed – just scale down the recipe accordingly.

Chicken and chorizo rice

There are various incarnations of one-pan chicken and rice dishes, originating from all over the world, and this version, which includes some lovely Spanish flavours, is one of my favourites. It's delicious and satisfying, with tangy sweet peppers and tomatoes, and spicy chorizo, to balance the soothing rice, chicken and brothy juices.

SERVES 6

1 large or 2 medium onions, sliced

3 red, orange or yellow peppers, deseeded and sliced

2 fat garlic cloves, sliced

100g chorizo, diced

1–2 tbsp olive or rapeseed oil

1 bay leaf

250g brown rice (such as basmati), well rinsed

1 small chicken, jointed, or 6 bone-in chicken thighs

200ml white wine

About 500ml well-flavoured chicken stock

200g cherry tomatoes, halved if large

Sea salt and black pepper

Preheat the oven to 190°C/170°C Fan/Gas 5.

Put the onion(s), peppers, garlic and chorizo into a large roasting dish with just a trickle of oil (the chorizo will release its own fat so you don't need much). Add the bay leaf and some salt and pepper and toss together well. Place in the oven for 25 minutes.

Tip the rice into a saucepan, cover with plenty of boiling water and bring to a simmer. Cook for 20 minutes, until almost *al dente* (still firm to the bite), then drain.

Heat a trickle more oil in a large frying pan over a medium-high heat. Season the chicken skin. Put half the chicken pieces into the pan, skin side down, and season their other sides. Fry the chicken for around 8 minutes, turning occasionally, until each piece is nicely browned. Transfer to a dish. Repeat with the remaining chicken pieces. Everything should be coming together at roughly the same time now: veg, rice and chicken! If the veg or rice get a few minutes more cooking, it doesn't matter.

When you've taken all of the chicken out of the frying pan, add the wine. Let it bubble while you scrape up any caramelised bits from the base of the pan, and simmer for 3 minutes or so, until reduced by about half. Add the stock and bring to a brisk simmer.

Take the tray of roast veg from the oven. Stir in the part-cooked rice then add the cherry tomatoes. Use tongs to place the browned chicken pieces on top, skin side up. Pour the hot stock around the chicken – it should just about cover the rice. Cover with foil and return to the oven for 30 minutes. Take off the foil, give the rice a gentle stir and finish in the oven for a final 15 minutes, or until everything is bubbling nicely and the chicken is cooked through.

Dish up the chicken, rice and veg with any juices from the tray spooned over. This is pretty much a complete dish, but some steamed greens, such as purple sprouting broccoli, cavolo nero or shredded Savoy cabbage, will go well with it.

Squash speltotto

Whole grains of nutty spelt are much higher in fibre than white risotto rice. I think they have more flavour and a nicer texture too, and they are generally well-behaved – it's harder to overcook them! This recipe is vegan-friendly – beating some of the soft roasted squash into the spelt grains slightly mimics the effect of beating in butter and cheese – though you can finish it with cheese if you like (see overleaf). I think you'll find this a very satisfying dish.

SERVES 5–6

250g pearled spelt or barley

About 1kg squash (butternut, Crown Prince and onion squash are great but you can use any winter squash)

8 large-ish garlic cloves in their skins, lightly crushed, plus another 2 cloves, finely chopped

1 mild red chilli, sliced, or a sprinkle of dried chilli flakes

A handful of sage leaves (or you can use thyme or rosemary)

3 tbsp olive or vegetable oil

1 medium onion, finely chopped

A glass of dry white wine

750ml–1 litre hot vegetable stock

Sea salt and black pepper

Put the spelt or barley in a bowl and cover with cold water. Leave to soak while you start the rest of the dish.

Peel and deseed the squash then cut the flesh into roughly 3cm cubes. You want about 700g prepared squash flesh.

Preheat the oven to 190°C/170°C Fan/Gas 5. Put the cubed squash in a large roasting tray with the lightly crushed whole garlic cloves, chilli and herbs. Trickle over half the oil and season well with salt and pepper. Toss together and roast for 35–40 minutes, stirring halfway through, until tender and caramelised.

While the squash is cooking, heat the remaining oil in a large saucepan over a medium heat. Add the onion and chopped garlic with a pinch of salt and some pepper. Stir well, then lower the heat, cover the pan and let the onion sweat gently for about 10 minutes, until soft, stirring occasionally.

Drain the soaked spelt or barley, rinse well and add to the pan, stirring it well with the onion. Cook for a minute then add the wine and let it bubble and reduce away to almost nothing.

Add 750ml of the hot stock and bring to a very gentle simmer. Cook, stirring regularly, until the spelt or barley is tender but not mushy, and most of the stock is absorbed. It should take around 25 minutes (or a little longer for barley). You can add a splash more stock or water if needed.

Take the tray of roasted squash, garlic and chilli from the oven and transfer about half of it to a separate dish.

Squeeze the soft garlic out of its skins onto the roasted squash still in the tray then use a fork to roughly mash the garlic and squash together.

Continued overleaf →

89

Add this mash to the pan of cooked spelt/barley and stir it in fairly vigorously so it breaks down and helps bind the grains together.

Add the remaining whole pieces of squash, and any remaining chilli and herbs in the roasting tray, to the speltotto and stir again – more gently this time, so you get chunkier pieces of squash, as well as the purée. Taste and add more salt and pepper if you think it is needed.

Spoon the speltotto into warmed dishes and finish in one of the following ways:

With crispy sage: Fry 12–20 fresh sage leaves in 2–3 tbsp olive or vegetable oil for a few minutes, until crisp. You can add a pinch of dried chilli flakes too, for an extra kick. Sprinkle the crispy sage leaves over the speltotto.

With walnuts: Scatter lightly toasted and bashed walnuts, a trickle of olive oil and some dried chilli flakes over each serving.

With pesto: Swirl some pestomega (see page 93) or a good shop-bought pesto into each dish of speltotto.

With Parmesan: Grate some Parmesan (or vegetarian alternative) over each serving.

With blue cheese: Crumble a few nuggets of tangy blue cheese into each dish before serving.

VARIATIONS

Courgette speltotto: Slice about 500g courgettes (instead of the squash). Heat 2 tbsp olive oil in a large pan over a medium heat and add the courgettes, 2 crushed or grated garlic cloves and some salt and pepper. Cook at a slow sizzle so that the courgettes soften but do not brown, stirring often as they become tender, to break them down into a rough purée. Stir this into the cooked spelt and finish with some grated Parmesan and fresh basil or parsley, or indeed any of the suggestions above.

Pea or bean and spinach speltotto: Bring a pan of water to the boil and add about 250g peas, broad beans or a combination of the two. Cook for a few minutes, then drain. Add to the hot cooked spelt with a few handfuls of baby leaf spinach and stir until the spinach wilts. Serve topped with pesto (or pestomega, page 93) or with diced fresh tomatoes dressed simply with olive oil and spooned over the speltotto.

Pasta 'pestomega', green beans and spuds

VgO

If you are one of the millions (I am) who love a bowl of pasta tossed with homemade pesto, then you are going to really enjoy this dish. Pasta with potatoes, green beans and pesto is a classic and comforting Italian combination, particularly associated with Liguria – I couldn't resist adding peas too, for extra green goodness. The delicious pesto is full of healthy oils, which is why I like to call it pestomega. The seaweed is optional, but adds a nice umami touch if you are leaving out the cheese (which will make this dish vegan).

SERVES 4

300g wholewheat pasta, such as penne

175g new potatoes, scrubbed and cut into thin wedges

150g frozen peas or petits pois

250g French beans, trimmed and halved

Sea salt and black pepper

'PESTOMEGA'

50g walnuts or pumpkin seeds, or a mix

50g hulled hemp seeds or sunflower seeds

1 small garlic clove, roughly chopped

50g flat-leaf parsley and/or basil leaves

50g Parmesan (or vegetarian alternative) or Cheddar, finely grated, or 10g dried seaweed flakes, rehydrated in water

Juice of ½ lemon, or to taste

Up to 150ml olive oil, hemp oil or virgin rapeseed oil, or a mix

TO SERVE

Finely grated Parmesan (or vegetarian alternative) or Cheddar (optional)

First make the pestomega. Lightly toast the nuts and seeds in a dry pan for a few minutes. Transfer to a food processor, add the garlic and process until chopped but still with some texture. Add the herb leaves, and grated cheese or seaweed, and blitz again to chop the leaves.

Add the lemon juice then begin trickling in the oil, pulsing the processor as you go. Stop blitzing when you have a loose but still pleasingly granular texture with flecks of the leaves still visible (i.e. before you have a green paste!). You can add more oil to loosen the pesto once you are happy with the texture. Taste and add salt, pepper and more lemon juice if you like. Set aside.

Bring a large pan of water to the boil and add salt. You're going to add the pasta first, then the spuds and lastly the peas and beans. So, note the cooking time of the pasta as it goes in, and add the new potatoes about 6–7 minutes before the pasta will be done, and the peas and beans about 3 minutes after that (i.e. for the final 3–4 minutes).

When the pasta and veg are tender, scoop out and reserve a mugful of the cooking water, then drain the pasta and veg and return to the hot pan. Add 3–4 tbsp of the pestomega and stir gently into the pasta and veg, trickling in a little of the hot pasta cooking water as you go, to help everything emulsify together. Taste and add salt and/or pepper if needed.

Serve straight away, piping hot with a further grinding of black pepper on top, and a sprinkling of cheese if you like.

The remaining pestomega can be stored in a sealed jar with a thin layer of oil over the surface to seal out the air. It will keep in the fridge for 2 weeks.

93

Spaghetti with clams and tomato sauce

This is inspired by the classic *spaghetti alle vongole*, where tender salty clams come together with pasta and tangy tomatoes. If you can get tarragon, the flavour is wonderful with the clams and tomato sauce; if not, flat-leaf parsley is also very good.

SERVES 4

1 quantity cooked tomato sauce (page 78)

1kg fresh live palourdes clams (or cockles or mussels)

300g wholewheat spaghetti or linguine

1 tbsp olive or vegetable oil, or butter, plus a dash of oil for the pasta

2 garlic cloves, chopped

A pinch of dried chilli flakes

100ml dry white wine

1 tbsp chopped tarragon (or parsley)

Sea salt and black pepper

Extra virgin olive oil, to finish

You'll need to wait until the tomato sauce is cooked before you cook the pasta and clams, as they don't take long. But you can prepare the shellfish while the sauce is cooking: put the clams (or cockles or mussels) in a colander and give them a good rinse, shaking them about a bit under cold running water. If you are using mussels, trim off any little wiry 'beards'. Discard any shellfish with broken or damaged shells, and any that are open and don't close when you tap them against the side of the sink.

When the tomato sauce is cooked, keep it hot. Bring a large pan of water to the boil, add salt and then the pasta. Cook until *al dente* (tender but firm to the bite).

Meanwhile, put the oil or butter, garlic and chilli in a large pan that has a tight-fitting lid. Over a medium heat, sizzle the garlic gently for a minute or two, then add the wine and bring to the boil. Add the clams (or cockles/mussels) and cover the pan tightly with the lid. Cook for 2–3 minutes, shaking once or twice. Lift the lid. If the shells are not all open, cover the pan and give them another minute. Tip the clams into a sieve over a bowl to catch the juices. Discard any that still aren't open at this stage.

Drain the spaghetti as soon as it is cooked and return to the hot pan with a dash of oil. If the tomato sauce isn't piping hot, give it a minute over a medium heat, then turn the heat off again. Pick around half of the clams out of their shells and stir them gently into the hot tomato sauce along with the tarragon (or parsley).

Add the clam cooking liquor to the sauce, pouring it in gently so you can stop before you get to any gritty bits at the bottom (if the shellfish have released a lot of liquor, which can happen with cockles, you don't need to add it all – taste as you go).

Serve the spaghetti in warmed large bowls. Spoon the clammy tomato sauce on top and arrange the remaining clams in shells on top as a garnish. Add a trickle of extra virgin oil and serve straight away.

94

Brown rice chicken biryani

A chicken biryani, where marinated chicken is layered in a pot with rice and a generous blend of fragrant spices, sealed and then baked to become something much more than the sum of its parts, is another much-loved manifestation of the spice, rice and chicken combination. One of the best versions thereof is to be found in the excellent book *Dishoom "From Bombay with Love"*, titled Chicken berry Britannia. This is my wholed-up homage to that recipe, with brown rice swapped in for white, a tin of chickpeas (I'm keen on the black ones) and extra toasted nuts.

SERVES 5–6

300g brown basmati rice

3 tbsp vegetable oil

1 large onion, halved and finely sliced

100g natural yoghurt, plus extra (optional) to serve

3cm piece of fresh ginger, finely grated

4 garlic cloves, finely grated

½– 1 tsp dried chilli flakes

Juice of ½ lime

2 tsp ground cumin

2 tsp garam masala

500g skinless, boneless chicken thighs, each cut into 4 pieces

A pinch of saffron threads

400g tin chickpeas, drained and rinsed, or 150g peas (defrosted if frozen)

20g butter

40g dried cranberries, raisins or sultanas

A handful (30g) of toasted flaked almonds (optional)

Sea salt and black pepper

Rinse the rice thoroughly and soak it in cold water to cover while you prepare the other ingredients.

Heat the oil in a small saucepan over a medium heat, add the sliced onion and fry for about 15 minutes until soft and golden. Scrape it out onto a small plate, along with the oil, and leave to cool completely. It's helpful to do this in advance if you can, because the onion needs to be completely cool before you add it to the yoghurt.

In a large bowl, combine the cold fried onion and its oil with the yoghurt, ginger, garlic, chilli flakes, lime juice, ground cumin, garam masala and 1 tsp salt. Stir in the chicken pieces, cover and leave in a cool place, or the fridge, to marinate while you prepare the saffron and rice.

Put the saffron into a small, dry frying pan and place over a low heat for a minute or so until the pan is hot, then take off the heat. When the pan has cooled, transfer the toasted saffron to a small bowl and crush it to a powder with a pestle or the end of a rolling pin, then add 1 tbsp boiling water and leave to infuse.

Bring a large pan of water to the boil and add salt. Drain and rinse the rice, then add to the boiling water. Bring to the boil and simmer for about 20 minutes, until the rice is almost done with just a bit of chalky bite left.

Drain the rice thoroughly, tip it into a bowl and add the chickpeas or peas. Toss to combine and set aside.

Preheat the oven to 200°C/180°C Fan/Gas 6.

Continued overleaf →

96

Put the chicken and its yoghurt marinade into a casserole pan – one that has a well-fitting lid and can go in the oven. Place over a moderate heat and cook gently for 5 minutes, stirring from time to time, to get the heat going into it. At the same time, melt the butter in a small pan.

Turn off the heat under the chicken pan. Tip the drained, part-cooked rice and peas/chickpeas on top of the chicken in a thick layer. Spoon the saffron and its soaking water over the rice. Dot over the dried cranberries, raisins or sultanas, and the flaked almonds if using. Finally, trickle over the melted butter.

Place a layer of foil over the pan and put the lid on to seal tightly. Put it back over a high heat for 2–3 minutes, then transfer to the oven to bake for 40 minutes.

Remove the pan from the oven and let the biryani stand for 10 minutes before taking the lid off and serving. You can bring it to the table in its dish or, if you're feeling brave, turn out the whole thing onto a warmed serving platter so the chicken sits on top. Either way, a little cool yoghurt is very nice alongside, but not essential.

VARIATION

Vg

Vegan biryani: This recipe works really well with mixed vegetables and plant-based yoghurt. Use the florets from ½ medium cauliflower, cut into bite-sized pieces, plus a large carrot and a medium potato, each peeled or scrubbed and chunkily chopped (combined veg weight about 700g). Prepare the onion marinade as for the main recipe but use coconut yoghurt. Add the veg to the marinade and set aside to marinate while you prepare the rice. Continue as above, trickling 20g melted coconut oil (rather than butter) over the biryani before it goes into the oven.

Green potato gnocchi

Don't make these lovely gnocchi with green potatoes! But do make them with lots of gorgeous greens – spinach, nettles, kale, or any combination thereof – *as well as* potatoes. These gnocchi are not just better for you than classic potato gnocchi (which can be quite leathery and heavy), they are also much more delicious – lighter, more tender and yielding.

SERVES 4

500g spinach, or about 350g kale, tough stalks removed, or well-washed nettle tips

500g floury potatoes, such as King Edward, peeled and cut into similar-sized chunks

150g fine plain wholemeal flour

50g ricotta or soft cheese (cream cheese)

50g Cheddar or Parmesan, finely grated

1 medium egg, lightly beaten

Sea salt and black pepper

TO SERVE

A knob of butter or trickle of olive oil

Cooked tomato sauce (page 78), pesto or pestomega (page 93)

A little chilli oil (optional)

A little extra grated Cheddar or Parmesan

Bring a large pan of water to the boil and drop in the spinach, kale leaves or nettle tips. Cook for 2 minutes, then drain thoroughly in a colander over a second saucepan to catch the water. Leave the greens until cool enough to handle then squeeze out all the moisture you can from them – you should end up with a fairly small, tight, squeezed-out green ball! Chop this finely.

Meanwhile, add the potatoes to the pan of greens' cooking water. Bring to the boil, lower the heat and simmer for about 10 minutes, until tender. Drain well.

Mash the potatoes (they can stay a little coarse – you don't need to reduce them to a smooth mash), then transfer to a bowl and leave to cool.

Add the chopped greens, flour, cheeses and beaten egg to the cooled mashed potatoes and season with plenty of salt and pepper. Mix thoroughly, then use your hands to bring the mix together into a firm dough. Knead this gently for a minute.

Now roll out the gnocchi dough on a clean surface into long sausages, about 2cm in diameter. Cut each one into 3cm lengths.

Bring a large pan of water to a simmer. Drop in about one-third of the gnocchi and cook for around 2–3 minutes. As they swell the gnocchi will rise to the top of the pan. When they have been at the surface for a minute or so, scoop them out with a slotted spoon or small sieve, letting them drain for a minute, then transfer to a lightly buttered or oiled warm dish; keep warm. Repeat to cook the rest, in another two batches.

Serve the gnocchi in warmed bowls with hot tomato sauce, pesto or my pestomega. Finish with a trickle of chilli oil if you like, and a scattering of grated cheese.

101

Venison ragu

It's great to include some wild meat in your repertoire, and venison makes a fantastic 'ragu' – a rich meat, veg and tomato sauce that is lovely with pasta. I like to serve this with homemade wild nettle pappardelle (see overleaf) but any wholewheat pasta is good.

SERVES 4–5

1 tbsp olive or vegetable oil

100g unsmoked streaky bacon, chopped, or bacon lardons

1kg diced venison shoulder

1 onion, finely chopped

2 celery stalks, finely chopped

2 carrots, scrubbed or peeled and chopped quite fine

2 garlic cloves, chopped

2 bay leaves

A few sprigs of thyme

150ml white wine

400g tin plum tomatoes, or about 500ml passata

500ml veg or meat stock

A dash of Worcestershire sauce (optional)

Sea salt and black pepper

TO SERVE

Pasta of your choice (see above)

Finely grated Parmesan or crumbled ricotta

Heat a large flameproof casserole over a medium heat and add the oil. Add the bacon and fry for a few minutes until golden. Scoop out the bacon onto a plate, leaving the fat in the pan.

Season the pieces of venison and add half of them to the casserole, frying on all sides to brown well. Remove the meat and add to the bacon. Repeat to colour the rest of the venison. Set aside.

Add the onion, celery, carrots, garlic and herbs to the casserole and sizzle for a few minutes, pushing the veg around to pick up any brown meaty bits on the base of the casserole. Turn down the heat and sweat the veg for 10 minutes until starting to soften. Pour in the wine and simmer until reduced by about two-thirds.

Return the bacon and meat to the pan, along with the tomatoes (crushing them first in your hands or with a fork) or passata, and the stock. The liquid should just cover the meat, so add a dash more water if it's needed. Bring to a low simmer, cover and cook very gently for about 1½ hours until the meat is tender.

Remove the venison from the casserole and set aside. Taste the sauce and add a dash of Worcestershire sauce if you like. If it isn't already deliciously rich, simmer uncovered for 15–20 minutes to reduce down and concentrate the flavour. Check the seasoning.

Meanwhile, cut the venison into smaller pieces with a knife and fork. Return the meat to the sauce and check the seasoning.

Serve on fresh nettle pasta or wholewheat linguine or spaghetti, with a dusting of Parmesan or a little crumbled ricotta... or both.

VARIATION

Rabbit and cider ragu: Use 1 rabbit, jointed, in place of the venison. Proceed as above, using 150ml dry cider instead of the wine. Once the rabbit is tender, lift the pieces out of the stew and take the meat off the bones before returning it to the pan. You can finish the ragu with 2 tbsp double cream or half-fat crème fraîche, if you like.

Fresh nettle pasta

If you're cooking for a special occasion, this homemade pasta, packed full of freshly foraged greens, is a fantastic thing to put on the table. (You could also use spinach in place of nettles.) Serve it with a ragu like the one on the previous page, or bolognese (page 81), or the mushroom filling from my cobbler (page 156), or a simple fresh or cooked tomato sauce (pages 108 and 78). It's also good left in larger sheets and cut to fit a homemade lasagne like the one on page 222. Whatever you choose, it's pretty much the epitome of good comfort.
Pictured overleaf

SERVES 4–6

300–400g nettle tops (or spinach)

250g fine plain wholemeal flour

250g pasta flour, plus extra to dust if needed

4 medium eggs, beaten

Salt

Wearing rubber gloves, wash the nettle tops thoroughly in cold water, picking out anything that isn't nettle.

Bring a large pan of water to the boil, add salt, then drop in the nettle tops and cook for 2–3 minutes. Drain and refresh the nettles in ice-cold water. Drain again and squeeze out the excess water into a bowl; keep this nettle water for now.

Put the wilted nettles into a food processor or blender and whiz to a relatively smooth purée. If the mixture seems thick, add a splash of the saved nettle water to help things along, but keep it to a minimum. You don't want a sloppy purée. Measure out 300g nettle purée.

Place the flours in a large bowl. Make a well in the centre and add the nettle purée and beaten eggs. Use a fork to slowly start to incorporate the flour, a little at a time, into the wet ingredients. When you have a soft dough, tip it out, along with any loose flour, onto a clean surface.

Knead the dough, stretching and folding it on your work surface for 8–10 minutes, until it is smooth and silky. If it seems too soft, dust the surface with more pasta flour. Wrap the dough and rest it in the fridge for 30–40 minutes.

Divide the dough into 4 pieces and shape each into a flattish rectangle in your hands. Now it's time to roll it out: you can do this using a rolling pin, which is hard work, but you'll get there – go as thin as you can.

It's easier, however, if you use a pasta machine. Take one rectangle and pass it through the machine on its thickest setting a couple of times. Fold the dough into three, as if folding a letter, and, still on the thickest setting, pass it through twice more (this gives the dough structure). Now, run the dough through all the settings on the machine, from thickest to thinnest (or second thinnest if it already looks very fine). Dust both sides of the pasta lightly with flour each time you roll.

Now lay the pasta sheets on a lightly floured large board and cut with a knife into long ribbons, about 1.5cm wide, to make the pappardelle. Hang the pasta ribbons over a clean broomstick, or the back of a chair, while you roll and cut the remaining dough.

To cook the pasta, bring a very large pan of water to the boil, and add salt. Drop in the ribbons of pappardelle and cook for 3–4 minutes, stirring once or twice, or until *al dente* (tender but firm to the bite). Drain well and serve straight away.

If you don't want to cook the pasta straight away, or it suits you to make it in advance, you can keep it semi-dried, in a sealed container in the fridge for a couple of days.

VARIATION

Plain half-wholemeal pasta: If you fancy a simple, plain homemade pasta – which is so good with tomato sauce or a lovely virgin olive oil, chilli and garlic – just leave out the nettle purée and add an extra egg instead (i.e. 1 egg per 100g flour). Mix and knead the dough, rest it in the fridge then roll and slice as above.

Pasta with fresh tomato sauce

In the summer when it's easy to find good fresh tomatoes – ideally grown locally or at least within the UK – it's great to use their special sweet-sharp deliciousness with cooked pasta. This recipe macerates the tomatoes for a little while so that their juices flow freely, before tossing them into piping hot pasta, which soaks those lovely juices right up. It's a gorgeous summer meal, and lovely to eat outside!

SERVES 4

500g cherry tomatoes or other flavourful tomatoes

2 garlic cloves, finely chopped or grated

3 tbsp extra virgin olive oil

A small bunch of basil, leaves roughly torn

300g wholewheat penne, or pasta shape of your choice

Sea salt and black pepper

Cut the cherry tomatoes into quarters (or eighths if they are larger ones, or rough dice if they are 'full size'). Put them into a large bowl with the garlic, olive oil, basil and some salt and pepper, and toss gently together.

Set the tomatoes aside to macerate for an hour (if you have time, if not they can just stand while you cook the pasta).

Bring a large pan of water to the boil, add salt and then the pasta. Cook until *al dente* (tender but firm to the bite), drain and return to the hot pan.

Tip the juicy, fragrant tomato mixture into the piping hot pasta and stir well. Serve straight away.

Stews, Hotpots and Curries

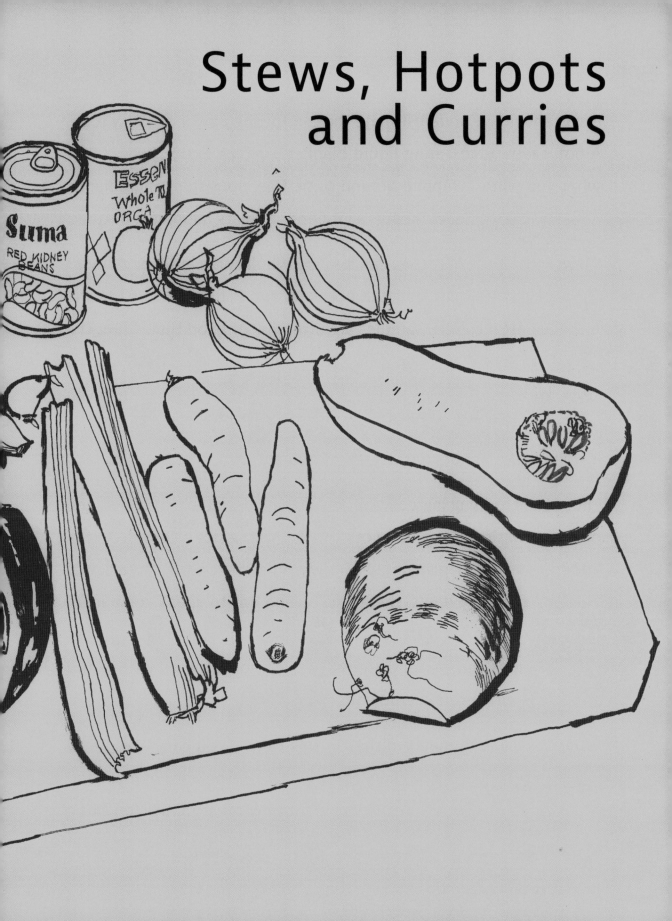

Never should we underestimate the comforting power of saucy food. A hot, savoury, cosseting liquid blanket – gravy, liquor, juice, call it what you will – wrapped around some fine, nourishing ingredients. It's a combination that presses a lot of our culinary happiness buttons.

Stews, hotpots and curries can be very wholesome indeed: many of the classics, like dhals, vegetarian curries and fish stews, already are. And the best meatier examples are often full of good things too. The sauce in these dishes may be boosted by liquids with intrinsic qualities: stock, wine, milk, coconut cream, sieved tomatoes and more. But even water can become a magical sauce when it takes on the flavours of a well-chosen set of characterful ingredients.

Those transforming ingredients will certainly include vegetables, and often aromatic herbs and spices too. Some classics also include the added comfort of pleasingly pillowy pulses – and if the original versions generally don't, there's no reason not to sneak them in. In short, the 'standards' of the genre are ready and waiting for tweaks and upgrades that extend the variety of good things within and increase their all-round wholeness.

When it comes to meaty dishes in this canon, you can take pretty much any existing family favourite and shift the balance of meat and veg within it. That's what I've done with my meaty Chilli con carne (page 114), Baked green chicken curry (page 124) and Beef and ale stew (page 136). There's so much richness in these dishes that a bit less meat and a bit more veg improves them.

If it's a vegetarian curry or hotpot you're after, I've increased the diversity of the ingredients in some of my favourites, adding more veg, as well as beans or lentils. It's important to realise that's it not just the amount of fruit and veg in our diet that matters, but the variety. We need a diversity to support a range of good bacteria in our gut – and here are great recipes to help deliver it.

Choosing what to serve *with* these stewy, saucy classics can also help you achieve that diversity and make them better for you. It's traditional to serve curries and chillies with white rice and puffy naan bread, and stews with lots of mash. Undeniably pleasing, yes, but really not necessary. Switch your carby accompaniments to wholer and higher fibre options – wholewheat pasta, brown rice, skin-on mash, a whole baked spud – and you'll be doing your body a favour without short-changing your taste buds. These wholer carbs tend to satisfy more even when you serve up less, which also works in your favour.

And don't forget the power of a final flourish or a bit on the side. This could be as simple as a fresh green salad, but might also be a refreshing raita or a scattering of toasted nuts or seeds. Such finishing touches up the interest as well as your veg count, enhancing both the goodness and pleasure of a dish.

Chunky chilli con carne

My beef chillies have been getting chunkier and veggier in recent years. This is my veggiest yet – and it still hits the 'comfort' spot so well. I particularly like the addition of swede, the brassica root which gives a pleasingly peppery savoury tone. But if you are not convinced, you can swap with parsnip...

SERVES 6–8

Olive or vegetable oil, for frying

200g free-range pork belly, pancetta or thick streaky bacon, sliced or cubed

800g chuck or stewing steak, in generous cubes

150ml red wine (optional)

2 medium onions, sliced

4 medium carrots, scrubbed or peeled, halved and sliced

About 300g swede (or 1 large parsnip), peeled and cubed

3 celery sticks, sliced

4 garlic cloves, finely chopped

1 tsp dried chilli flakes

2 tsp cumin seeds (or 1 tsp ground)

2 tsp coriander seeds (or 1 tsp ground)

1 tsp smoked paprika

1 red chilli, sliced (optional)

3–4 sprigs of thyme (optional)

400g tin plum tomatoes

About 700ml hot beef, chicken or vegetable stock

1 large sweet potato, or 400g squash, peeled and cubed

2 x 400g tins kidney beans, drained and rinsed

Sea salt and black pepper

Set a large heavy-based frying pan over a high heat and add a dash of oil. When hot, add the pork or bacon, with some salt and pepper. Cook briskly for several minutes, turning the meat from time to time, until browned all over. Transfer to a large flameproof casserole dish.

Repeat the browning process with the beef, doing it in two batches so as not to overcrowd the pan, seasoning it as you go and adding a dash more oil to the pan if necessary. Don't be shy of burning the meat a little bit – it enhances the flavour of the sauce.

When all the meat is browned and transferred to the casserole, reduce the heat under the frying pan to low and pour in the wine (or 150ml of the hot stock). It will bubble and hiss. Cook for a minute or so, stirring and scraping the pan with a spatula to release all the caramelised meaty bits from the base of the pan. Take off the heat and set aside.

Add the onions, carrots, swede (or parsnip), celery, garlic and chilli flakes to the casserole with the browned meat. Then add the spices, fresh chilli and/or thyme if using, a pinch of salt and some pepper. Cook over a medium heat, stirring often, for 8–10 minutes to soften the veg.

Tip the liquid from the frying pan over the meat. Add the tomatoes and hot stock; if that isn't enough to cover everything, add a little more stock or boiling water. Bring to a low simmer, cover and cook very gently for 1½ hours or until the meat is becoming tender.

Add the sweet potato or squash and the kidney beans, with a little more stock or water if needed, and cook for a further 30 minutes or so. Check that all the meat and veg are nice and tender, tweak the seasoning, and the chilli is ready to serve.

There are all sorts of options for accompaniments: a bit of brown rice, perhaps, or a baked potato, or some good bread, along with a fresh green salad and/or a bowl of guacamole (see page 177).

114

Porotos granados

This lovely Chilean bean, corn and squash stew proved one of the most popular recipes in *River Cottage Veg Everyday*. I've enjoyed playing with the dish since then, adding creamy beans, fresh tomatoes and basil (included in some Chilean versions), along with not-so-traditional celery, which adds a savoury note. I also ring the changes with courgettes in place of the squash. You can use whichever you prefer, or go half and half. It's an easy dish... and very more-ish.

SERVES 6

About 500g small–medium courgettes or peeled, deseeded squash, such as butternut, Crown Prince or onion squash

2 tbsp vegetable or olive oil

1 medium onion, sliced

2 celery sticks, sliced

2 garlic cloves, chopped

2 tsp sweet smoked paprika

A handful of oregano leaves, roughly chopped (or you can use thyme)

1 litre vegetable stock

1 bay leaf

200g green beans, trimmed and cut into 2cm pieces

400g tin beans, such as kidney, borlotti or butter beans, drained and rinsed

About 200g sweetcorn kernels (you should get this from 2 medium cobs, but frozen is also fine)

300g tomatoes, roughly chopped

6–8 basil leaves, torn

Sea salt and black pepper

Dried chilli flakes, to finish (optional)

If using courgettes, cut them into 1cm slices (first quartering them lengthways if they are very large). If you're using squash, cut it into 2cm chunks.

Heat the oil in a large saucepan or flameproof casserole over a medium heat. Add the onion, celery and garlic and sauté gently for 10–12 minutes. Add the paprika and chopped oregano (or thyme). Cook, stirring, for another minute.

Add the squash and/or courgettes, vegetable stock and bay leaf and bring to a simmer. Cook for 10–15 minutes until all the veg are almost tender.

Add the green beans, tinned beans, sweetcorn and tomatoes and simmer for 5 minutes or until all the veg are tender. Stir in the basil and season to taste with salt and pepper.

Serve the stew in warmed bowls, adding a pinch of chilli flakes for those who like a bit of heat.

117

Big roasted veg chilli

This is a wonderful chunky veg chill, which gets a great boost in flavour from the roasting of the veg. The zesty, herby, limey green yoghurt (see below) is a delicious contrast.

SERVES 6

1 large onion, chunkily chopped

1 large or 2 medium carrots, scrubbed or peeled and chunkily chopped

3 celery sticks, finely sliced

2 red, yellow or orange peppers, deseeded and sliced

1 garlic bulb, halved through the equator

2 bay leaves

2 medium-hot red chillies, sliced (deseeded for less heat if you prefer)

1 tsp cumin seeds

1 tsp dried oregano

½ tsp dried chilli flakes or to taste, plus extra to finish

2 tbsp olive or rapeseed oil

1 tsp cocoa or cacao powder

50ml strong black coffee

300ml tomato passata

400ml vegetable stock

150ml red wine

2 x 400g tins black beans or kidney beans, drained and rinsed

400g tin lentils, drained, or 250g cooked Puy or brown lentils

200g kale, cavolo nero or spring greens, tough stalks removed, shredded

Sea salt and black pepper

Preheat the oven to 180°C/160°C Fan/Gas 4.

Put the onion, carrots, celery, peppers, garlic, bay leaves and chillies into your largest roasting dish. Scatter over the cumin seeds, oregano, chilli flakes and a generous seasoning of salt and pepper. Trickle over the oil and toss everything together well. Roast in the oven for 30 minutes.

Add the cocoa/cacao powder, coffee, passata, veg stock, wine, beans and lentils and give everything a really good stir. Return to the oven for 30 minutes or so, until thick and bubbling. Stir in the shredded greens and cook in the oven for a further 10 minutes.

Taste and add more salt and pepper if needed, and more chilli flakes if you'd like it to be spicier.

Divide the chilli between warmed bowls, squeezing the soft garlic out of the skins and sharing it between servings. Serve the chilli as it is, or with a bowl of green yoghurt and wholemeal bread or pitta on the side.

VARIATIONS

You can add other roots to this: around 250g peeled and diced swede, celeriac, squash or sweet potato all work well. Put these into the tray at the beginning of roasting, with the other veg. There's no need to decrease the other ingredients, but you might need to stir in a little more hot stock at the end to keep things nice and saucy.

SIDE OPTION

Green yoghurt: Put 200g natural yoghurt (dairy or plant-based) into a blender with a finely sliced spring onion or a few chives, the grated zest of ½ lime and a squeeze of lime juice. Add the chopped leaves from a small bunch of coriander and some salt and pepper and blitz until blended. Alternatively, for a chunkier finish, you can just stir the ingredients together.

118

Cauli curry with spuds and cashews

We should all have a quick and easy, super-tasty, nice and saucy, veg-based curry in our repertoire, and this is one of my favourites. The cauli aside, it's largely made from store-cupboard staples. Using whole cumin and curry leaves, ground coriander, turmeric and garam masala is great, but if you want to switch in a couple of tablespoonfuls of curry powder or paste for these, that's fine – add to the onion, ginger and garlic while they are sweating.

SERVES 6

3 tbsp vegetable oil

2 tsp cumin seeds

6–8 curry leaves (optional)

1 large onion, chopped

2–3 garlic cloves, grated or crushed

5cm piece of fresh ginger, grated

1 tbsp grated fresh turmeric (or 1 tsp dried turmeric)

2 tsp ground coriander

2 tsp garam masala

½ tsp dried chilli flakes, or to taste

500g waxy or new potatoes, cut into 2cm cubes (no need to peel)

500ml hot vegetable stock

300ml tomato passata or cooked tomato sauce (see page 78)

500g cauliflower (1 small one or ½ large one), tougher parts of the stalk removed, cut into small bite-sized pieces

150g cashew nuts

250g frozen peas

Sea salt and black pepper

Heat the oven to 180°C/160°C Fan/Gas 4.

Heat the oil in a large pan or flameproof casserole over a medium-low heat. Add the cumin seeds, and curry leaves if using, and let them sizzle for a couple of minutes, keeping a close eye on the cumin so it doesn't burn.

Add the chopped onion with a good pinch of salt, increase the heat a little and cook for 8–10 minutes, until the onion is softening. Stir in the garlic, ginger and fresh turmeric if using, and cook for another minute. Add the ground coriander, garam masala, ground turmeric if using, and chilli flakes. Cook for another couple of minutes, stirring often.

Now add the potatoes and the hot stock to the pan, bring to a simmer and cook for 5 minutes, to get the potatoes on their way. Then stir in the tomato passata or sauce and the cauliflower. Season with a little more salt and some pepper. Bring to the boil, turn the heat down low, cover and simmer for about 10 minutes until the cauli is just tender but not too soft.

Meanwhile, scatter the cashew nuts on a baking tray and toast in the oven for 5–7 minutes.

When the veg are tender, stir in the peas and cook for 2 minutes, then stir through the toasted cashews. Taste for seasoning, adding more salt and pepper if needed.

Serve the curry with some brown rice. I like to serve a bowl of raita (see page 63 or 174) on the side too.

Baked green chicken curry

This is a deeply flavourful, richly saucy chicken curry. I like to use the greens on the side almost like pasta ribbons to pick up the sauce.

SERVES 6

1 chicken, jointed into 6 pieces, or 6 skin-on, bone-in chicken pieces

A little vegetable oil

3 shallots (or 1 medium onion), roughly chopped

400g tin coconut milk

300ml hot chicken stock

About 400g spring greens, roughly shredded

Sea salt and black pepper

GREEN CURRY PASTE

6 garlic cloves, peeled

4 small hot chillies, roughly chopped

About 30g fresh ginger, roughly chopped

2 lemongrass stems, tough outer layers removed and reserved, sliced

A 50g bunch of coriander, chopped, stalks and all

2 tsp cumin seeds

2 tsp coriander seeds

1 tsp ground turmeric

Finely grated zest and juice of 1 lime

2 tbsp fish sauce

1 tbsp soft brown sugar

TO FINISH AND SERVE

Coriander leaves

Lime wedges

Preheat the oven to 200°C/180°C Fan/Gas 6. Set the chicken breast pieces aside for now. Put the thigh and leg pieces, skin side up, into a large roasting tin or oven dish and season the skin. Bake in the oven for about 40 minutes until golden, while you make the curry paste and get the sauce started.

To make the curry paste, put all the ingredients into a blender and blitz to a pungent green paste. You will probably need to stop several times to scrape down the sides. The paste should be well amalgamated but doesn't need to be perfectly smooth – in fact, it's quite nice if it isn't!

Pour a trickle of oil into a large, wide frying pan and add the shallots (or onion). Fry, stirring often, for a few minutes. Scrape the curry paste into the pan and fry it with the shallots for about 3 minutes. Then add the coconut milk and chicken stock. Toss in the reserved lengths of lemongrass too. Stir well, bring to a simmer and cook for about 10 minutes.

Take the sizzling chicken leg and thigh pieces out of the oven. Pour the sauce (including the lemongrass) into the roasting tin or dish, surrounding the chicken pieces but not completely covering them (there's a lot of sauce, don't worry). Return to the oven and turn the setting down to 170°C/150°C Fan/Gas 3.

Wipe out the frying pan and return to a medium heat. Season the skin of the chicken breast pieces and put them, skin side down, into the pan. Cook for 3–5 minutes, until the skin is nicely coloured.

Take the dish from the oven and add the chicken breasts, skin side up. Return to the oven for 20 minutes, or until the chicken breasts are cooked through.

While the chicken is finishing, cook the greens. Bring a large pan of water to the boil, add salt then drop in the shredded greens. Cook for about 4 minutes, until tender; drain well.

Serve up the chicken in its spicy sauce with the greens on the side, and some brown rice if you like. Add a scattering of coriander and serve with lime wedges for squeezing over the curry.

124

Vegged-up dhal

A simple red lentil dhal is one of the most comforting foods there is and hard to improve on. But I do like elevating it from side to supper sometimes, with added vegetables and tomatoes to ramp up the variety and goodness. It's a store-cupboard, fridge-friendly affair that can accommodate a few omissions and tweaks. So, if you're missing the celery or there's no turmeric to hand, or you have a few greens you want to add, feel free to free-wheel. You'll still be cooking up a delicious, warming and well-balanced dish.

SERVES 4

TOMATO SAUCE

1 tbsp vegetable oil

1 onion, finely chopped

1 medium carrot, scrubbed or peeled and finely chopped

1–2 tender inner celery sticks, finely chopped

A pinch of dried chilli flakes

400g tin plum tomatoes

Sea salt and black pepper

DHAL

2 tbsp vegetable oil

1 tsp coriander seeds

1 tsp cumin seeds

1 bay leaf (optional)

2 garlic cloves, grated or crushed

3–4cm piece of fresh ginger, grated

3–4cm piece of fresh turmeric, grated, or 1 tsp ground (optional)

200g red lentils, well rinsed

650ml light vegetable stock (or water)

For the tomato sauce, heat the oil in a large saucepan over a medium heat. Add the onion, carrot and celery, the chilli flakes, a pinch of salt and some pepper. When all the veg are sizzling nicely, turn down the heat, cover the pan and let the veg sweat for 10 minutes or so, stirring every now and then, until they are starting to soften.

Add the tomatoes, crushing them in the pan with a fork, and cook, uncovered, for about 15 minutes, stirring occasionally, until pulpy and saucy.

Meanwhile, for the dhal, heat the oil in a second large saucepan over a medium-low heat. Add the coriander and cumin seeds, and the bay leaf if you have one, and fry briefly until they start to sizzle and pop. Add the garlic and ginger, and turmeric if using, and fry gently, stirring, for a minute.

Add the rinsed lentils, pour in the veg stock or water and bring to a simmer. Cook, uncovered, for 20–25 minutes until the lentils are soft and broken down, and the dhal is thick, stirring often to stop it sticking and burning, and to encourage the lentils to break down.

Combine the pulpy tomato sauce and the dhal in one of the pans – it doesn't matter which one. Stir well and cook very gently for a further 5 minutes to amalgamate. Leave to stand for 10 minutes or so. You can stir in a little hot water to loosen the dhal if you like. Taste and add more salt and pepper if needed.

Serve the dhal with brown rice, raita (see page 63 or 174) and, if you like, a salady salsa of sliced cherry tomatoes, a little thinly sliced onion and some torn coriander leaves.

126

Fish stew

This tomatoey fish stew has lots of lovely flavours going on, and plenty of veg and pulses with the saucy fish and shellfish. I use either celeriac or fennel, depending on what's in season. A finishing sprinkle of chopped preserved lemon is nice, but by no means essential.

SERVES 6

2 tbsp olive oil

1 large onion, thinly sliced

2 large or 3 medium fennel bulbs, cut into 1cm slices or wedges, or 250g peeled celeriac, chopped quite small

1 tsp fennel seeds

2 garlic cloves, sliced

1 tbsp harissa, or to taste

200ml dry white wine (plus an extra 2 tbsp if you're cooking mussels or clams)

300ml tomato passata

400g tin chickpeas, drained and rinsed

500ml fish stock

200g sustainably sourced prawns, or cleaned squid with tentacles (pouches sliced into rings), or 500g rinsed and de-bearded mussels or clams

500g sustainably caught white fish fillets, such as pollack, haddock or coley, skinned and cut into large bite-sized chunks

A pinch of dried chilli flakes (optional)

Sea salt and black pepper

TO FINISH

1 preserved lemon, chopped (optional)

1 tbsp chopped parsley (optional)

Heat the olive oil in a large saucepan or flameproof casserole over a medium heat. Add the onion and fennel or celeriac, with a good pinch of salt and some pepper. Stir well then add the fennel seeds, stir again, cover and reduce the heat. Let the veg sweat for up to 15 minutes, until the onion and fennel are nice and soft (the celeriac may not be quite there yet).

Add the garlic and harissa and cook for a couple of minutes then pour in the wine and bring to a simmer. Cook for a few minutes or until the wine is reduced by about half.

Add the tomato passata and simmer briskly for 5 minutes to reduce a little. Then add the chickpeas and pour in the fish stock. Bring to a simmer again and cook, uncovered, for 5–10 minutes.

If using mussels or clams, cook them now: put 2 tbsp each of wine and water into a large, wide pan that has a tight-fitting lid and bring to the boil over a medium-high heat. Add the mussels or clams and put the lid on. Cook for 2–3 minutes, shaking the pan once or twice. Lift the lid. The shells should all be open; if not, cover the pan and give them another minute. Discard any that do not open after this.

Check the stew, making sure the celeriac, if used, is now tender. Add the white fish, and the prawns or squid if using. Bring back to a gentle simmer and cook for just 3 minutes. Take off the heat. If using clams or mussels, add them now, scooping them out of their pan with a slotted spoon, then carefully pouring in their cooking juices so that any gritty residue is left behind in the pan.

Stir the stew again, then taste to check the seasoning and add a little more salt and/or pepper if needed. You might want a touch more harissa at this point, or a pinch of chilli flakes for an extra kick of heat.

Finish, if you like, with diced preserved lemon and/or chopped parsley. Ladle the stew into warmed bowls. I like to serve warm wholemeal pitta bread on the side – it's great for dipping.

129

Lamb tagine with apricots

This is a gorgeous tagine, wonderfully simple but rich and well flavoured, with a natural sweetness coming from the dried apricots. I prefer not to serve it with a mountain of white couscous, but with a more modest portion of cracked bulgur wheat or wholewheat couscous. It's also lovely with nutty brown rice. If you have a jar of good harissa to hand, a dab on the side goes well too.

SERVES 6

1 tsp coriander seeds

1 tsp cumin seeds

2 tbsp olive or vegetable oil

1 large onion, roughly chopped

1 large leek, trimmed and sliced (or use another onion)

2 medium carrots, scrubbed or peeled and thickly sliced

A large pinch of dried chilli flakes

1 tsp ground turmeric

3–4cm piece of fresh ginger, grated

2 garlic cloves, crushed or grated

2 tbsp tomato purée

About 750g trimmed lamb neck fillet or lamb shoulder, in large bite-sized chunks

400g tin chickpeas, drained and rinsed

200g unsulphured dried apricots

Sea salt and black pepper

Heat a dry frying pan over a medium heat. Add the coriander and cumin seeds and toast them gently for a few minutes until fragrant. Tip into a mortar (or just a sturdy bowl) and crush with the pestle or the end of a rolling pin.

Heat the oil in a large flameproof casserole or small stockpot over a medium heat. Add the onion(s), leek if using, and carrots with some salt and pepper and sauté for about 10 minutes, stirring a few times, until starting to soften.

Add the ground cumin and coriander, the chilli flakes, turmeric, ginger and garlic and stir thoroughly to mix with the veg, then stir in the tomato purée.

Add the lamb and stir it over the heat for a minute to coat with the spices. Add the chickpeas and some more salt and pepper. Then pour in enough water to just cover everything (around 500ml) and bring to a simmer.

Cover the pan and leave the tagine to cook for an hour, giving it a stir every now and then. Test the lamb – if it's nearly tender, you can add the dried apricots now. If the lamb seems tough, cook for another 30 minutes. Repeat if necessary – this really depends on the lamb you have!

Once the lamb is yielding and the apricots are in, return to a simmer and cook for about 20 minutes or until the apricots look moist and juicy.

Taste to check the seasoning and add more salt and pepper if needed. You can also add more chilli if you fancy a little more heat. Serve with cracked bulgur wheat, wholewheat couscous or brown rice, with a dot of harissa on the side if you like.

130

Spicy pork belly and butter bean hotpot

This aromatic one-pot wonder offers up a big bowlful of savoury, spicy richness. Along with the yielding pork belly and some sensational seasonings, it's packed with pulses and veg: butter beans, carrots and other roots, greens and spring onions. It'll warm every last cockle.

SERVES 4

750g pork belly

2 tsp vegetable oil

5cm piece of fresh ginger, cut into thin batons or slices

4 garlic cloves, finely slivered

2 hot red or green chillies, finely sliced (deseeded for less heat if you prefer)

50ml tamari or soy sauce

400ml hot chicken or vegetable stock

250ml cloudy apple juice (not from concentrate)

1 whole star anise

200g carrots, scrubbed or peeled and cut into 5mm thick slices on the diagonal

200g radishes, halved, or daikon (mooli), cut into thin quarter-moons, or baby turnips, thinly sliced

2 large pak choi or 2 Little Gem lettuce, or a bunch of choi sum or mustard greens

2 x 400g tins butter beans, drained and rinsed

A bunch of spring onions, finely sliced

2 tbsp rice wine vinegar or cider vinegar

Sea salt and black pepper

Dried chilli flakes, to finish (optional)

Cut the pork belly into roughly 3–4cm cubes and season them with salt and pepper. Heat the oil in a large flameproof casserole over a medium heat. Add the cubes of pork belly and brown them well all over – for at least 10 minutes, turning often. If you don't have a wide casserole pan, do this in two batches before returning all the pork to the pan.

Add the ginger, garlic and chillies to the pan and fry them with the pork for a minute or two. Combine the tamari/soy, stock and apple juice and pour into the pan, stirring and scraping to release any caramelised bits from the base of the pan. Add the star anise.

Bring to a simmer, partially cover the casserole pan with the lid and leave the hotpot to simmer very gently for about 1 hour. Add the carrots and radishes or turnips and simmer for another 10–15 minutes or so until just tender.

In the meantime, slice the pak choi or lettuce lengthways into sixths or roughly slice the choi sum or mustard greens. Add to the hotpot with the butter beans, spring onions and vinegar. Cook for another few minutes until the greens are wilted. Take the casserole off the heat.

Taste the hotpot – you want a nice balance of hot and sour, so adjust with some dried chilli or some more vinegar if needed. Ladle into warmed bowls and serve.

133

Cowboy bangers and beans

To justify the billing, this dish should be made in a cast-iron crock over an open fire. But the domesticated version is always a winner too! It makes a great family supper and scales up easily as a party dish. A crunchy coleslaw (see below) is a great accompaniment and a hunk of wholemeal bread for mopping up will be welcomed too.

SERVES 6

1 tbsp olive or vegetable oil

6 well-seasoned butcher's sausages

1 large or 2 medium onions, sliced

1 medium-hot red or green chilli, chopped (deseeded for less heat if you prefer), or a pinch of dried chilli flakes

1 large or 2 medium carrots, scrubbed or peeled and chunkily chopped on the diagonal

3 celery sticks, chunkily sliced

About 250g peeled and deseeded squash, or sweet potato, chunkily chopped

About 700g tomato passata

2 tbsp English mustard

1 tbsp molasses (or soft dark brown sugar)

1 tbsp cocoa or cacao powder

2 tsp sweet smoked paprika

1 garlic bulb, halved through the equator

2 bay leaves

1 sprig of thyme (optional)

2 x 400g tins kidney, borlotti or butter beans, drained and rinsed

Sea salt and black pepper

Heat the oil in a large flameproof casserole over a medium heat. Add the sausages and cook for 5–10 minutes, turning a few times, so that they take on some nice brown colour and firm up. Then use tongs in one hand and kitchen scissors in the other to pick up each sausage, snip it into 3 or 4 pieces and drop it back into the pan.

Add the onion(s), chilli, carrot(s), celery and the squash or sweet potato. Cook for a further 10 minutes, stirring often, to start softening the vegetables.

Add the passata, mustard, molasses (or brown sugar), cocoa or cacao, paprika, garlic, bay, thyme if using, some salt and pepper and the tinned beans. Pour on enough water to just cover everything, stir well and bring to a simmer.

Now reduce the heat, cover and cook for 30–40 minutes, or until the veg are tender. (While the stew is cooking, prepare the coleslaw, if serving.)

Taste the beans and add more salt and pepper if needed, then serve up, with a portion of coleslaw, if serving, on the side.

SIDE OPTION

Red cabbage slaw: Using a mandoline or a food processor (or just a sharp knife), finely shred ¼ large red cabbage and tip into a large bowl. Scrub or peel and coarsely grate 1 small–medium carrot and add to the cabbage with 4–6 finely sliced spring onions. Add 100g soured cream (or 50g each of natural yoghurt and mayonnaise), 1 tsp ground coriander (if you fancy) and some salt and pepper. Mix thoroughly, adding a little olive oil (1 tbsp or so) to loosen it as you go, then it's ready to serve.

Beef and ale stew with rooty dumplings

Here's a one-pot dish that's big on beefy flavour, but also big on veg. The herby root-veg dumplings are a lovely idea from my long-time collaborator Nikki Duffy. They up the comfort factor considerably.

SERVES 6

2 tbsp vegetable or olive oil

500g shallots or small onions, peeled but left whole (or halved if larger)

200g swede, celeriac or turnip, peeled and chunkily chopped

200g parsnip or carrot, scrubbed or peeled and chunkily chopped

750g chuck or stewing steak, trimmed and cut into generous chunks

500g chestnut or open-cap mushrooms, thickly sliced

500ml ale

500ml hot stock (meat or veg)

2 bay leaves

A sprig of thyme

Sea salt and black pepper

ROOTY, HERBY DUMPLINGS

150g fine plain wholemeal flour (or half white and half wholemeal flour)

1 rounded tsp baking powder

30g cold butter, grated or diced

1 small–medium carrot, about 100g (or use 100g of any of the other roots in the stew), grated

2 tbsp chopped chives and/or parsley

Heat 1 tbsp oil in a large flameproof casserole over a medium-high heat. Add the shallots and root veg and sauté briskly for about 10 minutes, or until they take on some good golden-brown colour. Scoop the veg out of the casserole and set aside in a large bowl.

Add a little more oil to the casserole. Add half the beef, season it well and fry until well browned all over – this is really important for creating flavour. Add the browned beef to the veg in the bowl. Repeat with the second lot of beef, adding it to the bowl too.

Now put half the mushrooms into the casserole, with a trickle more oil if necessary, and increase the heat a little. Fry, stirring, for a few minutes, until the mushrooms are coloured and have released their liquid, which will help to deglaze the casserole. Add to the bowl. Repeat with the second lot of mushrooms.

Pour in the ale, let it bubble for a few minutes, then return the beef, veg and any juices to the casserole. Pour on the hot stock, add the bay and thyme and bring to a simmer. Half-cover with the lid and reduce the heat to low. Simmer gently for about 1 hour.

Shortly before the hour is up, make the dumplings. Put the flour and baking powder into a bowl or a food processor and season well with salt and pepper. Add the butter and either rub into the flour with your fingers or pulse in the processor, until it resembles fine crumbs. Tip into a large bowl if it isn't already, then add the grated carrot/other root and chives or parsley and stir together.

Now add just enough cold water (about 2 tbsp) to lightly bring the mix together and form a firm, slightly sticky dough. With wet hands and a light touch, form it into 12 small dumplings. Don't overwork the dough or your dumplings may be dense.

Space the dumplings evenly apart on top of the stew. Cover with the lid and simmer very gently for a further 25 minutes or until the dumplings are puffed up and cooked through (test one with a skewer). To ensure they are juicy, baste or turn the dumplings 5 minutes before the end of cooking. I like to serve up some wilted greens or purple sprouting broccoli alongside.

136

Pies
and
Tarts

A steamy-centred savoury pie – with a little of the saucy middle trickling out from under the crispy golden pastry lid, perhaps – is a fine thing to put on the table. Lovely to look at and promising deep satisfaction, it speaks of comfort like few other dishes.

It's unfortunate, and unfair, that 'pie' has become a catch-all term for unhealthy food – after all, no one actually ate all the pies. Eating well certainly doesn't mean saying goodbye to pastry and the many good things we can wrap it around. But it might mean tweaking tradition a bit.

I'm going to start this chapter by adjusting that pie-defining pastry, dialling down the white flour and dialling up my much-favoured fine plain wholemeal. Now, you can make a 100 per cent wholemeal pastry, but for me you lose out a little too much in the ethereal texture department. A half white/half wholemeal mix of flour, however, delivers an excellent pastry, or rather two excellent pastries, as it works equally brilliantly for shortcrust and rough puff. You get goodness and fibre and a lovely tawny colour, while still retaining the authentically pleasing friable (shortcrust) or flaky (rough puff) texture.

With these two fail-safe half-wholemeal pastry recipes (on pages 143 and 144) up your sleeve, any pie, tart or pasty can be brought into the fold, and this genre of comfort food becomes a much healthier proposition. And that's before you pile up your pie filling with the extra veg (and sometimes fruit) on which you can really go to town. Note the lavish amount of leek in my chicken pie on page 152; the vibrant greens among the sweet and silky alliums in my otherwise pretty classic onion tart on page 148; the prunes and apples in my sausage rolls on page 146... you get the idea.

Not every pie has pastry, of course: the luscious fish pie on page 160 is topped with a chunky-textured mash of skin-on potatoes and butter beans, while my shepherd's pie on page 162 is crowned with an equally delicious celeriac and potato mash. And the rich mushroom cobbler (page 156) has a simple, dairy- and egg-free scone topping that keeps the whole thing vegan-friendly (though you can switch to buttery wholemeal rough puff pastry for this dish, if you prefer).

I've popped a pizza recipe into this chapter too (see page 167), once again showcasing the 50:50 wholemeal blend, this time in an easy one-rise dough, alongside a range of toppings that includes crispy kale for green goodness.

So really, there's no need to banish or demonise this crusted and trusted band of family favourites, when you can simply make them better than ever.

Half-wholemeal shortcrust pastry

This is a brilliant all-round short-textured pastry for tart cases and pie crusts, which can be tweaked from savoury to sweet with the addition of a little sugar.

MAKES ENOUGH FOR A 24CM TART CASE

125g fine plain wholemeal flour

125g plain white flour

A pinch of salt

125g chilled butter, cubed or coarsely grated

1 medium egg, beaten

Combine the two flours with the salt in a large bowl, or the bowl of a food processor. Add the cold butter and either rub in with your fingertips, or by pulsing in the processor, until the mixture resembles fine crumbs. Add the beaten egg gradually – either to the bowl, working it in with a table knife, or trickling it into the processor while it's running. Add a little cold water too, just enough to bring the pastry together into large clumps; don't overwork it.

Tip the pastry onto a floured surface and use your hands to bring it together, then knead it briefly into a ball. Flatten the ball into a thick slab. Wrap and chill in the fridge for at least 30 minutes, ideally an hour or two, before using. It will keep for 48 hours.

If you are making a tart that requires blind baking, preheat the oven to 180°C/160°C Fan/Gas 4. Roll out the pastry on a floured surface, as thinly as you comfortably can, turning once or twice and dusting with a little more flour. Use it to line a 24cm loose-based tart tin. If there are any cracks or it doesn't completely cover part of the tin's side, you can tear off some of the 'overhang' and patch it up. Leave the remaining excess pastry overhanging the edges of the tart tin (this helps to stop the pastry shrinking).

Place the tart tin on a baking tray. Prick the pastry in a few places with a fork. Line the pastry with baking paper or foil, then add a layer of baking beans or dried beans, lentils or rice. Bake for 15 minutes, then remove the paper or foil and beans and return the pastry to the oven for 5–10 minutes until it looks dry and cooked and is just starting to colour in places.

Leave the pastry case to cool a little, then with a small sharp knife, trim off the overhanging pastry (chef's perks!). You can do all this up to 24 hours in advance of making the filling.

> **VARIATION**
> **Sweet half-wholemeal shortcrust pastry:** Simply add 20g golden caster or soft light brown sugar to the flours at the beginning and stir in well before rubbing in the butter.

Half-wholemeal rough puff pastry

You can certainly use my half-wholemeal shortcrust pastry on the previous page as an all-round savoury pastry, but this lovely 'laminated' rough puff has a great flaky texture that is just perfect for savoury pie crusts, pasties and sausage rolls.

MAKES ENOUGH FOR 8 CHUNKY SAUSAGE ROLLS OR TO TOP 1 MEDIUM PIE

150g fine plain wholemeal flour

150g plain white flour, plus extra to dust

A pinch of salt

150g chilled unsalted butter, cut into roughly 1cm cubes

In a large bowl, mix the flours with the salt, then add the cubed butter and toss to coat the pieces in the flour. Mix in just enough very cold water (around 150ml) to bring the mixture together into a fairly firm, very rough dough – the chunks of butter should still be visible.

On a well-floured surface, shape the dough into a rectangle with your hands. Roll it out in one direction, away from you, to form a long rectangle, about 2cm thick. Generously sprinkling with more flour as you go, fold the furthest third towards you, then fold the nearest third over that (like folding a business letter), so that you now have a rectangle made up of 3 equal layers.

Give the pastry a quarter/90° turn, then repeat the rolling, folding and turning process three more times.

Wrap the rough puff pastry in baking paper and rest it in the fridge for at least 2 hours, and up to 48 hours before using. You can also freeze it, in which case remove from the freezer at least 4 hours before you want to use it.

Roll out the pastry, as required for your recipe, with generous sprinklings of flour as you go.

144

Prune, chestnut and apple sausage rolls

These fabulously festive, chunky sausage rolls are flirting with the enticing flavours of pigs-in-blankets and devilled prunes, and why not? The result is so tempting...

MAKES 8

1 quantity half-wholemeal rough puff pastry (page 144)

Flour, to dust

1 egg, beaten with a little milk, to brush

FILLING

4 butcher's large pork sausages

100g pitted prunes, roughly chopped

75g pre-cooked chestnuts, coarsely chopped

1 eating apple, cored and cut into small dice

1 tsp chopped thyme or sage, or both

Make the pastry ahead and have it chilling in the fridge.

Preheat the oven to 190°C/170°C Fan/Gas 5 and line a baking tray with baking paper (use a lipped baking tray rather than a flat baking sheet in case the pastry leaks a little butter).

For the filling, split the skins of the sausages and squeeze out the meat into a bowl. Add the prunes, chestnuts, apple and chopped herbs and mash together well.

Divide the pastry in two, cutting the rectangle in half crossways. On a lightly floured work surface, roll out one half into a rectangle, 35–40cm long and about 15cm wide. Arrange half the sausage meat in an even line down the pastry, positioning it slightly to one side of the centre.

Lightly brush one long edge of the pastry with beaten egg. Take the slightly wider side of the pastry and fold it over the top of the meaty, fruity mix, matching up the edges of the pastry. Press the edges together firmly to seal them together and leave a little 'handle' down one side (really these are more 'sausage fold-overs' than sausage rolls).

With a very sharp knife, slice the roll into 4 equal pieces then make 2 or 3 little cuts in the pastry on the top of each sausage roll. Place on the prepared baking tray. Repeat with the remaining pastry and sausage meat, to make 8 large sausage rolls.

Brush the tops of the sausage rolls with more beaten egg. Bake in the oven for 30–35 minutes, until the pastry is a rich golden brown colour and the meat is cooked through. Transfer the sausage rolls to a wire rack and allow to rest and cool down for at least 30 minutes before eating.

These sausage rolls are very good warm or cold. They will keep in the fridge in a sealed container for 3 days. You can reheat them in the oven preheated to 190°C/170°C Fan/Gas 5 for about 15 minutes, until hot right through. Let cool for a few minutes before serving.

VARIATION

Vegetarian sausage rolls: Put 300g chestnut mushrooms and 100g cooked chestnuts into a food processor and pulse almost to a paste. Heat 2 tbsp oil in a large frying pan and sauté 2 finely chopped banana shallots or 1 medium onion, 1 finely diced celery stick and 2 chopped garlic cloves with a little salt and pepper for 3–4 minutes. Add the mushroom and chestnut mix with some chopped thyme, and cook, stirring often, for at least 10 minutes until all the liquid released by the mushrooms is evaporated. Stir in 50g chopped prunes or dried apricots, then leave to cool. Make, fill and bake the rolls as described (opposite), checking after 25 minutes in the oven.

Onion tart with greens

I learned to make (and to love) a French onion tart from the recipe in Elizabeth David's classic *French Provincial Cooking*. This tart remains faithful to the spirit of that recipe, based as it is on lots of sweet, soft onion, but I've added greens, used my half-wholemeal shortcrust pastry and gone for a lighter custard based on half milk, half cream (and whole eggs, so there are no spare whites leftover for you to deal with). It's still gorgeous. And this is an endlessly adaptable tart template, as you'll see from the variations on the opposite page.
Pictured overleaf

SERVES 6–8

1 quantity half-wholemeal shortcrust pastry (page 143), chilled

Flour, to dust

FILLING

1 tbsp olive or vegetable oil

A large knob of butter

About 600g onions (red, brown or a combination), finely sliced

Nutmeg, for grating

200–250g cavolo nero, tough stalks removed, or about 300g spinach, very well rinsed

150ml double cream

150ml whole milk

3 medium eggs

50g mature Cheddar or Parmesan, grated

Sea salt and black pepper

Use the chilled shortcrust pastry to line a 24cm tart tin and bake blind as per the instructions on page 143. Trim the edges.

Preheat the oven to 180°C/160°C Fan/Gas 4.

To make the filling, heat the oil and butter together in a large frying pan over a medium-low heat. Add the sliced onions with some salt and pepper. Cook gently, stirring regularly, for about 30 minutes until soft, golden and tender. Grate over some fresh nutmeg, stir in and leave to cool a little.

While the onions are cooking, blanch the greens: bring a pan of water to the boil and add the cavolo nero or spinach. Return to a simmer then immediately tip the greens into a colander to drain and run under the cold tap to cool them quickly.

Now squeeze out as much moisture from the greens as you can, then chop coarsely and combine with the cooked onion.

Beat the cream, milk and eggs together in a bowl and season well with salt and pepper.

Arrange the onion and greens mix in the prepared tart case and carefully pour the beaten egg mixture over them. Scatter the grated cheese over the surface.

Bake in the oven for about 30–35 minutes until the filling is just set and golden. Leave the tart to cool, at least a little, before serving warm or at room temperature.

VARIATIONS

Onion and creamy courgette tart: Instead of the greens, finely slice about 500g small or medium courgettes. Heat a little oil and butter in a frying pan over a moderate heat, then add the sliced courgettes with a good pinch of salt. Sizzle and sweat, stirring regularly. When the liquid runs from the courgettes, you can turn up the heat a bit. Keep cooking, stirring regularly and crushing the courgettes, until they are very soft and pulpy, without too much browning. You can do this at the same time as you are cooking the onions, dividing your attention between the two pans. Finally, mix the pulpy courgettes with the sweet soft onions, adding a little roughly chopped basil, if you like. Pile into the tart case and spread evenly with a spatula, then pour on the custard, sprinkle over the cheese and bake as for the main recipe.

Onion and asparagus tart: Instead of the greens, trim 12–15 asparagus spears (of their woody ends) and blanch in a pan of well-salted boiling water for 3–5 minutes, until *al dente* (tender but firm to the bite). Drain and leave to cool. Make the tart as for the main recipe (leaving out the greens). Spread the cooked onions evenly in the tart case and pour on the custard. Arrange the asparagus spears randomly but evenly over the surface, pressing them lightly in, before sprinkling over the cheese. Or, if you prefer, arrange them in a symmetrical star, points to the centre. You might have to trim them to make them fit – but don't waste the trimmed-off bits, just push them further into the mix, out of sight! Bake as for the onion tart.

Chicken and leek pie

This warming pie is generous with the herbs as well as the veg, and still comes up trumps for sheer chickeny-ness too (I've specified chicken thighs, both for their flavour and their dependable juiciness). A single layer of my buttery half-wholemeal rough puff pastry tops it off beautifully. You'll probably have more pastry than you need; you can use the excess to make some Cheesy peasy swirls (page 155).

SERVES 4

1 quantity half-wholemeal rough puff pastry (page 144)

Flour, to dust

A little beaten egg or milk

FILLING

3 tbsp olive or vegetable oil, or about 30g butter

3 medium leeks (about 500g), trimmed and sliced

1 large or 2 slim celery sticks, finely sliced

1 bay leaf

About 500g skinless, boneless chicken thighs, cut into large chunks

2 tbsp fine plain wholemeal flour

1 tsp roughly chopped thyme (optional)

100ml dry white wine

300ml chicken stock

1 tsp English mustard

A small bunch of flat-leaf parsley, stalks removed (save these for stock) or a small sprig of lovage, leaves roughly chopped

A small bunch of chives, chopped

Sea salt and black pepper

Make the pastry ahead and have it chilling in the fridge.

For the filling, heat 2 tbsp oil or a big knob of butter in a large frying pan over a medium heat. Add the leeks, celery, bay leaf and some salt and pepper and stir to break up the leeks a little. Reduce the heat and sweat the veg gently for 10 minutes until the leeks are soft and silky. Transfer to a bowl.

Put the chicken into another bowl, add the flour, chopped thyme if using, and some salt and pepper and toss the chicken pieces to coat. Trickle a little more oil into the frying pan and place over a medium heat. Add the chicken and fry, turning, for about 5 minutes, until browning nicely.

Reduce the heat under the frying pan. Add the wine and let it bubble for a few minutes to reduce and thicken, stirring and scraping to release any tasty bits from the base of the pan. Return the leeks to the pan, pour in the stock and let it come to a simmer. Cook, stirring occasionally, for about 5 minutes, until the sauce is thickened. Stir in the mustard, parsley (or lovage) and chives.

Tip the filling into a pie dish, around 1.5 litre capacity, and leave to cool completely. If you're making it ahead, cover and refrigerate.

Preheat the oven to 190°C/170°C Fan/Gas 5. Roll out the pastry to about a 4mm thickness. Brush the rim of the pie dish with egg or milk. Lay the pastry over the dish and push firmly onto the rim. Trim off the excess pastry (use some to make decorations if you like, sticking them on the pie with a little beaten egg or milk).

Go round the rim of the pie one more time pressing with your thumb to get a good seal (you can also nick the pastry between each thumb print with the tip of a knife if you like). Brush the pie crust all over with egg or milk and make a couple of slits for steam to escape. Bake in the oven for about 30 minutes until golden brown. Serve with peas or buttered greens.

Cheesy peasy swirls

I originally came up with these cheeky, cheesy nibbles as a way to use up odds and ends of my wholemeal rough puff pastry. They turned out to be so tasty that these days I'm more likely to make a full batch of rough puff just so I can make lots of them for a party. You can easily make a half batch, or less, though – just scale down the pea and cheese quantities accordingly.

MAKES ABOUT 40

1 quantity half-wholemeal rough puff pastry (page 144)

Flour, to dust

FILLING

1 tsp olive or vegetable oil

1 garlic clove, grated or crushed

200g frozen petits pois or peas

80g grated mature Cheddar or Parmesan, or crumbled feta (or you can use any other well-flavoured cheese)

Sea salt and black pepper

TO FINISH

1 egg yolk or 1 whole egg, beaten with a splash of milk, to brush

Any or all of the following:

Sesame seeds

Black onion seeds (nigella/ kalonji seeds)

Pumpkin seeds

Extra grated cheese

Make the pastry ahead and have it chilling in the fridge.

For the filling, heat the oil in a small saucepan over a medium heat. Add the garlic and let it sizzle gently for 1 minute then add the frozen peas, 2 tbsp water and some salt and pepper. Cook gently for 5 minutes or so, stirring often as the peas defrost, until the whole panful is hot and the water is bubbling away.

Take the pan off the heat and use a stick blender to blitz the peas to a coarse purée, keeping some crushed pea texture. Spread the purée out on a plate to cool quickly then place in the fridge to chill.

Cut the chilled rough puff pastry into quarters. Roll out one quarter on a floured surface to a 4–5mm thickness – you should get a rectangle around 15 x 20cm. Spread one quarter of the cold pea purée over the pastry, leaving a 1cm clear margin all the way round. Scatter one-quarter of the grated or crumbled cheese all over the peas, then grind over some black pepper.

Carefully roll up the pastry, working from one of the shorter ends, keeping the roll as snug and neat as you can. Cover the roll and place back in the fridge. Repeat with the other 3 portions of the pastry and filling and rest in the fridge for about 20 minutes.

Preheat the oven to 200°C/180°C Fan/Gas 6. Line two baking trays with baking paper (or use one and bake in two batches).

Take the pastry rolls from the fridge and use a sharp knife to slice them gently across into 1cm thick slices. Turn these on their sides and use your fingers to gently shape them back into fairly even rounds. Place on the baking tray(s).

Brush the top of each swirl with the beaten egg and milk, and scatter with your choice of your seeds or more cheese. Bake for 20–25 minutes until golden and just starting to brown on the bases. Serve warm or at room temperature.

155

Mushroom cobbler

A richly savoury veggie pie can be just as comforting as a meaty one, and the full-flavoured umami richness of this mushroom filling proves the point admirably. The cobbler topping (which is vegan) bakes into a hearty pie roof and I've included little pieces of dried apricot in the cobbler batter to give a slightly sweet tang. (You could, however, use my half-wholemeal rough puff pastry on page 144 for a more traditional, non-vegan, pastry lid; see opposite.) *Pictured overleaf*

SERVES 6

100g pearled spelt or barley

30g dried mushrooms, such as porcini

3 tbsp vegetable or olive oil

1 large onion, chopped

2 medium carrots, scrubbed or peeled and chopped

1 large or 2 slim celery sticks, finely chopped

2 garlic cloves, finely chopped

1 bay leaf

A sprig of thyme

600–700g chestnut or open-cap mushrooms, thickly sliced (include some oyster mushrooms too, if you have some)

250ml red wine

1 tbsp tomato purée

500ml vegetable stock

2 tbsp tamari or soy sauce

Sea salt and black pepper

Put the spelt or barley to soak in a bowl of cold water. Place the dried mushrooms in a separate small bowl, pour on 300ml boiling water and leave to soak.

Heat 1 tbsp oil in a flameproof casserole then add the chopped onion, carrots, celery, garlic, bay leaf, thyme, a pinch of salt and some pepper. Sauté over a medium heat to soften.

At the same time, heat another 1 tbsp oil in a large frying pan over a fairly high heat and add a third or half of the fresh mushrooms (depending on the size of your pan) with a pinch of salt. Fry until they are well coloured and the liquid released by the mushrooms is evaporated, then add them to the casserole of sautéing veg.

Repeat with the remaining fresh mushrooms, adding a little more oil as you go. When all the mushrooms are browned and transferred to the casserole, pour the wine into the frying pan and cook briskly for a couple of minutes, stirring to release any bits of caramelised mushroom from the bottom of the pan. Add this liquid to the casserole. Stir in the tomato purée, too.

Drain the soaked dried mushrooms, reserving the liquid. Chop them roughly and add to the casserole. Pour the mushroom soaking liquid carefully into the casserole too, stopping just short of the end, so any gritty bits at the bottom stay in the bowl (or you can strain it through a cloth or coffee filter).

Drain and rinse the spelt or barley and add to the casserole, then pour in the stock. Bring to a gentle simmer and cook, uncovered, for 20 minutes or until the spelt or barley is just tender. Stir in the tamari/soy, then taste the mushroom stew and add more salt or pepper if needed.

Preheat the oven to 180°C/160°C Fan/Gas 4.

COBBLER TOPPING

125g fine plain wholemeal flour

2 tsp baking powder

2 tbsp olive oil

1 tsp chopped thyme (optional)

6 dried apricots, finely chopped (optional)

100ml milk (plant-based)

To prepare the cobbler topping, put the flour and baking powder into a bowl with a good pinch of salt and some pepper. Mix well. Trickle in the olive oil and stir in roughly with a fork, then switch to using your hands and rub in the oil thoroughly until the mixture resembles fine crumbs. Stir in the chopped thyme and/or dried apricots, if using. Add the milk and stir to create a very soft dough.

Drop heaped teaspoonfuls of the soft cobbler dough onto the mushroom stew, placing them around the edge of the dish (not quite or only just touching each other) then filling the gap in the middle. You should get 8–10 cobbles.

Bake, uncovered, in the oven for 30 minutes, until the cobbler topping is expanded and browned and a skewer poked into one of the cobbles comes out clean.

Serve the cobbler with a bright, colourful veg, such as kale, purple sprouting broccoli or peas.

157

PIE VARIATIONS

Mushroom pie: For a more traditional pastry-lidded pie (which will be veggie, but not vegan) use my half-wholemeal rough puff (page 144). Put the finished filling in a pie dish, wet the edges with a little milk, and cover with the rolled-out pastry. Use the trimmings to decorate the pie (with pastry mushrooms, perhaps!) and brush the whole crust with a little beaten egg and/or milk before baking in the preheated oven at 190°C/170°C Fan/Gas 5 for 25–30 minutes until golden.

Vegan mushroom cottage pie: Instead of the cobbler topping, try the two-root mash on page 162, made with plant milk and olive oil instead of milk and butter. This will give you a lovely cottage-style vegan pie.

My mum's fish pie

Fish pie has long been one of my favourite comfort foods and this rich, silky-sauced example is based on my mum's recipe, so it's full of happy, homey memories. These days I make it with stock rather than béchamel, so it's full flavoured without being too creamy. You can leave out the peas if you like, but for me they are, along with the hard-boiled eggs, a Proustian part of this gorgeous dish. I've topped the pie with a lovely skin-on spud and butter bean mash.

SERVES 6

3 medium eggs

A knob of butter

1 medium onion, chopped

1 large or 2 slim celery sticks, chopped

1 small parsnip, or a wedge of celeriac, peeled and chopped (optional)

100ml dry white wine

20g fine plain wholemeal flour

400ml hot fish or veg stock

300g sustainably caught haddock, cod or pollack fillets

300g sustainably caught smoked haddock, cod or pollack fillets

100g sustainably sourced peeled cold-water prawns

150g frozen peas, defrosted

2–3 tbsp chopped parsley

Sea salt and black pepper

SPUD AND BEAN MASH

750g floury potatoes, such as King Edward, scrubbed but not peeled

400g tin butter beans, drained

100ml warm milk

50g butter

For the topping, cut the potatoes into large chunks (no smaller than an egg), place in a large pan, cover with water and add salt. Bring to the boil, lower the heat and simmer for 15–20 minutes until completely tender. Drain and return to the hot pan. Add the butter beans, warm milk, butter and some salt and pepper. Stir together with a wooden spoon then use a potato masher to bash the mix into a coarse, chunky mash.

While the potatoes are cooking, boil the eggs: lower them into a pan of boiling water and simmer for 7 minutes. Drain, then run under cold water in the pan to cool. Crack the shells and set aside.

Heat the butter in a large saucepan over a medium heat. Add the chopped onion, celery, and parsnip or celeriac if using, with a pinch of salt and some pepper. When sizzling, lower the heat. Let the veg sweat for about 10 minutes, stirring once or twice.

Add the wine to the veg and let it bubble, uncovered, for about 5 minutes, until most of the liquid is evaporated. Add the flour and cook, stirring, for 2 minutes. Gradually stir in the hot stock, and bring to a simmer. Cook gently for a couple of minutes, stirring occasionally, until the sauce is silky and smooth. Take off the heat, taste and add a little more salt and pepper if needed. Set aside.

Preheat the oven to 200°C/180°C Fan/Gas 6. Slice the fresh and smoked fish fillets off the skin, removing any stray bones. Cut the fish into roughly 3cm chunks. Stir the fish, prawns, peas and parsley into the saucy veg and transfer to an oven dish. Peel and quarter the boiled eggs and press these into the fish mixture.

Spoon the beany mash on top and spread out to cover the filling, keeping it nubbly. Bake for about 30 minutes until the mash is golden and the filling is bubbling up around the edges. Serve as it is, or with greens such as kale, cabbage or spinach.

Shepherd's/cottage pie

This glorious comfort pie has a little less meat than traditional versions (lamb for a shepherd's pie, beef for cottage), but boasts plenty of veg, a good helping of lentils and a two-root topping (although you can revert to pure spuds if celeriac is not your thing). For a lovely vegan cottage pie, see the variation for my mushroom cobbler on page 157.

SERVES 6

A little olive or vegetable oil

700g lamb or beef mince

1 large onion, chopped fairly fine

1 large or 2 small leeks, trimmed and thinly sliced (or use another onion)

2 large carrots, or ½ small swede (about 250g), scrubbed or peeled, and diced

1 large or 2 slim celery sticks, sliced

2 garlic cloves, chopped

125ml red wine

1 tbsp tomato purée

1 tbsp Worcestershire sauce

400ml well-flavoured stock (ideally fresh meat stock, but pre-prepared stock is fine)

400g tin lentils, drained, or 200g cooked lentils

Sea salt and black pepper

ROOTY MASH TOPPING

750g floury potatoes, such as King Edward, Wilja or Maris Piper, scrubbed but not peeled, cut into large chunks

500g celeriac, peeled and cut into large chunks

50g butter

150ml milk

Place a large frying pan or flameproof casserole over a medium-high heat and add a trickle of oil (unless using mince that's reasonably fatty, in which case you won't need any oil). Add the mince with some salt and pepper and get the meat sizzling, stirring and prodding with a wooden spoon to break it up. Initially, it will release some liquid: let this simmer away and then the mince can start to brown. Keep cooking for at least 10–15 minutes until the meat has taken on some good brown colour.

Scoop the browned meat out of the pan and transfer it to a bowl. You want to leave some fat in the pan to sauté the vegetables, but minced lamb can be very fatty, so if there is a lot of fat, do drain some off.

Reduce the heat under the pan to medium-low. Add the prepared veg and sauté gently for 10–15 minutes, until the onion is soft. Add the garlic and cook for another minute, stirring.

Return the browned meat to the pan, along with any juices. Add the wine and let it bubble away for 2–3 minutes, until reduced significantly. Stir in the tomato purée and Worcestershire sauce.

Now add the stock. It may seem like a lot of liquid at this point but don't worry – it will reduce quite a bit. Bring to a simmer and cook, uncovered, for around 15–25 minutes.

When the juices are well reduced and gravy-like, stir in the lentils. Cook for another 5 minutes. The lentils will absorb and slightly thicken the juices – you can add a dash more stock or water if necessary.

Meanwhile, preheat the oven to 190°C/170°C Fan/Gas 5 and prepare the rooty topping. Put the potatoes and celeriac into a large pan, cover with water and add salt. Bring to the boil, then

Continued overleaf →

reduce the heat and simmer for 15–20 minutes until the roots are tender and mashable. Drain well. Add the butter and milk to the still-warm pan with a good twist of pepper and place over a low heat to warm the milk and melt the butter.

Remove from the heat and tip the potatoes and celeriac into the pan. Use a potato masher to bash them into a rough and chunky mash – don't overwork it or make it too smooth. Taste to check the seasoning, adding salt and pepper as needed.

Choose an oven dish of 2–2.5 litre capacity. Transfer the meat and all the juices to the oven dish. Spoon the mash over fairly evenly but keep the surface rough, forking it up into ridges if you like. Put the dish on a baking tray to catch any bubbled-up juices and bake for 30 minutes until bubbling and golden on top.

Leave the pie to stand for 10 minutes before you dig in. Serve with peas, greens or a simple salad.

165

VARIATION

You can make a delicious version of this pie using leftover roast lamb or beef – you'll need 400–600g meat, chopped small. You should still colour the meat well when you start to make the pie filling, to really maximise those crisp golden-brown bits. If you have any gravy left over from your roast, use that in place of some of the stock too.

Crispy kale-topped pizza

Kale pizza may sound like a contradiction in terms: the healthy green leaf imposed incongruously on unhealthy 'junk' food. But pizza is not inherently bad for you – it's only certain versions that can be: those with over-salty sauces, piles of processed meat and thick blankets of cheese. By contrast, this delicious version offers up a great half-wholemeal crust, a rich homemade tomato sauce, just enough cheese to make it yummy, a few 'tasty bits' to tweak the pizza to your liking and a final scattering of crispy kale.

The dough for the pizza bases is made with a 'no-knead' method, co-opted from my sourdough baking. If you have your own preferred technique for kneading dough, by all means use it. I just like this method as it means minimal input and mess. You do need to be around and about in the kitchen for a couple of hours, but the actual work you do takes moments.

SERVES 4

'NO KNEAD' DOUGH

200g strong white bread flour, plus extra to dust

200g strong wholemeal bread flour

7g sachet (or 2 tsp) easy-blend dried yeast

2 tbsp olive oil

5g fine sea salt

SAUCE

1 quantity cooked tomato sauce (page 78)

To make the dough, combine the flours and yeast thoroughly in a large bowl (don't add the salt yet). Trickle the olive oil over the flour. Measure out 300ml lukewarm water and gradually pour into the flour, stirring as you do so until you have a dough that is quite sticky and loose. Cover the bowl and leave to stand for 20 minutes.

Sprinkle the salt over the dough, then wet your hands and briefly work the salt into the dough by folding it over a few times, still in the bowl. Cover it again and leave for another 20 minutes.

To stretch and fold the dough, with wet hands and the dough still in the bowl, take one edge and stretch it upwards a bit, then fold it towards the centre, over the rest of the dough. (The whole dough may start to lift out of the bowl, which is fine.) Turn the bowl 90° and repeat. Repeat twice more, so you are folding the dough in north, south, east and west. Cover and leave for another 20 minutes. Repeat this process once or twice more, then cover the bowl and leave for an hour or until roughly doubled in size.

You can either make the pizza now, or knock the dough back and let it rise again for another 30–60 minutes.

While the dough is proving, you can make the tomato sauce. I like it to be nice and thick to top a pizza, so I simmer it to reduce it down until more than I would for a pasta sauce. And I prefer to

Continued overleaf →

1 red pepper, deseeded and sliced, or a few sliced mushrooms

A few scraps of leftover chicken, scraps of ham or slices of chorizo (optional)

Anchovies, olives or capers (optional)

1 ball of mozzarella (125g), torn or sliced

A little grated Cheddar or Parmesan (optional)

75g kale (or cavolo nero), picked over, tough stalks removed, washed and shaken dry

A little olive oil

Sea salt and black pepper

168

keep it a bit pulpy, but you can blitz it until smooth with a stick blender if you like. Leave to cool before you use it (you won't need it all but it keeps for a week in the fridge and freezes well too).

When you're ready to bake, preheat the oven to its highest setting: 250°C/230°C Fan/Gas 10 if it will go that hot, or at least 230°C/220°C Fan/Gas 8. Cover two large baking trays with baking paper.

Tip the risen dough out onto a floured surface. Don't knock it back but use a big knife or a dough scraper to cut it in half. Use floured hands to transfer one puffy, wobbly half to each baking tray. Now stretch each piece into a roughly even base, about 30cm in diameter (not that it needs to be round, an oval or rectangle is fine). You can do this with well-floured hands, gradually pressing and pushing the dough outwards (it does take a few minutes!), or you can use a well-floured rolling pin to get things started.

Once you have two nice big dough bases, place 2–3 tbsp of the tomato sauce in the middle of each. Use the back of the spoon to spread it out in a thin layer, almost to the edges of your bases.

Scatter over the red pepper or mushrooms and any tasty bits of meat, anchovies, olives or capers. Distribute the mozzarella over the pizzas, then add a scattering of grated Cheddar or Parmesan if you like – this is intended to act as a seasoning, not a blanket of cheese. You should still be able to see plenty of the sauce underneath. Put both trays into the hot oven for 8 minutes.

Meanwhile, tear up the kale (or cavolo) leaves into smallish pieces. Put them in a bowl and add a trickle of olive oil and some salt. Rub with your hands so that all the kale is lightly oiled.

After 8 minutes, take the pizzas from the oven and scatter the kale (or cavolo) loosely on top, so the leaves are almost joined up but not smothering the pizza. The natural curls of the kale should mean it 'sits' on the pizza, not settling into the cheese and tomato.

Return both trays to the hot oven, swapping them around so that the one previously on the lower shelf is now on top. Give them another 6–8 minutes until the edges of the dough are crisp and brown, the toppings are bubbling and golden and the kale is starting to brown and crisp at the edges. If you have a seriously fierce oven (at around 250°C), you can knock a few minutes off the cooking time. Cut the hot pizzas on a board and eat them straight away.

Pan and
Griddle

One of the lovely things about frying, grilling and barbecuing is the incredible flavours you get when hot metal comes into contact with good food. It's like you're adding a whole other ingredient to the mix. We sometimes call it caramelisation, but there's more to it than just burning the natural sugars in our meat, fish and veg. The scientific term is the 'Maillard' reaction.

When we 'sear' and 'char' veg, meat and fish on a grill or barbecue, those alluring char-stripes on the food tell us the Maillard reaction is at work: the sugars and amino acids on the surface of the food are reacting with the very high heat and with each other, in a complex interplay that creates new and enticing flavours. At the same time, intense heat is driving away moisture on the outside of the food, leading to the crisped browned surface that we find so appealing.

Can fried food find its place in the canon of Good Comfort? I think it can – within reason. Frying needs oil and, like all fats, oils are calorie-dense. So, if you deep-fry anything, or you use a lot of oil when shallow-frying or sautéing, those calories are going to start stacking up. And if your food is coated in batter or breadcrumbs – which can make things very delicious, of course – that will retain even more of the oil, and the calorie count stacks up further.

So, part of my strategy is to bring you delicious grilled and fried foods that use a bit less oil. Deep-frying, where ingredients are completely submerged in oil, is now, for me, a rare indulgence and you won't find recipes for it here. Shallow-frying batter-based or crumb-coated foods, as deployed for my pakoras and fish fingers for example, is a once-in-a-while thing. I am a little more relaxed about lightly oiled food, such as burgers, sausages and fish cakes. (As to the type of oil or fat you choose, see page 340.)

The key with these recipes, and the other prong of my better-for-you approach, is to grasp them as an opportunity to add more variety, more veg, and more fibre to your plate. This isn't merely about 'offsetting' the oil. It's about making the dishes even lovelier and more satisfying to eat. Well-chosen accompaniments, often leaning on crunchy raw veg (sometimes pickled or fermented!), bring not only goodness and balance, but zestiness and flavour to the party.

So, my burger (on page 183) is stacked up with gorgeous grilled veg, and my 'meatballs' are a version of the Italian polpette, boosted with courgette (see page 199). My fish fingers are coated with wholemeal breadcrumbs, my fish cakes with wholemeal flour, and both come with lovely veg-laden sides. And my spicy lamb kebab (on page 197) is augmented with lots of crunchy cabbage and saucy hummus.

As I've looked for ways to shift the balance of these indubitably treaty dishes in the direction of goodness, and away from guilt, I have been increasingly surprised by how easy and delicious it is to do so!

Cauliflower pakora with radish raita

If you're going to batter and fry something, you might as well make it a vegetable! And this is a really tasty way to dish up cauliflower. Fried snacks like this are a once-in-a-while treat but shallow- rather than deep-frying the pakora means you need far less oil. And a radish raita on the side boosts the goodness – you're getting four different veg in every well-sauced, crisp, golden mouthful!

SERVES 6 AS STARTER (OR 10–12 AS A NIBBLE)

1 medium cauliflower (about 800g)

1 large red or brown onion, quartered and thinly sliced

Vegetable oil, for frying

BATTER

175g gram (chickpea) flour

½ tsp baking powder

2 tsp ground cumin

2 tsp ground coriander

½ tsp ground turmeric

A pinch of dried chilli flakes

½ tsp black onion seeds (nigella/kalonji seeds)

½ tsp salt

RADISH RAITA

150g radishes, thinly sliced

200g piece of cucumber, seeds scooped out, diced small or grated and squeezed

150g natural (or plant-based) yoghurt

A scrap of garlic, grated or crushed (about ¼ clove)

1–2 tbsp finely shredded coriander or mint (optional)

Sea salt and black pepper

First make the raita: put all the ingredients into a bowl and stir to combine thoroughly. Set aside in a cool place, ready to serve.

To make the batter, put the flour, baking powder, spices and salt into a large bowl and whisk these dry ingredients together well. Measure out 200ml cold water and start whisking this into the flour. Stop when you have a smooth batter with the consistency of standard double cream. Set aside for a moment.

Remove any tough or dirty outer leaves from the cauliflower, quarter it and trim away the tough stalk base. Roughly chop the cauliflower so you end up with a chunky cauliflower rubble: break it into florets first, then chop these smaller so nothing is bigger than 2cm in any direction. Chop the stalk into similar-sized chunks.

Toss the cauliflower and onion together in a bowl, breaking up the slivers of onion as you go. Add these veg to the batter and stir together well so everything is coated. Preheat the oven to a low setting (so you can keep the cooked pakora warm).

Heat about a 1cm depth of oil in a frying pan over a medium-high heat. To test that it is hot enough, drop a little batter into the oil. It should fizz and bubble straight away, and turn a crisp golden brown in a couple of minutes.

Drop heaped teaspoonfuls of the battered veg into the hot oil. Each spoonful should flatten out a bit once in the pan, but you can help it gently with the back of a spoon. Leave a bit of space in between them and don't add too many or you will cool the oil down. Cook the pakora for 3–4 minutes, flipping them over once or twice, until they are a rich golden colour all over.

Scoop the cooked pakora out with a slotted spoon, place on a baking tray lined with kitchen paper and put into the oven to keep warm. Lift out any stray bits of veg or batter in the oil between each batch, so they don't burn.

174

TO SERVE (OPTIONAL)

Lemon or lime wedges

Continue to cook spoonfuls of the battered veg, making sure you keep the oil temperature fairly consistent. You can turn the heat down if it is starting to get too hot and burn the batter. If, on the other hand, you think the oil is cooling down, give it a little time in between batches to come back up to heat.

Serve the hot, crisp pakora as soon as they are all ready, with a little sprinkling of salt if you wish, the bowl of raita to dip them in, and some lime or lemon wedges on the side if you like.

Fish tacos

Inspired by the street food of Baja California in north-west Mexico, these tacos are bursting with good things. The fish is spicily seasoned and dipped in beaten egg, but not battered. You can use white fish such as cod, haddock, pollack, hake or coley, or flat fish like dab or flounder. Richer fish like bream and mackerel are good too. Soft corn or wheat flour tortillas are traditionally used to wrap fish tacos, and I've included a quick recipe for half-wholemeal tortillas here. You can also buy wholemeal flour tortillas or wraps. *Pictured overleaf*

SERVES 4

About 600g sustainably caught boneless, skinless fish fillets, cut into large chunks

3 tbsp fine plain wholemeal flour

2 pinches of dried chilli flakes

2 pinches of ground cumin

2 pinches of ground coriander

2 medium eggs, beaten

Vegetable oil, for frying

Chilli sauce, such as Tabasco

Sea salt and black pepper

TORTILLAS

125g plain flour, plus extra to dust

125g fine plain wholemeal flour

1 tsp baking powder

½ tsp salt

50ml olive or vegetable oil

CABBAGE RELISH

¼ small red or white cabbage

150g radishes (optional)

A squeeze of lime (or lemon) juice

First make the tortilla dough. Put the flours, baking powder and salt into a bowl and whisk briefly to combine. In a jug, whisk the oil with 110ml water then add to the flour. Turn everything together with one hand until it forms a dough. Knead for a few minutes until it is smooth and even. Leave to rest for 10 minutes or so.

While the tortilla dough is resting, prepare the relish and salsa. For the relish, slice the cabbage, and radishes if using, as thinly as you can (use a mandoline if you have one). Combine them in a bowl, squeeze over a little lime juice and sprinkle with salt and pepper. Leave to soften slightly.

For the tomato and chilli salsa, combine the chopped onion, chilli and lime (or lemon) juice in a medium bowl (the citrus juice will slightly soften the sharpness of the onion). Cut the cherry tomatoes into quarters or eighths, depending on their size. Add them to the onion mix with a good couple of pinches of salt and some pepper and stir gently but thoroughly. Set aside.

To make the tortillas, divide the dough into 8 equal portions and shape each one into a smooth ball. Roll each out piece on a floured surface to a very thin round, just 1mm thick.

Heat a wide heavy-based pan over a high heat. Place a tortilla in the hot, dry pan, and cook for a minute or so, until puffing up in parts and speckled with dark brown spots. Then flip the tortilla over and cook for a minute to brown the other side.

Once cooked, place the tortilla on one half of a tea towel and fold it over – this will help to keep your tacos soft and foldable. Cook the other tortillas in the same way and stack them inside the tea towel. Keep warm while you finish the other accompaniments and cook the fish.

176

TOMATO AND CHILLI SALSA

1 small (golf-ball-sized) red
onion, or ¼ medium one,
finely chopped

1 medium-hot green or red
chilli, deseeded and very
finely chopped

Juice of ½ small–medium
lime (or ¼ lemon)

300g cherry tomatoes

1 tbsp olive oil

GUACAMOLE

1 red chilli, finely chopped
(deseeded for less heat if
you prefer)

2 tbsp finely chopped
coriander

Juice of 1 lime (or 1 small
lemon)

2 ripe avocados (ideally
organic)

For the guacamole, put the chilli, coriander and lime (or lemon) juice into a bowl. Halve, stone and peel the avocados, cut into chunks and drop into the bowl. Add some salt and pepper. Mash the lot together: keep it rough and chunky, or mash until smooth if you prefer. Taste to check the seasoning and citrus flavour; adjust as necessary.

Before cooking the fish, bring the guacamole, salsa and cabbage relish to the table, and have the stack of warm tortillas ready (reheated in the oven if you've made them well in advance).

When you are ready to cook, season the flour with a good pinch each of chilli flakes, ground cumin, coriander and salt. Season the beaten eggs with the same seasonings. Have ready a plate lined with kitchen paper. Toss the fish in the flour, shaking off the excess.

Put a large, non-stick frying pan over a medium heat and cover the base in a thin film of oil. When the oil is hot, dip a piece of floured fish into the beaten egg, hold it for a second or two over the bowl to let the extra egg drip off, then place in the pan. Repeat with a few more pieces for the first batch – don't crowd the pan. Fry the fish pieces for 2–3 minutes on each side, until lightly browned and cooked through. Lift out onto the paper-lined plate.

Repeat with the remaining fish, adjusting the heat under the pan if you need to. As soon as all the fish is done, transfer it to a bowl or basket and take straight to the table.

Now you are ready to dig in! A small, hand-sized tortilla is perfect for a simple 'roll-up', with one or two pieces of fish down the middle, and all your trimmings loaded on as you like. Larger wraps and tortillas can be torn in half or into quarters, and you can improvise from there.

Mussels with leeks (and fennel)

Mussels are a delicious and sustainable seafood, rich with good things including omega-3 oils. Simply cooked with wine or cider, garlic and leeks, they release their juices to form an irresistibly salty-savoury liquor. And I love to add fennel when I have it. In Belgium, they would insist you mop up the liquor with *frites* – and the ripped chips on page 188 will indeed go very well. But I'm equally happy with a slice of lovely wholemeal bread.

SERVES 2

1kg live mussels

1–2 tbsp vegetable or olive oil

A small knob of butter

1 slim leek, trimmed and finely sliced

1 fennel bulb, trimmed, halved vertically and sliced (or another leek)

1 bay leaf

A sprig of thyme

2 garlic cloves, slivered

200ml dry white wine or cider

1 tsp English mustard

1–2 tbsp half-fat crème fraîche (or single cream)

Chopped parsley, to finish

Put the mussels into a colander and give them a good rinse, shaking them about a bit under cold running water. Trim off any little wiry 'beards' on the mussel shells. Discard any mussels with broken or damaged shells, and any that are open and that don't close when you tap them against the side of the sink.

Put the oil and butter into a large pan that has a tight-fitting lid and place over a medium heat. When the butter is melted, add the leek, fennel if using, bay leaf and thyme. Sweat for about 5 minutes, stirring now and then, until almost tender, then add the garlic and cook for a couple of minutes more.

Pour in the wine or cider and bring to the boil, then stir in the mustard and crème fraîche (or cream).

Add the mussels to the pan and put on the lid tightly. Cook for 2–3 minutes, shaking the pan once or twice. Lift the lid. The mussels should all be open; if not, cover the pan and give them another minute. Discard any that do not open after this.

Ladle the mussels, leek, fennel and all their juices into two warmed bowls, dividing them evenly. Scatter over the chopped parsley. Bring to the table with some wholemeal bread and a dish to put the empty shells in, and enjoy! When you've eaten all the mussels, finish the liquor with a spoon, and bread for dunking.

VARIATION

Lightly curried mussels: Simply add a teaspoonful or two of good curry powder or paste (according to heat, and your taste) to the oil and butter just before you add the leeks. You can finish with fresh coriander instead of parsley if you like.

180

A pair of dirty burgers... Veggie...

Everyone knows that a great burger is about more than the actual burger and with deliciously dirty (but still good for you!) extras, this pair takes everything to the next level. The veggie combo below features a beetroot burger, a juicy, garlicky mushroom, fermented or pickled veg and cheese (or hummus). Feel free to add or swap in some of the griddled veg from my beefy burger opposite. Just don't expect to finish your burger with a clean shirt... *Pictured overleaf*

MAKES 6

BURGERS

1 tbsp olive or vegetable oil, plus extra for frying

1 onion, chopped

1–2 garlic cloves, chopped

400g tin white beans or chickpeas, well drained

100g cooked beetroot, roughly chopped

25g fine wholemeal breadcrumbs

1 tsp ground cumin

1 tsp ground coriander

Sea salt and black pepper

TO ASSEMBLE

2 tbsp soft butter or olive oil

2 garlic cloves, grated

6 large open-cap mushrooms

6 wholemeal baps

12 crisp lettuce leaves

Sliced mozzarella, Cheddar or other cheese, or hummus

6 tbsp kimchi or sauerkraut, or pickled cucumbers, sliced

3 tbsp mayonnaise mixed with 3 tbsp natural yoghurt (optional)

6 thick tomato slices (optional)

182

To make the burgers, heat the oil in a frying pan over a medium heat. Add the onion, with a pinch of salt and some pepper, and fry for about 10 minutes until golden brown. Add the garlic and fry for another minute. Take off the heat and leave to cool.

Put the drained beans or chickpeas into a food processor. Add the cooked beetroot, fried onion and garlic, breadcrumbs, spices and some salt and pepper. Blitz the ingredients to a coarse paste – not a completely smooth one. You want to see some little chunks of bean and vegetable in there. You'll probably need to stop and scrape down the sides of the processor once or twice.

With slightly wet hands, form the mixture into 6 patties, about 8cm in diameter. Put them on a plate lined with kitchen paper and place in the fridge to chill.

Meanwhile, preheat the oven to 190°C/170°C Fan/Gas 5. Combine the soft butter or olive oil and garlic and spread roughly over the upturned mushrooms. Place them in a small oven dish and bake in the oven for 20 minutes until bubbling and fragrant.

Heat a large non-stick frying pan over a medium heat and add enough oil to just cover the base. When hot, add the burgers. Let them cook for 3–4 minutes, until a good crust has formed on the base, then flip them over and repeat. Cook for a few minutes more, turning once or twice, until piping hot all the way through.

Split each bap and toast the cut surfaces lightly. Lay a couple of lettuce leaves on each bap base. Place a hot, garlicky mushroom, juicy side up, on top and then add a hot burger. Add the cheese, if using, or hummus, then a little drained kraut or other fermented veg. Spoon on the mayo and yoghurt mix, if using, and top with a tomato slice if you like. Put the burger lids on top, press down lightly and serve.

...and Beefy

If you can, I think it's worth buying best-quality organic minced beef and making your own burgers. I like to form the meat, unseasoned, into patties, about 120g each, and then season it well on the outside with salt and pepper as it griddles. The hot bars of a grill are unrivalled in their ability to bring out sweet, caramelised flavours from fresh veg as well as meat, and the two go together brilliantly here. As with the veggie burger opposite, the 'dirty' extras can be mixed and matched according to what takes your fancy. *Pictured overleaf*

MAKES 4

4 plain beef burgers, ideally organic (about 120g each)

2 or 3 veg from the following, including a crunchy veg and something oniony:

1 large fennel bulb, top trimmed, or ¼ cauliflower

½ Hispi or 'sweetheart' cabbage, or 1 Little Gem lettuce

1 medium courgette, or 1 small or ½ large aubergine, trimmed (optional)

12 spring onions, trimmed, or 2 medium onions, sliced

About 1 tbsp vegetable or olive oil, plus extra to cook the burgers

Sea salt and black pepper

TO ASSEMBLE

½ quantity tomato and chilli salsa (see page 177)

2 tbsp mayonnaise mixed with 2 tbsp natural yoghurt

4 wholemeal baps

Sliced pickled cucumbers (optional)

Have your burgers at room temperature, ready to cook. Have the salsa made and the yoghurt and mayo mixed, ready for serving.

Cut the fennel or cauliflower into thin slices, no more than 1cm thick, keeping them joined at the root or stalk end. Cut the cabbage into slim wedges, keeping them joined at the stalk, or quarter the lettuce lengthways. If using courgette or aubergine, cut into 3mm thick slices. Put *all* of the prepared veg into a large bowl, add 1 tbsp oil and toss to coat. (You might need a little more oil if using aubergine.) Sprinkle with salt and pepper and toss again.

Set the oven to a low heat and heat up a ridged grill pan (or your barbecue). Use tongs to place the oiled and seasoned veg on the grill. Let the veg cook, turning now and again, until charred on the outside and just tender. The time it takes will depend on the veg and the heat of the grill, and whether you can cook everything at once or not, but allow for 6–8 minutes per batch. Transfer the cooked veg to a plate and pop in the oven to keep warm.

When all the veg are done, cook the burgers. Brush them lightly with oil and season with salt and pepper just before cooking. Make sure the grill/barbecue is still good and hot, then add the burgers and cook, turning now and then, seasoning a little more as you go, until well browned on the outside and cooked through. To be well done with no pink meat remaining, burgers should reach 72°C inside, as registered on a digital meat probe – this will take about 7–9 minutes. You go rarer, and shorter, at your own risk! Transfer the burgers to a warm plate to rest for 5 minutes.

Meanwhile, split open the baps and briefly grill the cut sides. Distribute the griddled veg between the baps, add a burger to each, and some pickled cucumber if you like, top with a spoonful of mayo yoghurt mix and another of tomato salsa, and pile in.

183

Bangers, onion mash and sauerkraut

This dish is conceived as a cross between two comfort classics, which kind of overlap anyway: good old-fashioned British bangers and mash, and traditional Alsatian *choucroute* – sausages and boiled bacon with pickled cabbage and potatoes. In this case I'm suggesting you use a good live sauerkraut, and instead of serving it hot, just bring it to room temperature so it stays 'live' and you don't destroy its beneficial bacteria.

SERVES 4

About 200g sauerkraut

A little olive or vegetable oil

8 well-seasoned butcher's sausages

ONION MASH

1 large onion, chopped

750g floury potatoes, scrubbed but not peeled, halved or quartered depending on size

30g butter

Up to 100ml milk, warmed

Sea salt and black pepper

TO SERVE

Mustard

Transfer the sauerkraut to a plate or bowl and set aside at room temperature while you prepare the rest of the meal.

Preheat the oven to 180°C/160°C Fan/Gas 4.

Heat about 2 tsp oil in a large frying pan over a medium heat, add the sausages and sizzle for a few minutes, turning regularly, to start them browning nicely. Then lift them out and transfer to a small ovenproof dish. Bake for 15–20 minutes, until nicely coloured and cooked right through. You can keep the sausages in a warm place, or a low oven, when they're done.

While the sausages are baking, add a little more oil to the frying pan if you think it needs it (you might well have enough from the sausages) then add the onion and get it sizzling. Turn the heat down a bit and cook, stirring often, for 15–20 minutes. You want the onion to colour to a nice golden brown, but not burn, so keep an eye on it.

Cook the potatoes at the same time as the onion and sausages: put into a pan, cover with boiling water, add salt and bring to the boil. Cook for about 20 minutes until tender. Drain well and leave to steam off in the pan for a few minutes. (If the onion is cooked before the spuds, keep it warm over a very low heat.)

Tip the potatoes into the frying pan with the onion and add the butter with a little salt and pepper. Mash roughly, adding some warm milk as you go, to get a texture you are happy with. This rough mash will be flecked with the sizzled onion and broken-up potato skin, so it might not be the prettiest mash you've ever made, but it may well be the tastiest!

Spoon the mash onto warmed plates and add a couple of sausages to each plate. Spoon the sauerkraut alongside and serve with a pot of mustard on the table.

187

Steak, ripped chips and garlicky greens

A delightful alternative to steak and chips, this dish is big on veg and on flavour. There are a lot of greens, but don't panic, they cook down and are then cunningly deployed to pick up the caramelised residues from the steak pan – it's such a treat. *Pictured overleaf*

SERVES 2

2 small sirloin steaks (175–200g each), about 2cm thick

400g small new or waxy salad potatoes, scrubbed

2 tbsp vegetable oil, plus extra for the steaks

About 300g kale or cavolo nero, leaves torn from the stalks, or 200g spring greens, thickly sliced (stems and all)

1 garlic clove, chopped

1 tbsp half-fat crème fraîche or a knob of butter

½ tsp English mustard, plus extra to serve if you like

Sea salt and black pepper

Preheat the oven to 200°C/180°C Fan/Gas 6. Have your steaks at room temperature, ready to cook.

Put the potatoes in a pan, cover with boiling water and simmer for around 10 minutes until just tender. Scoop the potatoes into a colander to drain (save the water in the pan to cook the greens) and steam off until cool enough to handle. Meanwhile, heat the oil in a roasting tray in the oven for a few minutes.

Take each potato and squeeze lightly in your hand, or press on a board, so it just starts to give, then pull apart to expose a rough 'ripped' surface that will crisp up in the oven. Add the potatoes to the hot tray, turn them in the oil and sprinkle with salt and pepper. Bake for 40–45 minutes until golden and starting to crisp.

Towards the end of the baking time, bring the pan of potato water back to the boil and drop in the prepared kale/greens, pushing them down into the water. Return to a simmer, cover and cook until the leaves are just tender – around 5 minutes for kale, a little less for greens. Tip them into a colander and leave to drain.

Start cooking the steaks when the spuds are almost ready. Put a dish in the oven to heat up. Heat a large, heavy-based frying pan over a high heat until good and hot but not smoking.

Brush the steaks with a little oil, season one side and lay, seasoned side down, in the pan. They should hiss and sizzle immediately. Season the surface of the steaks, then leave to cook for 1 minute before flipping them over. Repeat this – cook for 1 minute, flip and season – until the steaks are done to your liking. In total:

For rare steaks – about 3 minutes

For medium-rare – 4–5 minutes

For medium – 6–7 minutes

For well done – about 10 minutes

Continued overleaf →

188

(If you're cooking steaks medium or well done, stop seasoning after 3–4 minutes to avoid over-seasoning.)

To finish cooking, you can hold the steaks upright with tongs, pressing the fat against the base of the pan to help it crisp up. Transfer the cooked steaks to the warmed dish and set aside to rest while you finish the greens. The steaks need at least 5 minutes' resting time.

Reduce the heat under the steak pan to medium and give it a minute to cool a little. Then add the chopped garlic and stir briefly for 20 seconds or so to colour before tossing in the cooked greens. Stir them around with the garlic. The residual water clinging to the greens will deglaze the pan, picking up the caramelised residue from the base. Cook the greens like this for a couple of minutes, then push them to one side of the pan.

Dollop the crème fraîche or butter and mustard into the space you've just created and stir them together as the crème fraîche or butter melts. Then stir the greens back in, coating them evenly.

190

Tip the juices from the resting steaks back into the pan with the greens. Stir well and cook for a minute or so. Taste the greens – they're unlikely to need further seasoning because there will be plenty in the pan already, but it's best to check.

Transfer the steaks to two warmed plates, heap the greens and ripped potatoes next to them, and serve. If you really enjoy mustard, add another dot on the side of the plate too.

Hot fish (finger) pitta sandwich

You don't have to serve these crumb-coated fish fingers in a sandwich; dishing them up with roasted veg and freshly crushed green peas would also be a treat. But there is something very satisfying about the combination of bread, fish, slaw and salad. Any good fish fillets will do here but make sure the fish is sustainably caught – ideally scoring 1–3 on the Marine Conservation Society Good Fish Guide. If kimchi isn't your thing, use the lovely quick tomato and chilli salsa on page 177, or a dash of chilli sauce.

SERVES 2

About 300g skinless, boneless white fish fillets, such as sustainably caught haddock, pollack, cod, hake, coley, dab or flounder

1 heaped tbsp (about 20g) fine plain wholemeal flour

1–2 medium eggs, beaten

75–100g fine wholemeal breadcrumbs (from 1 medium slice of wholemeal bread, or bought ready-made), or half crumbs, half porridge oats

Vegetable oil, for frying

Sea salt and black pepper

KIMCHI SLAW

About 2 tbsp 'live' kimchi

1 tbsp natural yoghurt

1 tbsp mayonnaise (or another 1 tbsp yoghurt)

TO ASSEMBLE

¼ cucumber or ½ small red onion

A few lettuce leaves

2 wholemeal pittas (or 4 slices of wholemeal bread)

A little butter (optional)

½ lemon

First, prepare your kimchi slaw and salad for serving. Strain the kimchi of any liquid (which can go back in the jar) and combine it with the yoghurt and mayo in a bowl. Slice the cucumber into thin quarter-moons or thinly slice the onion and shred the lettuce; set aside on a plate.

Cut the fish fillets into large, rough 'fingers'. Put the flour into a shallow dish or on a plate and season well with salt and pepper. Put the egg into another dish (start with one egg and add a second if you find you need it) and beat with some seasoning. Have the breadcrumbs ready on a third dish or plate.

Dip each fish finger first into the seasoned flour, shaking to remove excess, then in the beaten egg, holding it above the dish for a moment to allow any extra egg to drip off. Finally press the fish finger into the breadcrumbs, turn over and lightly press again to coat all over. Place the crumbed fish finger on a board, ready for frying. Repeat to coat the rest of the fish.

Heat a large non-stick frying pan over a medium heat and add enough oil to just cover the surface. When hot, add the crumbed fish fingers and fry for 2–3 minutes on each side until cooked through and golden. Transfer to a warm dish.

Toast the pittas lightly, then split them open. (If you're using bread, butter it lightly.)

Divide half the kimchi slaw between the pittas (or 2 slices of bread), then add a layer of cucumber/onion and lettuce. Add a few hot fish fingers then dollop in the rest of the kimchi slaw. Give your pitta pocket a spritz of lemon juice (or spritz the sandwich filling and put the lid on top). Cut your sandwich in half if you like, and tuck in.

Smoked mackerel fish cakes

The versatility of smoked mackerel is under-appreciated, and who doesn't love a fish cake? This recipe offers up a tasty take on the fish patty – bursting with flavour as well as a healthy dose of omega-3s. The beetroot and soured cream salad is great alongside (use ready-cooked if you haven't time to boil beetroot), but if you don't like beetroot, the tomato and chilli salsa (on page 177) also goes well.

SERVES 4 AS A LIGHT LUNCH, 2 FOR SUPPER

300g floury potatoes, scrubbed or peeled

25g butter

1 tbsp hot horseradish sauce (or 1 tsp freshly grated horseradish root)

1 tsp English mustard

300g smoked mackerel fillet

1 tsp baby capers, coarsely chopped (optional)

Finely grated zest of ½ lemon

1 tbsp chopped chives or parsley

Fine plain wholemeal flour or spelt flour, to dust

Vegetable oil, for frying

Sea salt and black pepper

BEETROOT SALAD

About 300g beetroot, trimmed and scrubbed

1 tbsp olive oil

A scrap of garlic, grated or crushed (about ¼ clove)

2–3 tbsp soured cream or half-fat crème fraîche

1–2 tbsp snipped dill or chives

Start with the beetroot salad (making it well in advance if you like). Cut up any larger beetroot so they will cook in the same time. Put them all in a saucepan with a good pinch of salt, cover with boiling water, put the lid on and bring to the boil over a high heat. Lower the heat and simmer until tender – about 30 minutes, depending on the beetroot. Drain and leave to cool completely.

Use your thumb to push the skin off the beetroot, then crush or 'tear' them into rough-edged chunks and drop into a bowl. Combine the olive oil, garlic, soured cream or crème fraîche, herbs and some seasoning. Add to the beetroot and toss gently. Set aside (if you're not serving it straight away, put the salad in the fridge, but bring up to room temperature before serving).

To make the fish cakes, cut the potatoes into chunks and put into a saucepan. Cover with boiling water, add salt and bring to the boil. Cook until tender, then drain in a colander and leave to dry for 10 minutes. Tip the potatoes back into the pan, add the butter, horseradish, mustard and some seasoning and mash roughly.

Peel the mackerel fillets off their skins and flake into the pan of mash, removing any stray bones you come across. Add the capers if using, lemon zest and herbs and stir together, keeping the mix fairly coarse, with big bits of fish. Taste and add more mustard, horseradish, capers, lemon zest, salt and/or pepper if you like.

Tip some flour onto a plate and season well with salt and pepper. With floured hands, form the mixture into 4 fish cakes, dusting them with the seasoned flour as you go. Heat a large non-stick frying pan over a medium heat and add enough oil to cover the base. Fry the fish cakes for about 8 minutes in total, turning a few times, until golden brown. Drain on kitchen paper.

Serve the fish cakes with the beetroot salad and a crisp leafy salad or some lightly cooked purple sprouting broccoli.

194

Lamb kebabs with all the trimmings

'Getting a kebab' may be shorthand for indulging yourself after an evening in the pub, but beautifully spiced, grilled meat, tucked into a wholemeal pitta with plenty of fresh veg, hummus, yoghurt and a shot of chilli sounds like a balanced meal to me. I like to make my own hummus because I love it loose and lemony, but you can modify a ready-made one by adding a spritz of lemon juice and a little water.

SERVES 4

½ tsp each of ground cumin, coriander, turmeric and allspice, or 1 tbsp shawarma paste or powder

1 large or 2 medium lamb leg steaks (400–450g in total)

A little olive oil

¼ Hispi or 'sweetheart' cabbage

1 small red onion or spring onion, finely sliced (optional)

A squeeze of lemon juice

Sea salt and black pepper

LEMONY HUMMUS

400g tin chickpeas, drained (save the liquor)

Juice of ½ lemon

About ¼ garlic clove, grated

1 tbsp tahini or nut butter

1–2 tbsp extra virgin olive oil

A pinch of paprika

TO ASSEMBLE

Natural yoghurt (or half and half yoghurt and mayo)

A little chopped mint (optional)

Hot chilli sauce (Tabasco, Sriracha, Buffalo etc.)

4 wholemeal pittas

In a small bowl, combine the cumin, coriander, turmeric and allspice (or spice mix/paste) with a good pinch of salt and a generous grinding of black pepper. Put the lamb steak(s) into a dish, brush very lightly with oil then rub the spices all over it and set aside to marinate for about 30 minutes.

To make the hummus, put the chickpeas into a food processor with the lemon juice, garlic, tahini or nut butter, olive oil and some salt and pepper. Add about 25ml water or liquid from the chickpea tin. Blitz to a coarse, loose hummus, retaining some texture. Adjust with a little more water, lemon juice, garlic, oil, salt or pepper to your taste. Set aside until needed (refrigerate if you're making it ahead and bring back to room temperature to serve).

Finely shred the cabbage and toss in a bowl with the onion if using, a trickle of olive oil and a squeeze of lemon juice. Set aside.

Heat a heavy-based frying pan or griddle pan over a high heat. When the pan is hot, add the spiced lamb steak(s) and fry for about 3 minutes on each side – this will give you nicely pink meat. Cook it for a little longer if you like your lamb more well done. Set aside on a warm plate to rest for 5 minutes.

Flavour the yoghurt with a little mint if you like and sprinkle the hummus with paprika. Place both on a board with the shredded veg and chilli sauce. Warm your pittas in the toaster or a low oven, split them and place on the board. Slice the spiced lamb fairly thinly and serve in a bowl so everyone can build their own kebab.

> **VARIATION**
>
> **Veggie kebab:** Replace the spiced lamb with the vegetarian polpette on page 199, made with 1 tsp ground cumin and/or 1 tsp curry powder added to the mix. Serve up in warmed pittas with all the above trimmings.

197

Lamb and courgette polpette

I love these polpette browned and then baked in a rich tomato sauce, but you can serve them with the sauce on the side as I have here – frying them until cooked through. They are also delicious tucked into warm pittas with the same trimmings as my kebab on page 197.

SERVES 4

300g courgettes, diced into roughly 1cm pieces

Finely grated zest of 1 lemon

2 tbsp finely grated Parmesan (or other well-flavoured hard cheese)

1 ball of mozzarella (125g), diced

50g brown breadcrumbs

1 tbsp chopped parsley

1 tbsp chopped mint

2 garlic cloves, finely chopped

400g lamb mince (not too fatty)

1 medium egg, lightly beaten

2 tbsp vegetable or olive oil, for cooking

Sea salt and black pepper

1 quantity cooked tomato sauce (page 78), to serve

Toss the diced courgettes with 1 tsp salt and put into a colander. Leave for 30 minutes, then rinse off the salt under the cold tap. Put the courgette into a clean tea towel, twist the ends together and squeeze hard to get rid of the moisture.

Tip the courgettes into a bowl and add all the other ingredients for the polpette (except the oil), seasoning with some pepper. Mix well, ideally with your hands, until well combined.

Take pieces of the mix, about the size of a small egg, and form into little patties. Don't worry if courgette cubes need pushing back into the mixture. Even if some come out in the pan, the overall mix will still be delicious.

Heat a trickle of oil in a large non-stick frying pan over a medium heat. Add the patties to the pan and fry for several minutes on each side or until nicely golden brown and cooked through. Add a little more oil to the pan if you need to. Transfer the polpette to a warmed serving dish.

When the patties are done, heat the tomato sauce: add it to the frying pan in which you've just browned the patties and bring up to a simmer, scraping to release any bits stuck to the pan.

Serve the polpette with the tomato sauce, wholewheat couscous or bulgur wheat and a fresh leafy salad.

199

VARIATION

Vegetarian polpette: Leave out the lamb and increase the courgettes to 500g, diced small; don't salt them. Fry the courgettes in 2 tbsp olive oil for 10 minutes until golden. Drain on kitchen paper and allow to cool slightly. Combine with the rest of the ingredients as above (using vegetarian cheese). Form into roughly 12 balls and bake on a lined tray at 200°C/180°C Fan/Gas 6 for about 15 minutes, until golden.

Bakes and Roasts

Food that is hot and delicious and inherently filling; dishes that are golden and gorgeous, possibly crispy on top to boot, satisfying to the eye as well as the stomach; meals that are shared – and therefore good for the soul as well as the body. Put all these things together and you have sumptuous centrepieces that you will be proud to feed your friends and family. That's what this chapter is all about: dishes to widen everyone's eyes and rumble their tummies as they gather round the table.

Even these big-hearted favourites can make room for some extra goodness, and, of course, the best tweaks and additions only make the offerings more generous and delicious. You'll find a roast chicken dinner laden with lovely roast veg on page 208 (and you should get a cockle-warming broth from the leftovers). I've got a stunning vegetarian lasagne for you on page 222 that beautifully balances greens and 'shrooms. And I've expanded the metaphorical amphibians in my toad-in-the-hole (see page 212) to include some fruit and veg, which just happen to be great companions to the mighty banger.

Sometimes starches are an integral part of these recipes – pasta in my macaroni cheese (see page 204), for example, or potatoes in my gratin (see page 232). The fact that you don't need more carbs on the side means there's room on your plate – for extra greens or salad! And some of these steaming, satisfying dishes cry out for something crisp and fresh to complement them – bitter radicchio or chicory with your sweet, earthy stuffed squash, perhaps, or steamed purple sprouting broccoli with your meaty moussaka. Bringing some clean and colourful veg to the party only adds to the sense of occasion.

And these dishes are well suited to entertaining: some may take a little work to put together, but they can then be slid into the oven and left to their own devices, giving you time to potter about. They're very well-behaved too – once cooked, leaving them in a warm oven or standing on the side for a bit won't hurt them at all. That's an asset you'll appreciate when a friend has a good story to finish, or an empty glass to fill.

So, gather in some great ingredients – veg and pulses, fruit and herbs, perhaps some well-chosen meat – then roll up your sleeves and enjoy putting together a dish of delicious goodness that will grace your table and delight your guests.

Macaroni cheese, peas and greens

This recipe turns the traditional starchy macaroni cheese into something more vibrant and bursting with good green stuff. The baked garlicky cherry tomatoes are a lovely tangy accompaniment.

SERVES 4–5

500ml whole milk

1 bay leaf

½ small onion or some onion trimmings (optional)

200g spinach, well washed (stalks retained unless coarse)

30g butter

30g fine plain wholemeal flour

125g mature Cheddar or other strong-flavoured hard cheese, coarsely grated

1 tsp English mustard

250g wholewheat macaroni or penne

150g frozen peas

1 tbsp baby capers (optional)

Sea salt and black pepper

TO ACCOMPANY

500g cherry tomatoes (on-the-vine if you like)

3–4 garlic cloves, bashed

2 tbsp olive oil

Pour the milk into a pan and add the bay leaf, onion if using, and a twist of pepper. Bring almost to the boil, turn off the heat then leave to infuse for 10 minutes or so while you cook the spinach.

Bring a large pan of lightly salted water to the boil. Add the spinach, submerge in the water and leave in the pan for 2 minutes only. (It doesn't need to come back to the boil.) Drain the spinach in a colander and run under cold water until cool enough to handle. Squeeze out the excess water and chop, but not too finely.

Melt the butter in a large saucepan over a medium heat. Add the flour and stir to make a smooth, thick paste (i.e. a roux). Cook, stirring, for 2–3 minutes (it's fine if it browns a little). Take the pan off the heat. Remove the bay and onion from the hot infused milk and tip about a quarter of it onto the roux. Stir vigorously to form a thick paste. Add the rest of the milk in 3 or 4 lots, stirring each in to get the mixture smooth before you add the next.

Return the pan to a low heat and stir the sauce until starting to bubble. Cook for a couple of minutes, stirring often, until thickened. Set aside 2 tbsp of the grated cheese and add the rest to the hot sauce, stirring it in until melted. Take the pan off the heat and stir in the mustard. Season with salt and pepper to taste. Set aside.

Preheat the oven to 190°C/170°C Fan/Gas 5. Add the pasta to a big pan of boiling salted water and cook for a couple of minutes less than suggested on the pack. Then add the frozen peas and bring back to a simmer. Drain the pasta and peas and stir through the sauce, with the chopped spinach, and capers if using.

Tip the mixture into a lightly oiled oven dish (2-litre capacity) and spread out. Scatter over the reserved cheese.

Put the cherry tomatoes and bashed garlic cloves into a separate ovenproof dish, trickle with the olive oil and season well. Put both dishes into the oven for about 20 minutes until the pasta is bubbling and golden on top and the tomatoes are blistered. The tomatoes may take a few minutes longer, which is fine as the macaroni cheese benefits from a brief 'sit' before serving anyway.

204

Chick-chouka

Chachouka (also called *shakshuka*) is a delicious, saucy tomato and egg dish enjoyed in North Africa and the Middle East. It's often served for breakfast, but I've vegged up my version with chickpeas and aubergine, for a more substantial suppery (or brunchy!) version. (If you're not a fan of aubergine you can use an extra pepper.)

SERVES 2 GENEROUSLY (OR 4 AS A SNACK)

1 large or 2 medium onions, halved and sliced

2 red, orange or yellow peppers, deseeded and sliced

1 medium-large aubergine (250–350g), cut into 3cm cubes (or use another pepper)

2 garlic cloves, sliced

1 tsp cumin seeds, roughly bashed

2 tbsp olive or vegetable oil

680–690g jar tomato passata

400g tin (regular or black) chickpeas, drained and rinsed

1 tsp sweet smoked paprika, or curry powder

A pinch of saffron threads (optional)

A pinch of dried chilli flakes or cayenne (optional)

4 medium eggs (at room temperature)

Sea salt and black pepper

Preheat the oven to 190°C/170°C Fan/Gas 5.

Put the sliced onions and peppers, and the aubergine if using, into a medium-small oven dish (about 22 x 32cm); you don't want one that is too large, as there needs to be a bit of depth to the sauce once it's all in. Add the garlic, bashed cumin, oil and some salt and pepper, toss together well and roast for 40–50 minutes, stirring once or twice, until tender and just starting to colour.

Add the passata, chickpeas, sweet smoked paprika, and saffron if using, to the dish of roasted veg. Stir well. Return the dish to the oven for 15–20 minutes until everything is hot and bubbling.

Stir the saucy mixture, taste it and add more salt, pepper and/or paprika if needed. You can add a pinch of dried chilli flakes or cayenne now, if you fancy a bit more heat.

Make four hollows in the surface of the tomatoey veg and carefully break an egg into each one. Sprinkle the eggs with salt and pepper, and a pinch more chilli flakes if using.

Return the dish to the oven and bake for 8–10 minutes, until the egg whites are set but the yolks are still runny (remembering that the eggs will continue to cook once the dish is out of the oven).

Serve straight away with some green leaves, such as watercress, lamb's lettuce or butterhead lettuce, on the side.

Two-tray roast chicken dinner

For omnivores, there aren't many meals more deliciously comforting than roast chicken. And it's not a dish that needs much justification in terms of wholeness and goodness either, as long as the balance is right. Here are my suggestions for the best kind of chicken dinner: keep your portion of well-seasoned, golden-skinned meat moderate (leftovers are always welcome in a broth, see page 242), and add a good portion of roasted veg and something green on the side. A rich homemade gravy brings it all together, of course, and having some previously made chicken stock helps with that.

SERVES 4, WITH LEFTOVERS

VEG TRAY

2 large onions, each cut into 8 wedges

About 600g floury potatoes, scrubbed and cut into roughly 4cm pieces

About 300g carrots, scrubbed or peeled and chopped into chunky pieces

About 300g parsnips, peeled and cut into pointy pieces

1 garlic bulb, separated into cloves (unpeeled)

2 tbsp olive oil

Sea salt and black pepper

CHICKEN TRAY

1 free-range or organic chicken (1.5–2kg)

4–5 bay leaves

A sprig of thyme (optional)

½ onion (from the veg tray)

1 celery stick (a stringy outer stem is fine), roughly chopped

1 tbsp olive oil or softened butter

A glass of white wine (or water)

Preheat the oven to 200°C/180°C Fan/Gas 6.

Set aside half an onion and put the rest into a large roasting tray with the potatoes, carrots and parsnips, half the garlic cloves, the olive oil and some salt and pepper. Toss together thoroughly and set aside.

Put the chicken into a separate roasting tray (suitable for use on the hob because you'll be making the gravy in this). Untruss the bird and discard any elastic or string. Pull the legs gently away from the body so there is space for air to circulate. Pop the remaining whole garlic cloves, skin-on, into the cavity of the bird, along with a bay leaf or two.

Put the remaining bay leaves into the chicken roasting tray, along with the thyme if using. Scatter the reserved onion wedges around the bird, along with the celery (this will help flavour the bird and gravy). Rub the oil or butter all over the chicken and sprinkle the skin generously with salt and pepper, then turn the bird breast side down in the tray.

Put the veg roasting tray on a lower shelf in the oven and the chicken tray on an oven shelf above it. Roast for 30 minutes.

Take the chicken out of the oven and turn it breast side up. Use a large spoon to baste the breast with any buttery juices. Pour the wine (or water) around the bird (not over it). Return the chicken tray to the oven. Give the veg a stir now and place back in the oven. Roast the veg and chicken for a further 40–50 minutes, until the skin of the bird is crisp and golden and the veg are nicely coloured too.

Continued overleaf →

208

1 level tbsp fine plain
wholemeal flour

200–300ml strong, hot
chicken stock (ideally
homemade, but an organic
ready-made stock is ok too)

Transfer the veg to a warmed serving dish and keep in a low oven while you fix the gravy for the chicken.

Take the chicken out and test to see if it's cooked: poke a skewer into one side, where the thigh meets the body, and check that the juices run clear, with no trace of pink. If you have a probe thermometer, push it into the same part: it should register 72°C or more. If the bird isn't cooked, return it to the oven for another 10 minutes and test again.

Transfer the chicken to a warmed plate and keep warm (by the cooker or in a low oven). This is the time to cook whatever greens you'd like with your roast, and to get on with the gravy. Pour most, but not all, of the juices out of the chicken roasting tray into a jug (discarding the herbs but retaining the veg in the tray, to serve with the rest of the veg).

Put the roasting tray over a medium heat, sprinkle in the flour and stir it into the chickeny juices with a spatula, scraping up any burnt bits as you go. Cook over the heat for a couple of minutes, letting it bubble gently and stirring with the spatula.

211

If there's a lot of fat on top of the juices in the jug, pour or skim some of it off, then gradually pour the remaining juices back into the roasting tray, stirring them into the flour paste. Then slowly stir in the hot stock. Whisk everything together and bring to a simmer so the gravy thickens a little.

Taste the gravy now: if it is full-flavoured and rich, pour it through a sieve into a warmed jug. Add a little more salt and pepper if needed. If the gravy flavour isn't quite intense enough for you, simmer it in the tray to reduce and concentrate the flavour, then strain as above.

Bring the chicken, gravy, roast veg and greens to the table. Carve the chicken (ideally everyone gets something on the bone – a thigh or a drumstick or a wing, and some breast meat and crispy skin). Serve up on four warmed plates with the roasted roots and plenty of greens, to each plate. Pass around the piping hot gravy.

Toad-in-the-hole with shallots and apples

A classic toad-in-the-hole is utterly delicious but it's not contributing much to your five-a-day. This recipe changes all that, with onions, apples and prunes upping the fruit and veg count – and working so well with the sausages. Serve it with greens and a tasty gravy (see page 214) and you really can have virtue with classic comfort.

SERVES 4

2 tbsp vegetable oil

6 large butcher's sausages (or veggie sausages)

6 shallots, peeled, or 2 medium onions, peeled and quartered

2 medium eating apples, cored and quartered

About 12 pitted prunes (or dried apricots)

1 tsp English mustard

About 2 tsp roughly chopped sage, plus a few extra whole leaves (optional)

HALF-WHOLEMEAL BATTER

75g plain white flour

75g fine plain wholemeal flour

3 medium eggs

200ml whole milk

Sea salt and black pepper

TO SERVE (OPTIONAL)

Vegan onion gravy (page 214)

Start with the batter: put the flours, eggs and milk into a food processor and add some salt and pepper. Blitz to form a smooth batter, stopping once and using a rubber spatula to scrape down the inside of the processor. (Alternatively, put the flours and seasoning into a large bowl. Whisk the eggs and milk together in a jug. Make a well in the centre of the flour and slowly pour in the milk mixture, whisking as you go, until smooth.)

Cover the batter and let it stand for at least 30 minutes – up to several hours. If you put it in the fridge, bring it back up to room temperature before cooking.

Preheat the oven to 210°C/190°C Fan/Gas 6–7.

Trickle the oil into a roasting tin, about 35 x 25cm. Add the sausages and the whole shallots or onion quarters and toss in the oil. Put into the hot oven for 10 minutes.

Meanwhile, toss the apple pieces and prunes (or apricots) with the mustard, chopped sage if using, and some salt and pepper. Re-whisk the batter – it will probably have thickened up a little, in which case, whisk in 1–2 tbsp milk or water to just 'let it down' a touch.

Take the roasting tin out of the oven and turn the sausages over. Arrange the prunes and apples around and between the sausages and onions, scatter in the whole sage leaves if you have some, then quickly pour in the batter and get the whole thing back in the oven pronto. Bake for about 25 minutes until the batter is risen, crisp and golden.

Serve the toad-in-the-hole straight away, with buttered steamed greens, and (my vegan) gravy if you like.

Vegan gravy

Great gravy is a real sauce of comfort (sorry!). I serve this meat-free gravy with all kinds of meals, vegan and otherwise, including my toad-in-the-hole on page 212 and the stuffed squash on page 216. It gets its rich, umami taste from the browned mushrooms and onions, and the background flavours of red wine (or beer for a slightly bitter note), soy and a hint of coffee.

SERVES 6–8

2 tbsp olive or vegetable oil

About 100g dark-coloured mushrooms, such as chestnut or open-cap, roughly chopped

200ml red wine or dark beer

1 medium onion, roughly chopped

1 medium carrot, scrubbed or peeled and sliced

1 celery stick, roughly chopped

1 tsp fine plain wholemeal flour

About 500ml light vegetable stock

2 bay leaves

A large sprig of thyme (optional)

1 tbsp strong coffee, such as espresso

1 tbsp tamari or soy sauce

Sea salt and black pepper

Heat 1 tbsp oil in a wide, heavy pan over a high heat. Add the mushrooms and fry 'hard' for 6–7 minutes, without stirring, until they start to develop some good brown colour. After that, you can stir from time to time: keep cooking until the mushrooms are a rich dark brown. Use a wooden spatula to loosen any bits sticking to the base of the pan from time to time. Tip the mushrooms into a bowl, then add a splash of the wine or beer to the pan, scraping to deglaze it as it simmers. Add this liquor to the mushrooms.

Give the pan a wipe and add the remaining 1 tbsp oil. Toss in the onion, carrot and celery and sizzle pretty hard until the veg are well browned (almost a bit burnt). Sprinkle in the flour and cook, stirring, for a couple of minutes. Add another splash of wine or beer, giving the pan a good stir-and-scrape with a spatula.

Stir in the stock, remaining wine or beer, and the herbs. Bring to a simmer and cook for a few minutes to make sure the veg are tender. Add the coffee and tamari/soy and return the mushrooms to the pan. Take off the heat, discard the herbs and tip the contents of the pan into a blender. Blitz thoroughly until smooth, then pour into a small pan and reheat gently, adding a little extra stock or water to get a pouring consistency. Season with salt and pepper to taste.

Serve the gravy straight away or cool and refrigerate until needed (it also freezes really well).

> **VARIATION**
>
> **Vegan onion gravy:** Finely slice 1 large onion and fry it in 1 tbsp oil in a covered pan over a medium-low heat with some salt and pepper, stirring often, until well reduced, soft and golden. This might take 20 minutes or so. Add to the finished vegan gravy and stir well. This is excellent with sausages (either veggie or meat) and mash, and with the toad-in-the-hole on page 212.

Stuffed squash

Winter squashes are being produced in Britain more and more these days, both by home gardeners and larger-scale growers. The variety and quality just gets better and better and that makes me very happy! By all means, use the very available butternut for this warming, filling and undeniably cheering dish – but you might enjoy it *even* more if you try one of the other squash I suggest here.

Sizing squash takes a bit of trial and error with unfamiliar varieties, as you never quite know how thick the 'walls' are. So err on the side of generosity when choosing – and bear in mind that you are looking for half a squash to either feed one person, or two. *Pictured overleaf*

SERVES 4

2 relatively small squashes (or 1 medium), such as Crown Prince, kabocha, delicata, red onion or butternut (about 1.5kg in total)

About 2 tbsp olive oil

1–2 garlic cloves, peeled and halved

A few sprigs of thyme, rosemary or sage

2–4 bay leaves

1 large onion, chopped

250g chestnut mushrooms, sliced

1 medium fennel bulb or ¼ medium cauliflower, roughly chopped

200g frozen peas or sweetcorn (or half and half)

100g blue cheese, crumbled, mozzarella, chopped, or Cheddar, grated

A pinch of dried chilli flakes or cayenne (optional)

Pumpkin seeds, or a handful of crumbled cooked chestnuts or bashed walnuts

Sea salt and black pepper

Preheat the oven to 190°C/170°C Fan/Gas 5.

Wash any earth off the squash(es). Slice them in half through the centre as cleanly as you can then use a spoon to scrape out all the seeds and any soft fibres around them.

Put the squash halves, cut side up, in a roasting tin. Brush all the cut and scraped-out surfaces with olive oil and sprinkle with salt and pepper. Drop half a garlic clove, a sprig of herbs and a bay leaf into each cavity. Roast for 45 minutes–1 hour, until the flesh is quite tender when pierced with a knife.

Meanwhile, heat 2 tbsp olive oil in a large frying pan over a medium heat. Add the chopped onion, season with some salt and pepper and get it sizzling, then turn down the heat and sweat for about 10 minutes to soften.

Turn up the heat again and add the sliced mushrooms to the pan. Cook, stirring, until the liquid they release is evaporated. Keep cooking for a few minutes to get some colour on the mushrooms and onion.

Now add the chopped fennel or cauliflower. Cook for another 10–15 minutes or so, until everything is fairly tender. Stir in the peas and/or sweetcorn 5 minutes before the end.

Take the squash halves from the oven and discard the herbs. Set the garlic aside for a moment. Starting in the middle of the squash, scoop out around half of the hot, roasted squash flesh with a teaspoon and put it into a large bowl. Leave a good 1–2cm-thick 'wall' all around the inside so the squash can hold its shape.

TO SERVE (OPTIONAL)

Vegan gravy (page 214)

Add the vegetable mix and the reserved garlic to the hot scooped-out squash in the bowl, along with about three-quarters of the cheese, and stir together to form a rough mash. Add more salt and pepper, and a pinch of chilli flakes or cayenne, if you like, to taste. Heap this mix back into the half squash shells.

Sprinkle the pumpkin seeds or nuts and the remaining cheese on top of the filling and return the stuffed squash to the oven for 15–20 minutes until everything is molten and the exposed surface of the squash is browning nicely.

Give everyone a squash half (or if you've baked two halves from a larger squash, cut these in half again and put a squash quarter on each plate). Serve straight up, or with a crisp salad on the side. (If you really want to make an occasion of it, you can serve it with my vegan gravy too!)

VARIATIONS

Vegan 'festive' stuffed squash: For a vegan stuffed squash, leave out the cheese and add sliced olives or baby capers to the stuffing mix. Served with the Vegan gravy on page 214, and sprouts and roasties on the side, this makes a great vegan Christmas dinner.

Vg

Spicy stuffed squash: Leave out the thyme, rosemary or sage. Add 1 tbsp curry powder or paste to the sweating onion. Leave out the cheese and stir 2 tbsp half-fat crème fraîche or soured cream into the stuffing before putting it back into the squash. Sprinkle with chopped coriander to serve.

Haggis, neeps and dhal

I'm partial to a good haggis – a true comfort food – and it is often surprisingly spicy. That's what gave me the idea of serving it alongside a lentil dhal, as well as the more traditional peppery, buttery swede (or 'neeps' as it's named in Scotland). It's not remotely traditional but it works, and I'd really like haggis-lovers to try it! The protein-rich lentils take the place of mashed tatties, and I add a serving of greens – to strike just the right balance of comfort and goodness.

SERVES 4

1 haggis (about 500g)

About 500g swede, peeled and cut into smallish cubes

25g butter, plus a knob for the greens

1 small onion, chopped

1 tsp chopped sage

About 400g kale, or 2 heads of spring greens or 1 small green cabbage, shredded

Sea salt and black pepper

DHAL

2 tbsp vegetable oil

1 tsp coriander seeds

1 tsp cumin seeds

1 bay leaf (optional)

2 garlic cloves, grated or crushed

3–4cm piece of fresh ginger, grated

3–4 cm piece of fresh turmeric, grated, or 1 tsp ground turmeric (optional)

200g red lentils, well rinsed

Preheat the oven to 180°C/160°C Fan/Gas 4. Remove the packaging, but not the natural casing, from the haggis then wrap it in foil and place in an ovenproof dish. Pour in enough boiling water to give a 2cm depth and cook in the oven for about 1¼ hours until the haggis is piping hot. (Or, put it into a large pan, cover with boiling water and simmer gently for 30 minutes or until heated through.)

At the same time, cook the swede in a pan of simmering salted water, with the lid on, for about 30 minutes until mashably soft.

Meanwhile, for the dhal, heat the oil in a second large saucepan over a medium-low heat. Add the coriander and cumin seeds, and the bay leaf if you have one, and fry briefly until they start to sizzle and pop. Add the garlic and ginger, with the turmeric if using, and fry gently, stirring, for another minute or two.

Add the rinsed lentils and 650ml water and bring to a simmer. Cook, uncovered, for about 20 minutes until the lentils are soft and broken down and the dhal is thick, stirring often to stop it sticking and burning. Season with salt and pepper to taste.

In the meantime, heat the butter in a small pan and add the chopped onion and sage. Sauté for about 15 minutes until the onion is soft and golden. When the swede is cooked, drain it thoroughly then roughly mash with the fried sage and onion, some salt and lots of black pepper.

Put the shredded kale, greens or cabbage into a pan of boiling salted water and cook for about 5 minutes until tender. Drain well then toss with a small knob of butter.

Slice into the hot haggis with a sharp knife and spoon it out of the casing onto four warmed plates. Add a generous dollop of mashed swede to each plate and another of dhal, and finish with a pile of buttered greens. Serve straight away.

Kale and mushroom lasagne

I love this dish! It is such a generous, hearty thing to share and having a layer of creamy greens and a layer of umami-rich mushrooms works brilliantly. It's just as popular with omnivores as vegetarians. If you like you can add a tin of beans to the mushrooms for more texture and goodness, but it isn't vital.

SERVES 4

2–3 tbsp olive or rapeseed oil

750g chestnut or open-cap mushrooms, thickly sliced

2 garlic cloves, chopped or coarsely grated

2 sprigs of thyme

150ml red wine

400g tin beans (black, borlotti or cannellini), drained and rinsed (optional)

1 tbsp tamari or soy sauce

100g mature Cheddar, grated

400–500g curly kale or cavolo nero, tough stalks removed

250g wholewheat lasagne sheets (or enough for 3 layers in your dish)

A little oil or butter, to grease the dish

BÉCHAMEL SAUCE

700ml whole milk

½ onion or some onion or leek trimmings

1 bay leaf

A few black peppercorns

40g butter

40g fine plain wholemeal flour

1–2 tsp English mustard

Preheat the oven to 190°C/170°C Fan/Gas 5.

Start by infusing the milk for the béchamel: pour the milk into a saucepan, add the onion, bay leaf and peppercorns and bring to just below the boil. Turn off the heat and leave to infuse while you prepare the mushrooms.

Heat a large frying pan over a fairly high heat and add 1 tbsp oil. Add a third or half of the mushrooms with some salt and pepper and fry them 'hard' for a few minutes until well coloured and the liquid they release is driven off. Tip into a bowl. Repeat with the remaining mushrooms, using more oil with each batch, and adding the garlic and thyme towards the end of cooking the last batch.

Return all the mushrooms to the pan and cook together for a few more minutes. Add the wine and let it bubble away until it is reduced to a nice saucy coating, then stir in the beans, if using, along with the tamari/soy. Take the pan off the heat.

To make the béchamel, melt the butter in a large saucepan over a medium heat. When it is starting to foam, add the flour and stir well to make a smooth, thick paste (i.e. a 'roux'). Cook, stirring, for 2–3 minutes (it's fine if this browns a little, but don't let it burn). Take the pan off the heat for a moment. Strain the infused milk to remove the bay leaf, peppercorns and onion then tip about a quarter of it onto the roux. Stir together vigorously to form a thick paste. Add the rest of the milk in 3 or 4 lots, stirring each in to get the mixture smooth before you add the next.

Once all the milk is added and the sauce is smooth, return the pan to a low heat and stir the sauce until it starts to bubble. Cook for a couple of minutes, stirring often until thickened. stir in the mustard and some pepper. Set aside 2 tbsp of the grated cheese and add the rest to the sauce, stirring it in until melted. Take the pan off the heat and taste to check the seasoning. Set aside.

Continued overleaf →

Roughly shred the kale or cavolo nero. Bring a pan of water to the boil, add the shredded leaves and cook for 3–4 minutes until just tender. Tip into a colander to drain and run under the cold tap until cool enough to handle, then squeeze out excess liquid and chop the greens roughly.

Set aside about half of the cheesy béchamel. Stir the chopped kale into the remainder. Taste to check the seasoning and add more salt and pepper if needed.

Bring another large pan of water to the boil so you can blanch the pasta – the pack may well tell you no pre-cooking is necessary but I've learned to ignore that!

Cook the pasta sheets in the simmering water, 3 or 4 at a time, for 3 minutes or so, just until they soften and become flexible. This will help to make sure your pasta is silky and tender, and enable you to cut the sheets to fit your dish if needed. Lift them out with tongs, let them drain for a moment then transfer to a large plate or board, ready to build the lasagne. If stacking them, brush or rub them with a little oil so they don't stick to each other.

Lightly oil or butter an oven dish around 20cm square and at least 6cm deep. Spread a couple of spoonfuls of the béchamel on the bottom of the dish then add a layer of lasagne sheets, trimmed to fit if needed. Spread the creamy kale evenly over the pasta. Then lay down another layer of lasagne sheets and another of béchamel. Now add the mushrooms in a layer. Top with the final lasagne sheets and spread with the last of the béchamel.

Sprinkle with the remaining cheese and bake in the oven for about 30 minutes until golden and bubbling. Leave to stand for a few minutes before serving.

224

VARIATIONS

Meaty green lasagne: For a more meaty (but still kale-y) lasagne, replace the mushroom layer with bolognese sauce (see page 81). Or you could go for a mighty triple-layered lasagne of kale, meat and mushrooms – you will need to up the amount of the béchamel and lasagne sheets by about a third and use a slightly deeper dish. (It will serve at least 6.)

Vg

Vegan lasagne: Make the béchamel sauce using oil and plant-based milk instead of butter and milk. Use vegan cheese instead of Cheddar.

Cheat's cassoulet

A traditional French cassoulet is full of good things, and the crisp crust and creamy beans make it a comfort classic. Typically it includes pork belly and confit duck or goose legs, as well as dried beans that need cooking for hours, but some good butcher's bangers instead of the poultry and pre-cooked tinned beans make for a fine and easy version. Whole cherry tomatoes give bursts of tangy sweetness.

SERVES 6–8

3 tbsp olive or veg oil

About 500g free-range pork belly (pre-sliced is fine), cut into chunky 4–5cm pieces

6 butcher's sausages (ideally herby and/or garlicky ones)

1 large or 2 medium onions, sliced

1 large or 2 medium carrots, scrubbed or peeled and chunkily chopped

4 garlic cloves, crushed

200ml white wine

250g cherry tomatoes

2 bay leaves

A sprig of thyme (optional)

3 x 400g tins white beans, such as cannellini or butter beans, drained and rinsed

About 150ml hot chicken stock

75g slightly stale wholemeal bread, ripped into chunks

Sea salt and black pepper

Preheat the oven to 170°C/150°C Fan/Gas 3.

Heat 1 tbsp oil in a large frying pan over a medium heat, add the pieces of pork belly, season with salt and pepper and brown well all over. Tip into a large casserole or stockpot. Add the sausages to the frying pan and brown them well all over too. Cut each sausage in half and add to the casserole.

Now add the onion(s) and carrot(s) to the frying pan and cook for 12–15 minutes until the onion is softened and golden. Stir in the garlic and cook for half a minute, then add the wine and simmer until reduced by about half. Add to the casserole and stir in.

Put the cherry tomatoes into the frying pan with a trickle more oil and cook for about 5 minutes until they start to soften and colour. Tip into the casserole, add the herbs and stir to combine.

Add the beans to the frying pan with the stock and seasoning. Bring to a gentle simmer, then tip them over the ingredients in the casserole to form a layer on top of everything. The beans should be barely covered with the liquid, but if the ones at the top are bit high and dry, trickle in a little more stock or water.

Cover and cook in the oven for 40 minutes. Remove the lid and bake for another 20 minutes. At the same time put the bread on a baking tray and toast in the oven until it is dry and crisp. Let it cool, then blitz in a food processor to crumbs. Take out the cassoulet and turn the oven up to 190°C/170°C Fan/Gas 5. If there's still liquid on top of the cassoulet, ladle some off now, before you add the crumbs. (Getting that perfect crust is a bit of a knack.)

Scatter the breadcrumbs evenly over the top of the cassoulet in a thick layer. Trickle over 2 tbsp oil. Return to the oven, uncovered, and bake for 30–40 minutes until the breadcrumbs are browned and nicely crisp on top. A watercress, celery and orange salad on the side will cut the richness of the cassoulet beautifully.

227

Moussaka

I had to include a moussaka in this book – my mum used to make it and I've always loved it. This is similar to the one in *River Cottage Meat* but I've reduced the meat, added a handful of wholegrains (spelt or barley goes brilliantly with lamb anyway), and boosted the veg element a bit. It all comes together very nicely. If you haven't made a moussaka for a while (or ever!) I'm sure you'll love this one.

SERVES 5–6

100g pearled spelt or barley

3–4 medium aubergines (about 750g), cut lengthways into 5mm thick slices

2 tsp fine salt

2–3 tbsp olive oil

About 600g lamb mince (or about 500g leftover cooked lamb, chopped fairly fine)

1 large onion, chopped

2 medium carrots, scrubbed or peeled and chopped quite small

2 celery sticks, thinly sliced

2 garlic cloves, crushed or finely grated

2 tsp ground cinnamon

2 tsp dried oregano

2 tbsp tomato purée

400g tin plum tomatoes

125ml red wine

About 300ml chicken, lamb or vegetable stock (or water)

Sea salt and black pepper

TOPPING

300g Greek-style yoghurt

2 medium eggs

50g grated Cheddar or crumbled feta

Put the pearled spelt or barley in a bowl, cover with cold water and set aside to soak.

Sprinkle the aubergine slices lightly all over with the salt and layer them in a colander. Leave for 30 minutes to draw out excess liquid.

Meanwhile, put a large frying pan or flameproof casserole over a fairly high heat and add a trickle of olive oil. Add the meat (raw or cooked) and cook, stirring, until the meat is browned. This will take a bit longer with raw mince than with cooked, and you'll need to allow a bit of time for some of the liquid the meat releases to cook off.

When the meat has some colour, assess how much fat is in the pan. Lamb mince can be very fatty, so if it's released a lot of fat strain or spoon some of it off. Add the onion, carrots and celery with a pinch of salt and some pepper. Get them sizzling then reduce the heat and let the veg sweat down with the meat for around 10 minutes, until they are softened.

Add the garlic, cinnamon, oregano, tomato purée, tinned tomatoes and wine. Crush the tomatoes with a fork to help break them down. Bring to a simmer and let the mixture bubble for a minute or two, then add the drained spelt or barley. Add just enough hot stock (or water) to almost cover everything. Bring to a simmer and let the sauce cook gently for about 20 minutes or until the spelt or barley is tender.

While the meat and veg are cooking, roast the aubergine slices. Preheat the oven to 200°C/Fan 180°C/Gas 6. Lightly oil two large baking trays. Rinse the salt off the aubergines and pat them dry. Place on the baking trays more or less in one layer (they can overlap a bit) and brush with olive oil. Roast for about 20 minutes until tender. Season with pepper (they won't need any more salt). Lower the oven setting to 180°C/Fan 160°C/Gas 4.

228

To make the topping, whisk the yoghurt and eggs together. If using Cheddar, stir it in (if using feta, it's nicer crumbled on top).

Choose a large, deep oven dish, around 20 x 25cm. Lay a third of the cooked aubergine slices over the base. Cover with half of the meat sauce. Add another third of the aubergines, then the remaining meat sauce. Top with the remaining aubergines then pour over the yoghurty topping. Crumble on the feta, if using.

Bake for 35–40 minutes until bubbling and set on top. If it isn't colouring much, turn the oven up 5–10 minutes before the end.

Leave the moussaka to settle for 10 minutes before serving, with plenty of crisp green salad on the side.

Roast red ribs and smoky slaw

These delicious pick-up-and-nibble pork ribs are coated with a tangy, piquant glaze and served with a lovely smoky slaw and cornbread. There's no standing on ceremony with a dish like this: roll up your sleeves, load your plate and get stuck in!

SERVES 4

2–3 racks of pork ribs, (1–1.5kg, depending on size/meatiness)

Hot veg stock (to cover)

2 bay leaves

Sea salt and black pepper

SAUCE

300ml tomato passata

2 tbsp tamari or soy sauce

3 tbsp soft light brown sugar

3 garlic cloves, grated

1 rounded tbsp English mustard

A pinch of dried chilli flakes

2 tbsp cider vinegar

SMOKY FENNEL SLAW

1 large fennel bulb, quartered

¼ small white cabbage (120g)

1 medium carrot, scrubbed or peeled and coarsely grated

3 spring onions, finely sliced

¼ garlic clove, crushed

1 tsp sweet smoked paprika

A good pinch of hot smoked paprika or cayenne

1 tbsp olive oil

½ lemon

1 tbsp natural yoghurt

1 tbsp mayonnaise (or another tbsp yoghurt)

Preheat the oven to 190°C/Fan 170°C/Gas 5.

Find the tough membrane that covers the inner surface of the ribs, grab it with a tea towel and pull it off – with luck it will come away in one piece. (You can ask your butcher to do this for you.) It's important as it exposes the meat close to the bones and makes it more available to the glaze – and to you when you eat it!

Put the pork ribs into a large baking tin or dish, cutting them up into smaller racks if necessary. Pour in enough veg stock to just cover the meat. Add the bay leaves and season with a little salt and pepper. Cover the dish with foil and bake for 1 hour.

Take the ribs out of the liquor, drain for a minute or two (or pat dry with a cloth when cool enough) and transfer to a baking tray lined with foil or baking paper. (You can prepare the ribs to this stage and refrigerate for up to 2 days before finishing the dish.)

You're left with a dish of excellent pork stock that you can use in another dish, such as a soup or risotto. Let it cool and skim off any fat before refrigerating or freezing.

Heat the sauce ingredients together with some seasoning, in a small pan for a few minutes, stirring to dissolve the sugar. Brush the ribs generously all over with the sauce, saving a third. Return to the oven for about 50 minutes, basting the ribs twice during cooking with more sauce, until richly coated and tender.

Meanwhile, make the slaw. Finely slice the fennel and cabbage and combine with the carrot and spring onions in a large bowl. In a smaller bowl, mix together the garlic, paprika or cayenne, olive oil, a squeeze of lemon, the yoghurt/mayo and some salt and pepper. Pour over the shredded veg and toss well. Taste and add more salt, pepper, lemon or paprika as needed.

Slice up the sticky ribs and serve with the smoky fennel slaw and Carrot and chive cornbread (page 236) or buttered corn-on-the cob, plus napkins!

230

Creamy potato gratin

A gratin dauphinois is the pinnacle of comfort cooking. This version uses stock in place of most of the cream, but still leaves enough for a bubbling, creamy finish. Some tender sweet red onion adds to the indulgence too. Peeling the spuds is optional: if you've got firm, freshly dug potatoes with clean, thin skins, it's nice not to; but if they've been stored for a while the skin will tend to separate on cooking so you might want to peel them.

SERVES 4–6

1kg floury potatoes, scrubbed or peeled

1 large onion, very thinly sliced

350ml vegetable stock

150ml double cream

1 garlic clove, grated

Nutmeg, for grating

Sea salt and black pepper

Preheat the oven to 190°C/Fan 170°C/Gas 5. Have ready a medium oven dish.

Slice the potatoes very thinly, using a mandoline if you have one, or a food processor or sharp knife. Rinse the sliced potatoes well then arrange fairly carefully in the oven dish, overlapping in flat layers, and scattering the slices of onion between the layers.

Put the stock and cream into a small pan, add the grated garlic and some salt and pepper, and bring to just below the boil. Carefully pour the creamy stock all over the gratin. Use the blade of a knife to lift the potatoes a little here and there to ensure the liquid gets around and in between them. Finish with a final scattering of salt and pepper and a good grating of nutmeg.

Bake in the oven for 1 hour, or until bubbling and golden. If the potatoes aren't perfectly tender, put the gratin back into the oven for 10 minutes or until they are. If by now you haven't got some lovely golden brown patches on the top, place under a hot grill for 5 minutes (or right at the top of the oven for 10 minutes). Leave to settle for a few minutes, then serve.

Some simply cooked Puy lentils and a good salad turn this much-loved side dish into a gorgeous main course.

VARIATION

Porky potato gratin: You can 'main up' the gratin by frying some bacon lardons or slices of chorizo and scattering them with the slices of onion amongst the potatoes, before pouring over the cream and stock and baking your gratin.

Three-root roast chips and ketchup dip

These three-root chips are fantastic as a tapas or starter. They are great with this tasty 'ketchup' dip, adapted from my tomato sauce on page 78. They're also lovely with guacamole (page 177) or hummus (page 197). Of course, you can do a two-roots only version, as I have when I've been down to a couple of spuds and a few carrots.

SERVES 4

2 medium floury potatoes, scrubbed and cut into thick chips (1–2cm across)

2 medium carrots, scrubbed or peeled and cut into thick chips

1 medium or 2 small parsnips, scrubbed or peeled and cut into thick chips

2 tbsp vegetable or olive oil

Sea salt and black pepper

KETCHUP DIP

1 quantity cooked tomato sauce (page 78)

1–2 tsp soft light brown sugar

1 tbsp cider vinegar

1 tsp ground mixed spice

Any (or all) of the following:

A good pinch of hot smoked paprika or cayenne

A pinch of celery salt

½ tsp ground cumin

½ tsp ground coriander

Start by preparing your ketchup. Make the tomato sauce according to the recipe, but keep simmering until it is reduced by at least half and is thick enough to hold its shape on a spoon.

Add 1 tsp brown sugar, the cider vinegar, mixed spice and any of the other seasonings you fancy, and cook gently for a few more minutes. Taste and add a bit more sugar and/or seasoning to your liking. Remove the bay leaves. If you want you can blitz or sieve the sauce to make it smoother. Keep warm.

While the sauce is cooking, preheat the oven to 220°C/Fan 200°C/Gas 7.

Put the potatoes, carrots and parsnip(s) into a large saucepan. Pour on enough boiling water to cover, bring to a rolling boil and cook for 2 minutes, then drain well. Tip the root chips back into the pan, season with salt and pepper and toss together (don't worry if they break up a bit).

Trickle the oil into a large baking tray and place in the oven for a couple of minutes to heat up.

Take the baking tray out, tip in the chips and turn them carefully or use a brush to coat them with the hot oil. Return to the oven and roast for 30 minutes, stirring once halfway through, until the chips are golden brown.

Serve the oven-roast chips with the warm ketchup. A rocket salad on the side is a lovely accompaniment.

235

Carrot and chive cornbread

This quick bread is a great partner to saucy stews or sticky ribs and I've packed the recipe with veg to boost the fibre content and balance out cornmeal's inherently starchy nature. There's a good measure of light wholemeal flour in there too – for fibre, flavour and texture.

MAKES 12 PIECES

A knob of butter (optional)

200g fine polenta (not quick-cook) or fine cornmeal

100g fine plain wholemeal flour

1 tsp salt

2 tsp baking powder

½ tsp bicarbonate of soda

100g sweetcorn kernels (frozen is fine)

100g grated carrot

2 tbsp snipped chives or 4 spring onions, thinly sliced

150ml natural yoghurt

150ml milk

50g butter, melted, or 2 tbsp rapeseed or olive oil

2 medium eggs

Preheat the oven to 190°C/Fan 170°C/Gas 5. Lightly butter a cake tin or baking dish, around 20cm square (or round), or line with baking paper.

Put the polenta or cornmeal, flour, salt, baking powder and bicarbonate of soda into a large bowl and mix together. Add the sweetcorn, carrot and chives or spring onions and mix through.

In a separate bowl or jug, thoroughly combine the yoghurt, milk, melted butter or oil and the eggs, then beat this liquid into the dry ingredients to form a batter.

Tip the cornbread batter into your prepared baking tin or dish and spread out evenly. Bake for about 30 minutes until risen and golden brown.

Turn out the cornbread and leave to cool slightly for a few minutes on a wire rack. Slice and serve while still warm.

VARIATIONS

This recipe is ripe for all kinds of customisation and improvisation. You can use other grated roots such as parsnip or celeriac instead of the carrot, and/or peas instead of the sweetcorn – or spice it up a bit, or make it cheesy or meaty:

Chilli cornbread: Add 2 finely chopped red chillies to the batter, along with the chives.

Cheesy cornbread: Add 75g strong cheese, such as grated Cheddar or a crumbled blue cheese, along with the chives.

Chorizo cornbread: Fry about 50g diced chorizo or bacon bits in 1 tsp oil until crisp. Leave to cool, then fold into the batter with the chives.

Leftovers

As you will have gathered, knowing the route my ingredients have taken to get to my plate is a key part of the pleasure of eating. And if I know that my supper not only uses the best local (maybe even homegrown) ingredients, but also represents a thrifty, zero-waste approach to cooking *as well*, then that's something from which I take *extra* comfort. This is part of the joy of making meals from leftovers. The other part is that the second outing for some ingredients is often even more delicious than the first!

However, dishes based on leftovers are rarely the same twice so, you might wonder, can they really be encapsulated in a recipe? Well, yes... when it's the sort of flexible, easy-going recipe that you'll find in this chapter. A clear idea of what you're shooting for, and a range of options for leftover and store-cupboard ingredients to help you get there, is often instruction enough in these feel-your-way endeavours. I've given you some ball-park weights and measures for key ingredients, but please don't be shy of trying these recipes if what you have to hand happens to fall outside these margins. Feel free to free-wheel further on my already imprecise prescriptions.

And be in no doubt that, despite being both second-hand and variable, these recipes include some of the stone-cold (but reheated!) classics of comfort eating: chicken broth; egg-fried rice; bubble and squeak; bread and butter pudding. Why do we love these make-do, standby suppers so much? I think it's something to do with the rustled-up nature of them, the conjuring of comfort out of the seemingly spent and surplus. And perhaps it also connects with our memories of who, in our formative years, was doing the rustling.

Charged as they may be with emotional connotations, these are also dishes to take the anxiety out of everyday cooking. What you have leftover should never be a burden – it's already on the way to solving your next supper dilemma. Cooked rice or roast carrots, cold chicken, even leftover porridge: these are undoubtedly assets. So much so that it's actually quite smart to deliberately over-cater these things sometimes. You'll be saving work for yourself tomorrow!

It also helps to have certain staples in your cupboard, fridge or freezer most of the time: eggs, frozen peas, tins of perennially useful beans and tomatoes, any kind of cheese... They partner up with your surplus veg and/or meat and/or carbs and help to make memorable meals appear as if by magic.

As a nation, we still waste too much food. Happily, our awareness around this problem has grown in recent years. We are getting smarter at shopping and better at not chucking things out. And if I can add just a few useful recipes to your own repertoire of recycled goodness then that will be another layer of comfort for me to enjoy.

Post-roast chicken broth

Your roast chicken leftovers are clearly a meal-in-waiting for the next day or the day after. And if there's enough meat left on the bird, you might get a tasty chicken sandwich as well as a fantastic broth. I love how *different* this dish is from the original roast chicken dinner (on page 208). Different, but every bit as good.

Some may find this questionable, but for me it's totally acceptable to recover bones (from wings, drumsticks and thighs, for example) from people's plates and put them into your chicken stock. Bringing it to the boil makes them completely safe.

SERVES 4

STOCK

A leftover roast chicken carcass and bones (ideally with a fair bit of meat still on)

1 fairly large onion

1 large or 2 medium carrots

Celery trimmings (tough outer stalk or the base of a whole head)

1 medium leek

1–2 bay leaves

A sprig of thyme and/or a few parsley stalks (optional)

A few black peppercorns

A glass of dry white wine (optional)

TO FINISH THE BROTH

1 tbsp olive or rapeseed oil

About 75g wholewheat spaghetti, broken into small pieces, or wholewheat macaroni or other small pasta

100g frozen peas or petits pois

Sea salt and black pepper

Chopped herbs (optional)

Start by making the stock, which you can do any time from when your roast is finished to about 3 days afterwards. Pick all the remaining bits of meat off the chicken and place in a covered container in the fridge. Put the chicken bones into a stockpot or large saucepan, along with any bits of skin or gristle.

Use the veg trimmings to flavour the stock, keeping the veg for the finished broth: peel the onion, remove the outer couple of layers of the onion and put these in the stockpot with the end bits (I don't put the papery outer brown skin in as it can make the stock bitter). Peel the carrot(s), making the amount of peelings quite generous, and drop the peelings into the pot. Roughly chop the celery trimmings and green top of the leek and add these, along with the bay leaves and parsley or thyme if you have some. Add a few peppercorns too. Pack everything into the pot as snugly as you can, so you'll need minimum water to submerge everything.

Put the peeled onion and carrot(s), and the topless white leek in a covered container in the fridge. You can store them for up to 48 hours like this.

Add the wine, if using, to the stockpot then pour in enough water to just cover all the ingredients. Bring to a simmer over a medium heat, then partially cover with the lid and reduce the heat. Let the stock simmer very gently for 2–4 hours until the brothy liquor tastes deliciously savoury.

Strain the stock through a sieve or colander into a clean bowl, pushing and pressing the bones and veg in the colander to extract as much flavour as possible. You should have about 1 litre stock.

Continued overleaf →

Discard the spent bones and veg trimmings. The stock can be used straight away, or cooled and refrigerated for 3–4 days, or you can freeze it. You can easily remove any set fat from the surface of the chilled stock before using it. Otherwise skim as much liquid fat as you can from the surface of the warm stock before making the broth.

When you are ready to cook your broth, finely chop the peeled carrot(s) and onion and finely slice the leek. Heat 1 tbsp oil in a large saucepan. Add the chopped onion, carrot(s) and leek, with some salt and pepper, and get them sizzling. Then reduce the heat, cover the pan and let the veg sweat for 10–15 minutes, stirring from time to time, until soft and fragrant.

Pour the stock onto the softened veg and bring to a simmer. Add the spaghetti or other small pasta and simmer until it is almost *al dente* (tender but firm to the bite), then add the frozen peas and cook for another couple of minutes.

While the veg are cooking, roughly chop the reserved chicken meat. Add this to the broth and bring back to a simmer, then take off the heat. Taste the broth and add more salt and/or pepper if needed. Ladle into warmed bowls. You can serve the broth just as it is or sprinkle it with a few chopped herbs if you like.

VARIATION

Chicken noodle broth with ginger, soy and greens: Cut 2–3 garlic cloves into slivers, slice a 3cm piece of fresh ginger into matchsticks and thinly slice a red chilli (or use a pinch of dried chilli flakes). Add all of these to the sweating veg before you pour in the stock. You can add a couple of makrut lime leaves, and/or a bashed lemongrass stem too, if you have them. Leave out the pasta and the peas, but add 100–150g shredded pak choi, choi sum, cavolo nero or spring greens to the broth and cook until tender. Season the broth with tamari or soy sauce rather than salt. Meanwhile, cook about 150g wholewheat or brown rice noodles, according to the pack instructions, drain and toss with 1 tsp sesame oil. Put these into warmed bowls. Ladle the broth and veg over the top. Finish with fresh coriander leaves if you like, and serve with lime or lemon wedges for squeezing.

Egg-fried brown rice

Cooked rice, tossed in a hot pan with peas (I always want peas, for some reason) and any other veg you have, then enriched with a bit of omelette-y egg and a generous splosh of soy and chilli, it's a dish so reviving and comforting that it's worth cooking too much rice the night before deliberately (with a proviso, see note, below).

The secret to this dish is to let the egg cook in the middle of the pan until set, like an omelette, before you start breaking it up and combining it with the grains. This is a dish to cook for just one or two people – more than that and the pan can get a bit crowded.

PER PERSON

A splash of vegetable oil

Any (or all) of the following:
A few mushrooms, finely sliced; a handful of tender rocket, shredded lettuce, watercress or spinach or leftover cooked greens, such as kale or cabbage; 1–2 broccoli stems, sliced into slim florets; thinly sliced red, yellow or green pepper

2–3 spring onions, sliced

50g frozen peas or petits pois

1 garlic clove, finely chopped

½ red chilli, sliced (deseeded for less heat if you prefer), or a pinch of dried chilli flakes (optional)

Up to 100g cold, cooked brown rice

1 medium egg (maximum 2 eggs for a panful of rice, otherwise you're making a rice omelette!), beaten

Sea salt and black pepper

TO FINISH

1 small red chilli, deseeded and finely sliced, or a pinch of dried chilli flakes (optional)

Tamari or soy sauce (optional)

Heat 2 tsp oil in a wok or large non-stick frying pan over a medium heat. If using raw mushrooms or pepper, add them a couple of minutes before anything else to start cooking. Toss in the spring onions, peas and any other veg bits. Stir-fry until the peas are defrosted, the spring onion is softened and any other veg is cooked or wilted or heated through. Add the garlic, and the chilli if using, and cook for another minute, stirring.

Add the cooked rice and stir-fry for 2 minutes, or until thoroughly heated and well mixed with the veg. Now push all the rice to the sides, leaving a space in the middle of the pan. Pour the beaten egg into this space. Wait for 30 seconds or so until the egg is set underneath then use a spatula to stir it. Stop and let it cook a bit more, then stir again. Keep cooking like this, part scrambling, part omeletting the egg, but not mixing in the rice, for 2 minutes.

When the egg is fairly well set, mix it into the rice with a chopping and folding motion. Keep frying, seasoning to taste with a little salt and pepper, until the rice and veg are combined with lots of 'bobbly bits' of cooked egg.

Take the pan off the heat and either bring it to the table as is, or transfer to a warmed serving dish. Sprinkle with a little fresh chilli or dried chilli flakes if you fancy, and a splash of tamari or soy sauce. Serve more tamari/soy sauce on the table if you like.

Note: You need to be careful with cooked rice as it can harbour toxic bacteria if left at room temperature for too long. Any leftover cooked rice should be spread out on a cold plate to cool quickly, then transferred to a container and refrigerated. Use within 2 days and reheat only once.

247

Frittata

This deep, Italian-style omelette is another great way to re-purpose a whole range of leftovers. It can happily hold all sorts of different cooked veg, as well as bits of meat or even fish. The best frittatas usually include some sort of allium at the beginning and some sort of cheese at the end but in between it's entirely up to you: this recipe includes a list of the many things you could use, but you only need choose one or two.

SERVES 4–5

8 medium eggs

1 tbsp olive or vegetable oil

Allium element (essential):
1 sliced onion, 1 sliced leek or a chopped trimmed bunch of spring onions

Meat/fish elements (optional):
Bits of bacon or ham or chorizo, or smoked fish (50–100g)

Starchy elements (desirable):
Cold cooked potato, carrot, parsnip, squash, swede, celeriac or sweet potato (or any combination of these (300–500g in total), cut into cubes

Green elements (optional):
200–300g cooked kale or cavolo nero, cauliflower, spring greens or cabbage, or a couple of handfuls of raw spinach or lettuce

Seasonal treats (optional):
A few sliced and fried baby courgettes, 8–10 blanched asparagus spears, 6–8 purple sprouting broccoli spears

Cheese elements (desirable):
30–50g grated Cheddar or any other hard cheese, crumbled ricotta, goat's cheese or blue cheese, or torn mozzarella

Sea salt and black pepper

In a bowl, beat the eggs together thoroughly, seasoning with plenty of salt and pepper.

Heat a 25–30cm non-stick ovenproof frying pan over a medium heat and add the oil. Start with your allium element: onion, leek or spring onions. Add this to the oil and sweat gently for 5–10 minutes (depending on the vegetable), until just tender.

Add any bits of bacon, ham, chorizo or fish – giving them a few minutes to cook through if they aren't already cooked.

Now add any vegetable elements you like – starchy, green or seasonal – and cook for a few minutes, stirring occasionally, until everything in the pan is hot (and any raw greens are wilted).

Spread out all the ingredients fairly evenly in the pan then carefully pour the beaten egg over and around them. Cook, without stirring, allowing the egg to set from the base up. Meanwhile, heat up your grill (or preheat the oven to 180°C/ 160°C Fan/Gas 4).

When the frittata is about two-thirds set but still has a layer of liquid egg on top, which should take 5–7 minutes, scatter the cheese over the surface. Slide the pan under the grill (or put it in the top of the hot oven) and cook until the top is golden and the egg set firm – if you poke a knife into the middle of the frittata there shouldn't be any liquid egg oozing out.

Leave the frittata to cool at least a little before serving – although it's also good eaten at room temperature. Serve, if you like, with a simple salad of lettuce, radicchio and watercress, or finely sliced raw fennel, and/or any kind of fresh tomato salad.

Squeak and bubble

Good old bubble and squeak is a much-loved dish in my house. Rather than one ingredient being 'bubble' and one 'squeak', the name is thought to refer to the sounds emanating from the frying pan as the dish is cooking. Nevertheless, I thought I'd reverse the title, to acknowledge that I've tipped the balance in this recipe towards greens rather than spuds. As so often, a handful of frozen peas can make up any shortfall of green goodness. A fried egg goes very nicely on top too...

SERVES 2–3

1 tbsp olive or vegetable oil (or lard or beef dripping)

1 large onion, thinly sliced

1–2 garlic cloves, chopped (optional)

About 150–200g cooked potatoes or cold mash (you can also use a mixture of roots such as spuds and celeriac or parsnips), ideally still skin-on

Sea salt and black pepper

VEG AND FLAVOURINGS

Flavour bombs (optional):
1–2 tsp curry paste or powder, or sliced olives, capers and/or chopped anchovies

Cooked greens:
About 150–250g cooked kale, cabbage, Brussels sprouts, cauliflower and/or broccoli, roughly chopped or shredded

Uncooked greens:
A handful of raw spinach, rocket or lettuce and/or 100g frozen peas

Herbs (optional):
1–2 tbsp chopped parsley, chives or chervil, or a tiny bit of lovage

TO SERVE (OPTIONAL)

2–3 fried eggs

Heat the oil or other fat in a non-stick frying pan over a medium heat. Add the onion with a pinch of salt and some pepper and fry gently for about 10 minutes until it starts to colour. If you're adding garlic and/or curry paste/powder, stir them into the onions now and cook for a minute or two.

Tip the spuds into the pan. If they aren't already mashed, crush them roughly with a fork or masher, but keep the texture quite chunky. Let the heat penetrate the potatoes for a minute or two then add all the other veg, and any herbs or flavour bombs, with a little more seasoning. Stir together then press the whole lot down into a rough cake.

Now leave the veg cake to cook for several minutes, so that it can form a good golden-brown crust on the base. It's tempting to move it but try not to: it's better that the base is a little over-browned than that the whole thing is underdone and sticks to the pan. (It still might stick a bit, but you should get some really good colour this way.)

When the cake is nicely browned underneath, flip it over with a spatula and cook the other side. (If you are scaling up quantities, and making a larger cake – one that pretty much fills the pan – you can cut it into halves or quarters when the first side is crisped, and flip over each half or quarter, one at a time.) Start to finish, your S and B might take 20 minutes or more.

Serve hot, topped with a fried egg if you like. Mustard or chilli sauce are also very good on the side.

250

Rooty toasty

This is a nifty way to use up any spuds and roots left from a roast dinner. Hot, savoury, creamy and lightly cheesed, it's a substantial lunch, made in minutes, that will set you up for the afternoon ahead. If you happen to have any leftover cheese sauce or béchamel, it makes a brilliant replacement for the crème fraîche here. And if you are really on the leftovers warpath, then a handful of cooked spinach or greens, or even peas and beans, won't go amiss either.

SERVES 1

1 tbsp olive or vegetable oil

1 small onion or 1 shallot, sliced

1 small garlic clove, chopped

About 100g mixed cold cooked root vegetables (potatoes, carrots, parsnips, celeriac, swede etc.), thickly sliced

A handful of cooked spinach, greens, peas or beans (optional)

1 tbsp half-fat crème fraîche or soured cream

1 thick slice of wholemeal bread

English mustard, to taste

About 30g grated, crumbled or thinly sliced cheese (Cheddar, Brie, goat's cheese, blue cheese etc.)

Sea salt and black pepper

Salad leaves, such as lettuce, chicory, rocket and/or watercress, to serve

Heat the oil in a small frying pan over a medium heat. Add the onion or shallot with a pinch of salt and some pepper and sweat gently for 5–10 minutes, until softening. Add the garlic and cook for another minute.

Add the cold cooked roots to the pan and fry gently for a few minutes until heated through and starting to colour. Add any green veg you're using and heat through briefly, then stir through the crème fraîche or soured cream. Taste to check the seasoning, adding more salt and/or pepper if needed, then take off the heat.

Preheat the grill. Toast the bread and spread it very thinly with mustard. Heap the cooked, creamy veg on top. Sprinkle with the cheese and put under the grill until golden and bubbling.

Serve straight away with a salad of lettuce and bitter leaves such as chicory and rocket or watercress on the side.

253

Meat and multi-veg pasties

I'm going to skip the arguments about pasty authenticity and get straight to the point: my lovely half-wholemeal rough puff pastry makes a great wrapping for a hearty combo of leftover meat and handy standby veg. This recipe is just a guide – you know what's in your fridge and should feel free to bring it into play. You can be similarly free-wheeling with the seasonings too...

MAKES 4

1 quantity half-wholemeal rough puff pastry (page 144)

1 tbsp vegetable or olive oil, or a knob of butter

1 medium onion or leek, finely chopped or sliced

1 large carrot or parsnip, or 150g swede, peeled and chopped

2 celery sticks (if handy)

A few mushrooms (if you like)

150–300g cooked meat: chicken, ham, beef, lamb etc., cut into bite-sized pieces

100g frozen peas, or ½ x 400g tin beans or chickpeas, drained

Any other veggie leftovers (that you like the look of)

100ml leftover gravy or sauce (tomato, curry or béchamel all work), or about 30ml cider, white wine, stock or water

1 tsp curry powder or paste, or a dash of Worcestershire sauce (optional)

Milk or beaten egg, to glaze

Sea salt and black pepper

Once you have made the pastry, put it into the fridge to chill. Preheat the oven to 190°C/170°C Fan/Gas 5. Choose a lipped baking tray rather than a flat baking sheet (the pasties may leak a little liquid) and line it with baking paper.

Heat the oil or butter in a frying pan over a medium heat and add the prepared fresh veg with some salt and pepper. Sweat for 12–15 minutes or so until softened and lightly coloured.

Add the meat, peas or pulses, any other cooked veggie bits, plus the gravy or sauce (or wine, cider, stock or water), along with the curry powder/paste or a good splash of Worcestershire sauce if you fancy. Cook for a few more minutes until everything is piping hot. Remove from the heat, taste to check the seasoning, and leave to cool down.

Divide the pastry into 4 equal pieces. Roll each out to a rough circle, about 15–20cm in diameter and 3–4mm thick. You can leave them a little rough-edged – which means no pastry waste – or use a plate or saucer to trim them into fairly tidy circles.

Spoon about a quarter of the filling onto each pastry round, placing it just to one side of the centre. Filling quantities may vary a little with a recipe like this but if you have some filling left over, consider its suitability for a toasty (see page 253) or frittata (page 248).

Brush a little water around the edge of each circle and fold the pastry over the filling, to form a half-moon shape. Pinch the pastry edges firmly together to seal. Make a small hole in the pastry to allow steam to escape.

Put the pasties onto the prepared tray. Brush with a little milk or egg and bake in the oven for around 35 minutes, until golden on top and crisp underneath. Eat hot, warm or cold.

254

Day two stew

It may be never quite the same twice, but the second outing of a stew can be just as delicious as the first. Try this with the leftovers of my Beef and ale stew with rooty dumplings (page 136), or Venison ragu (page 102). The post-roast hash below is also very fine fare.

SERVES 2 (PROBABLY)

Leftovers from a meaty/ veggie stew

1 tbsp olive or vegetable oil

1 large onion, sliced

Cold cooked potato (including mash) or dumplings, roughly chopped, or cooked rice or spelt

Any other leftover cooked veg you can find in the fridge

Sea salt and black pepper

Take the meat and veg out of the stew and chop them up a bit more if the pieces are very large.

Heat the oil in a large, non-stick frying pan over a medium heat. Add the onion with a pinch of salt and some pepper and fry gently for about 10 minutes until it starts to colour. Now add the meat and stew veg and fry 'hard' until everything is starting to crisp and colour nicely.

Add the cold cooked potato, dumplings or grains, along with any other leftover veg you may have, and fry until hot.

Tip the leftover sauce/gravy from the stew into the frying pan and bring to a simmer, scraping any caramelised bits from the base of the pan as you do so. Transfer to warmed plates and serve straight away.

VARIATION

Post-roast hash: Heat 1 tbsp olive or vegetable oil (or chicken fat or beef dripping from the roast) in a frying pan. Fry a sliced onion as above. Add up to 300g leftover chopped roast beef, chicken, lamb or pork etc. Fry until well coloured (even verging on burnt in places). Tip in up to 200g chopped cooked potatoes or cold mash (or a mix of roots such as spuds and celeriac or parsnips), and any leftover veg and greens from your roast, roughly chopped or shredded. Fry hard for a few minutes so that the veg gets some good colour too, then add a shake of Worcestershire sauce, and more seasoning if necessary. Tip onto warmed dishes. Pour any leftover gravy into the still-hot frying pan and get it quickly up to a simmer, scraping the base of the pan as you do so to release any bits of caramelised meat or veg. Pour over the hot hash and eat straight away.

Porridge soda bread

I find it's easy to over-cater porridge, and painful to throw it away!
Porridge soda bread to the rescue. This recipe makes a relatively
small loaf, using roughly 250g cold porridge (which I equate to a
half-eaten bowl plus that bit left in the pan). But use these basic
proportions and you can scale your bread up or down. This is also a
great way to use half a pot of yoghurt – and again, if you don't have
the exact quantity here, you can make it up with milk or water.

MAKES ABOUT 12 PIECES

About 250g cold leftover
porridge (it's fine if there are
a few seeds, raisins or traces
of honey in it)

200ml natural yoghurt or
buttermilk

300g wholegrain spelt flour
or fine plain wholemeal flour,
plus extra to dust

1 tsp bicarbonate of soda

½ tsp fine salt

TO FINISH (OPTIONAL)

A splash of milk or natural
yoghurt

Mixed seeds, such as
pumpkin, sunflower and
sesame seeds

TO SERVE (OPTIONAL)

Butter, for spreading

A little honey or jam

Preheat the oven to 200°C/180°C Fan/Gas 6. Line a baking tray
with baking paper.

Put the porridge and yoghurt or buttermilk into a large bowl and
beat together to combine thoroughly and get rid of any big lumps
of porridge.

Measure the flour into a bowl, add the bicarbonate of soda and
salt and whisk thoroughly to evenly distribute the bicarbonate.

Add the flour mix to the wet porridge mix and mix well (without
overworking) to create a ball of sticky dough: it should be thick
enough to hold its own shape but it shouldn't be tight or dry. Add
a little more flour or a little more milk to adjust the consistency
if you need to.

Scatter the lined baking tray with flour. Thoroughly flour your
hands or a spatula and scoop the sticky dough onto the floured
tray. Sprinkle the dough with more flour and use your hands to
pat it into a rough domed loaf.

Use a floured knife or dough scraper to cut a deep cross in the
middle of the loaf. The loaf looks great if you brush it lightly with
milk, or a milk and yoghurt mix, and sprinkle it with mixed seeds,
but don't worry if you don't have seeds to hand. Bake the loaf in
the hot oven for about 35 minutes until risen and golden brown.

Transfer the loaf to a wire rack and leave it to cool for at least
20 minutes before slicing. Serve still warm, with butter, and/or
honey or jam if you like, or leave to cool completely then eat
toasted over the next couple of days. The soda bread also freezes
well – whole or in quarters.

259

Brown bread and butter plum pudding

However tradition may have it, there's absolutely no reason not to make a bread and butter pudding with brown rather than white bread. The result is nuttily tasty and seriously satisfying. The 'plums' in this recipe are actually prunes (dried plums, after all), which give it a tangy sweetness and reduce the amount of sugar required.

SERVES 6

150g pitted prunes (or unsulphured dried apricots), roughly chopped

150ml cloudy apple juice (i.e. not from concentrate)

50g butter, softened

6 slices of slightly stale brown bread (about 275g in total)

4 medium eggs

50g soft light brown sugar, plus 2 tsp to finish

1 tsp vanilla extract

About 300ml whole milk

Finely grated zest of 1 lemon

Cream, to serve (optional)

Have ready an oven dish, about 2-litre capacity. Put the prunes and apple juice into a small pan, bring almost to the boil then take off the heat. Leave to soak for at least 20 minutes, ideally an hour.

Meanwhile, preheat the oven to 180°C/160°C Fan/Gas 4. Use the butter to butter the slices of bread on one side only. Cut the slices into pieces – triangles if the slices are square, or halves if they are rounded. Arrange the bread in overlapping rows in the oven dish, following the shape of the dish.

Tip the soaked prunes into a sieve set over a measuring jug to save the juice. Dot the prune pieces over and between the bread.

In a large bowl, whisk the eggs thoroughly, then whisk in the brown sugar and vanilla extract until well combined. Add enough milk to the pruney apple juice in the jug to make it up to 400ml, then add to the whisked egg mix and whisk again until smooth.

Pour this custard over the bread and prunes, making sure all the bread gets custard over it. Leave to soak for at least 10 minutes – ideally a bit longer, especially if your bread is quite stale. Use your hands to press the bread down into the custard a little, then scatter the lemon zest over the top, followed by 2 tsp brown sugar.

Bake the pudding in the oven for 30–35 minutes, until golden brown on top and the custard is just set but still a little wobbly. Leave to cool for 10 minutes before serving. You could have a trickle of cold cream with this, if you like!

VARIATION

Christmas boozy bread and butter plum pudding: Replace 50ml of the apple juice with brandy and add 50g chopped candied peel to the prunes. Add 1 tsp ground mixed spice to the custard and grate both orange and lemon zest over the top of the pudding before sprinkling with the sugar and baking.

Puddings

Pudding: even the word is comforting. It speaks of a dish designed to make you feel good: a special treat, a bountiful bonus, a warm, sweet hug. Some of those pudding hugs, however, can be *extremely sweet* – absolute sugar-fests, in fact. That can be gratifying, but it can also be alarming, prompting the question, do we really need to put in so much sugar to get the pleasure from these puds that we hope for? No, we definitely don't!

Once you start cooking in a lighter and wholer way, you may well find yourself baulking at the sheer quantities of sugar in conventional pudding recipes (including, I admit, a few of mine from back in the day). Happily, you may also find yourself warming to a better way of doing puds. That's where I'm at.

I'm a huge pudding fan, and for some time now I have been tweaking the classics to become lighter, wholer and often more fruity. And I can promise you that taking the sugar down in even the most indulgent puds, swapping in light wholemeal flours, and sometimes adding extra nuts and fruit, doesn't diminish them in any way. Quite the contrary, they often become better – not just in the sense of better for you, but actually more enjoyable to eat.

Fruit is often the key: many great puds are built around fresh or dried fruit, so it's relatively simple to shift the balance of ingredients a little more in that direction. Then there is the flour element – which I am happy to make at least half wholemeal and, in some cases, to swap in some ground almonds, as in my Hot chocolate pudding on page 289. And I have a few other tricks up my apron. Ingredients such as lemon zest and real vanilla can naturally enhance the sweetness of a pud while adding their own pleasing character. And natural sugars, like the lactose in milk, can be called into play too, for example in my warming Stovetop spelt pudding on page 299. Even a pinch of salt in a dessert recipe can emphasise the contrasting sweetness that is already there.

Then there's the matter of that little extra something to serve with your puds. Double cream – fridge-cold and lusciously rich – is lovely with so many puddings. And frankly, why not? A trickle of single cream (or even a spoonful of double!), ideally organic, now and then, is, to my mind, no sin. There are lighter options too: I'm a fan of organic half-fat crème fraîche (see page 338) and whole natural yoghurt. Both have the same contrasting appeal on a hot pudding as cream does. Combining double cream 50:50 with natural yoghurt is a good option too. I've also got a recipe for you for a lighter custard on page 275.

We don't *need* pudding and we shouldn't expect it every day. But when made with the best whole ingredients and a little (or a lot) less sugar, and enjoyed when the moment calls for it, it will always spread joy. The recipes that follow are hugs as warm as you could wish for, and quite sweet enough to delight.

Old-school apple pie

This is straight-up gorgeous. The lightly sweetened version of my half-wholemeal pastry is a delight with the silky apple filling which, these days, I make with far less sugar. I find that citrus zest and juice is so delicious with apple and, despite the tartness, seems to enhance the fruit's sweetness.

SERVES 6–8

Finely grated zest and juice of 1 lemon

Finely grated zest and juice of 1 orange

1.5kg cooking apples, such as Bramley's (or, for a more textured filling, about 1kg cookers and 500g eaters)

40–60g golden caster sugar, plus extra to finish

2 x quantity sweet half-wholemeal shortcrust pastry (page 143)

Flour, to dust

2 tbsp ground almonds (optional)

Custard (page 275), crème fraîche, cream or yoghurt, to serve

Put all the citrus zest and juice into a large bowl. Peel, core and thinly slice the apples, dropping them into the bowl as you do so, and tossing the apples in the juice occasionally.

Transfer the apples and juice to a fairly large saucepan and add the sugar. Cook over a medium heat, stirring often, for around 15 minutes until the apples collapse into a silky golden purée (if you use some eating apples, they will stay chunkier). Taste for sweetness and stir in a little more sugar only if you think it needs it. Allow to cool completely before you make the pie.

You can make the pastry while the apple is cooling. Wrap and place it in the fridge to rest.

Preheat the oven to 220°C/200°C Fan/Gas 7. Put a baking tray inside to heat up. Have ready an oval pie dish, about 28 x 19cm.

Divide the pastry into two pieces: roughly one-third for the top and two-thirds to line the base and sides of the dish. On a lightly floured surface, roll out the larger piece to the shape of your pie dish, until about 3mm thick. Use this to line the pie dish, allowing the excess pastry to overhang the rim.

Scatter the ground almonds, if using, over the base of the pastry case, and lightly press in. They aren't essential but they are a nice touch of flavour and texture in the base of the pie. Tip the cooled apple purée in and level it out.

Roll out the other piece of pastry for the pie lid, again to about a 3mm thickness. Brush the rim of the pie dish with water. Lift the piece of pastry over the pie, trim off the excess from around the edge, then press the pastry edges together firmly to seal, all the way round, using a knife, a fork or your fingers.

If you want to roll out the pastry trimmings to cut out leaves – or even an apple – to decorate the top of the pie, do so now, sticking

Continued overleaf →

266

them on with a little water (or just spread the trimmings on a lightly floured small baking tray and bake as a little treat).

Scatter another 1 tbsp sugar all over the pastry lid, and cut a few slits in the top to allow steam to escape. Place the dish on the hot baking sheet in the oven and cook for 10 minutes, then lower the oven setting to 180°C/160°C Fan/Gas 4 and cook for a further 30 minutes or until the pastry is a rich golden brown.

Let the pie sit for at least 15 minutes before cutting into it. Serve with my lighter custard, crème fraîche, cream or yoghurt.

VARIATIONS

Festive apple pie: Add boozy dried fruit to the cooked apple purée: about 100g raisins, chopped dried apricots, dried cranberries or chopped prunes, or a mix. Soak them in a small glass (about 50ml) of rum or brandy for an hour or so before stirring into the apple filling.

Spicy apple pie: Add 1 tsp ground mixed spice or ground cinnamon to both the apple filling and the flour for the pastry.

Apple and berry pie: Blackberries are, of course, a great addition to an apple pie, and autumn raspberries are also a delicious partner to apples. Swap 200–400g fresh berries for some of the apples, stirring them raw into the cooked apple filling just before you assemble the pie.

Quince and apple pie: Quince has a gorgeous aromatic flavour that complements apple beautifully. Replace 200–400g of the raw apple with peeled, cored and thinly sliced or coarsely grated quince and cook to a purée (as above).

Rhubarb crumble

There are many fruits that can make a lovely crumble (see a few variations opposite), but for sheer joy and happy memories of both my granny's and my mum's finest crumbles, I will always come back to rhubarb. If you sweeten the rhubarb with sugar, rather than honey, and use coconut oil for the crumble topping, then this recipe is vegan. And if a big crumble for eight is more than you need, you can simply halve all these quantities. But don't forget that fridge-cold leftover crumble – especially this nutty, oaty, seedy crumble – makes an excellent breakfast. *Pictured overleaf*

SERVES 8

ROAST RHUBARB

About 1.2kg rhubarb

Finely grated zest and juice of 1 large orange

Honey, or golden caster sugar, to taste

CRUMBLE TOPPING

100g fine plain wholemeal flour

100g ground almonds

100g porridge oats

50g soft light brown sugar

A pinch of salt

150g cold butter, diced, or 120g chilled coconut oil

100g mixed seeds, such as poppy, flax and sunflower

TO SERVE (OPTIONAL)

Custard (page 275), crème fraîche, cream or yoghurt

Preheat the oven to 180°C/160°C Fan/Gas 4.

Trim the rhubarb and chop it into roughly 5cm lengths. Place in a large baking dish (about 3-litre capacity – to accommodate the crumble later, too). Add the orange zest and juice, then trickle over 3 tbsp honey or add 4 tbsp sugar (which is a bit less sweet than honey) and toss together. Bake in the oven for 15–20 minutes, or until the rhubarb is starting to soften, but not quite collapsing.

Meanwhile, make the crumble. Put all the ingredients except the seeds in a food processor and blitz to form a crumbly mixture, then transfer to a bowl. Alternatively, put the ingredients into a large bowl and rub together with your fingers until the mixture comes together as a crumbly mix. Either way, stir in the seeds. Place in the fridge until needed.

Take the rhubarb from the oven and give it a gentle stir. Taste it and assess the sweetness. The tartness of rhubarb can vary a lot throughout the year; add more honey or sugar to taste, but keep the fruit a little tart, not overly sweet. Pat the rhubarb down a little to form a fairly level surface. Let it cool slightly – or leave to cool completely and refrigerate if you want to bake it later.

Squeeze the crumble mix into big lumps in your hands, then crumble these over the rhubarb in a generous layer. (If you have a bit more crumble mix than you need to cover your dish, you can freeze it, or bake it separately to make 'independent crumble', see opposite.)

Bake for 25–30 minutes, until the topping is golden and the fruit bubbling. Serve hot, with my lighter custard, crème fraîche, cream or yoghurt, if you like.

270

Strawberry and rhubarb crumble: In the summer, when the main-crop rhubarb and strawberry seasons overlap, replace half the rhubarb with hulled, halved strawberries. Don't pre-cook these but mix them into the cooked rhubarb before the crumble topping goes on.

Plum crumble: Roast 1.5kg halved plums or greengages with a little honey (as described for the cobbler on page 296), then proceed with the crumble topping as for the main recipe.

Apple crumble: Prepare about 1.5kg cooking apples (or a mix of cookers and eaters) as for the apple pie recipe on page 266. Pile this purée into the crumble dish and level off. Leave to cool at least a little before adding the crumble topping. Bake as for the rhubarb crumble.

Independent crumble: You can bake the crumble separately in a roasting dish for about 30 minutes, stirring twice (after about 15 minutes and again around 25 minutes) until golden brown and crunchy. Leave to cool and store in a tin – it will keep for about a week. This is a great sprinkle for fruit compotes and improvised 'fumbles' (see page 277).

A lighter custard

This is a very simple and pleasing custard, with less sugar than most recipes. Gently scented with vanilla (which also enhances the sweetness), it has a lovely rich flavour and a gorgeous silky texture. It can be served hot or cold, goes brilliantly with crumbles, pies and sponges, and is a key element of the gooseberry fool that follows. The cornflour is optional but provides a 'safety net' against scrambling your custard.

MAKES 500ML

300ml whole milk

200ml double cream

1 vanilla pod, split and seeds scraped, or 2 tsp vanilla extract

4 medium egg yolks

25g golden caster or soft light brown sugar

2 level tsp cornflour (optional)

If you plan to serve the custard cold, or use it to make a fruit fool, prepare it several hours in advance, or the day before, so it has time to chill.

Put the milk and cream into a saucepan with the vanilla pod and seeds, if using. Bring to just below the boil, then take off the heat and leave to cool for 10 minutes.

Beat the egg yolks, sugar and cornflour, if using, together in a bowl. Slowly pour on the warm milk, whisking as you do so, then tip in the vanilla pod, if using. Return the mixture to the pan and place over a medium-low heat. Cook, stirring fairly constantly with a wooden spoon, until the custard is steaming and has thickened noticeably (traditionally, it should 'coat the back of the spoon'). Don't let it start to simmer, or it will split and curdle. (If you have used cornflour, you will be able to get it a bit hotter and thicker, but still don't boil it!)

As soon as the custard is thickened, take it off the heat and keep stirring for a minute or two longer to help it cool a little without cooking any further. If you haven't used the whole vanilla pod, add the vanilla extract now.

If serving hot and more or less straight away, pour into a warmed jug and take to the table (if you think it's a bit lumpy or has some threads of cooked egg in it, you can strain it through a sieve).

If you are serving the custard later, or cold, transfer it to a container (again, you can strain it if you like). If you want to stop a skin forming, cover the surface with a piece of baking paper. Leave to cool completely and keep in the fridge.

To serve hot, reheat very gently (don't let it simmer). Remove the custard from the heat as soon as it is hot and keep stirring to stop it cooking any further. Transfer to a warmed jug to serve.

275

Gooseberry fool

This is a beautiful old-fashioned fool, with a proper homemade custard swirled into the chilled gooseberry compote. The more modern element is a second swirl of natural yoghurt – a lovely light counterpoint to the rich custard.

SERVES 6

500g gooseberries, topped and tailed

50g caster sugar

2 strips of lemon zest

A few freshly picked heads of elderflower (optional)

About 300ml natural full-fat or Greek-style yoghurt

About 300ml cold custard (page 275)

Independent crumble (page 271), to serve (optional)

Put the gooseberries, sugar and lemon zest into a pan, with the elderflower heads (if you have some) and 2 tbsp water. Bring to a gentle simmer over a low heat and cook for around 5 minutes until the fruit is soft but not mushy. Set aside to cool, then remove the elderflower, if used. Put the compote into the fridge to chill.

To serve, put a couple of generous spoonfuls of gooseberry compote into each serving bowl, positioning them to one side. Spoon some of the yoghurt next to the fruit, then add a portion of chilled custard.

Using a fork, very lightly ripple your three fool components together. Or if you prefer, you can leave that fun action to those you are serving.

Serve the fool as it is or top with my independent crumble for a fumble finish. It's also lovely with a piece of wholemeal shortbread (see page 324) on the side.

277

VARIATION

Rhubarb fool: This lovely approach to the classic fool works brilliantly with rhubarb too. Wash and cut up about 500g rhubarb and put into a small saucepan with the juice of an orange, or a splash of water or apple juice, and about 50g sugar or honey. Bring to a gentle simmer and cook until tender but not completely collapsed. Transfer to a bowl and cool, then chill, before assembling your fool as above.

Chocolate mousse

Sometimes the best recipes are the simplest. Recipes for chocolate mousse come cooked and raw, spiked with booze or fruit or spices. But in the end, what we want for sheer indulgence is just a mousse that's *really* chocolatey. Here it is...

By all means add a contrasting finish if you like – take your pick from my suggestions below. But when it comes to the actual mousse, don't mess...

SERVES 6

100g dark chocolate, broken into pieces

50g butter

100ml whole milk

2 medium eggs, separated

40g soft light brown sugar

Cream, to serve (optional)

Melt the chocolate, butter and milk together in a heatproof bowl over a pan of simmering water. Set aside to cool slightly. When the chocolate is no more than tepid, stir in the egg yolks.

In a clean bowl, whisk the egg whites and brown sugar together until the mixture forms soft peaks. Gently fold into the melted chocolate mixture.

Divide the mousse between ramekins, teacups or other small individual dishes and refrigerate for a few hours until set.

My favourite way to serve the chocolate mousse is with a little jug of cream on the side to trickle on top.

SERVING OPTIONS

Summer berries: Spoon macerated strawberries and/or raspberries (see page 286) on top of the mousse before serving.

Orange segments: Slice off the pith and peel from 2 small oranges or clementines, then slice the segments out from between the membranes, catching any juice in a bowl. Toss the orange segments in the juice and spoon over the mousses.

Boozy fruit: Soak a few roughly chopped pitted prunes or dried apricots in a little rum or cider brandy (or apple juice) for a few hours. Spoon over the mousse.

Cheat's praline: Lightly toast a handful of hazelnuts or almonds in the oven, then chop roughly. Scatter over the mousses and finish with a good pinch of demerara sugar.

278

Raspberry jelly

Jewel-coloured and full of actual fruit, this is a world away from rubbery, artificially flavoured jellies made with cubes. Use organic gelatine if you can find it (I appreciate it's not always easy to do so). Alternatively, if you'd like to make a vegan jelly, there are various types of vegetarian 'gelatine' you can use. They all have slightly different properties, so follow the instructions on the pack carefully.

SERVES 6

A little vegetable oil, to grease the moulds

Leaf or powdered gelatine (about 7 sheets or 2 sachets)

500g raspberries (fresh or frozen)

Finely grated zest and juice of 1 lemon

100g icing sugar

Cream or yoghurt (dairy or plant-based), to serve (optional)

Very lightly oil 6 dariole moulds or ramekins (200ml capacity) or a 1-litre jelly mould. Follow the pack instructions to calculate how much gelatine, leaf or powdered, you need to set 900ml liquid (it's fine to cut leaves of gelatine in half to get the right amount).

If using leaf gelatine, pour some cold water into a shallow dish, add the gelatine sheets and leave for a few minutes to soften until floppy.

Meanwhile, put the raspberries, lemon zest and juice, and the icing sugar into a saucepan over a low heat. Cook very gently for a few minutes, crushing the berries lightly with a fork or potato masher to encourage them to soften and collapse. Take off the heat and tip the berry mix into a sieve set over a measuring jug. Rub through the sieve with a spoon or spatula to remove the pips. Add enough hot water to the purée to make it up to 900ml.

Lift the gelatine leaves from their water, squeeze out any excess water, then stir into the (still hot) raspberry liquid until fully dissolved. Leave to cool until tepid, stirring now and again.

If using powdered gelatine, transfer 300ml of the raspberry liquid to a saucepan and heat until steaming. Take off the heat, sprinkle the gelatine over the surface and stir until dissolved, then pour this liquid back into the rest of the raspberry liquid, stirring to incorporate fully. Leave to cool until tepid, stirring now and again.

Pour the tepid raspberry mixture equally into the mould(s). Let cool completely, then place in the fridge for several hours to set.

To turn out, dip the mould(s) in hot water for a few seconds then invert onto plates. If the jelly is reluctant to plop out, dip the mould back in the hot water for a few more seconds and try again. Serve with a little cream or yoghurt trickled over, if you like.

280

Blackcurrant fro-yo granita

Tangy, fruity frozen yoghurt, with more fruit than yoghurt, is a great way to push our frozen fruity treat buttons. And, as this is a granita version, there's no need to churn it in a machine. Served with extra yoghurt underneath, and a trickle of blackcurrant purée to finish, it's a simple but elegant and refreshing frozen pud.

SERVES 4

500g blackcurrants, fresh or defrosted if frozen (or you can use redcurrants, gooseberries or rhubarb)

100g golden caster sugar

Finely grated zest of 1 lemon and juice of ½ lemon

400g full-fat Greek-style yoghurt, or plant-based yoghurt

282

Put the blackcurrants (or other fruit) into a medium saucepan with the sugar, lemon zest and juice, and 100ml water. Bring to a simmer over a medium heat and cook, uncovered, stirring regularly, for 6–8 minutes or until the berries are soft and pulpy – you can squash them with the back of the spoon to help break them down into a rough purée. Leave to cool completely.

Press the cooled fruit purée through a sieve into a bowl to remove the pips. Set aside a quarter of it for serving.

Mix the other three-quarters of the purée with 250g of the yoghurt. Transfer to a shallow container and place in the freezer for at least 3 hours until frozen solid.

Transfer the fro-yo granita from the freezer to the fridge about 30 minutes before serving, so it softens slightly.

Divide the remaining yoghurt between 4 serving glasses or small bowls. Scrape the frozen berry mix into shards with a fork and put a generous pile of this granita on each portion of yoghurt. Trickle over the reserved fruit purée and serve straight away.

VARIATION

Fresh berry fro-yo granita: Use 500g fresh berries, such as raspberries, strawberries or blueberries, or a mixture. No need to cook them: just blend with 50–100g golden caster sugar (strawberries and blueberries need less sugar than raspberries), using a stick blender or jug blender. You can leave the pips in or sieve them out if you prefer. Proceed as above, using this mix in place of the cooked berries.

Basque-style cheesecake

You may have come across recipes in recent years for the lovely 'Basque burnt cheesecake', made famous by chef Santiago Rivera of La Viña restaurant in San Sebastián, Spain. Baked in a fairly fierce oven so it becomes richly burnished on top, this cheesecake is as good to look at as it is to eat; it's also easy to make. This is my version, with moderate sugar and a hint of orange zest. Serve it in small slices, either straight up or with any kind of fruit compote or some crushed fresh berries.

MAKES 10 SLICES

500g full-fat soft cream cheese (or make the labneh on page 316, starting with about 1kg yoghurt)

100g golden caster or soft light brown sugar

A pinch of salt

Finely grated zest of 1 orange

1 tsp vanilla extract

20g fine plain wholemeal flour

300ml half-fat crème fraîche or soured cream

3 medium eggs

Crushed fresh berries, plum compote (see page 21) or apple purée (see page 266), to serve (optional)

Preheat the oven to 220°C/200°C Fan/Gas 7.

Line the inside of a loose-bottomed 18cm round cake tin with a single piece of baking paper, first scrunching and unscrunching the paper to make it easier to manipulate. Leave the excess paper overhanging the rim of the tin. When peeled away, the wrinkled lining paper also gives the sides of the finished cheesecake a characteristic finish.

In a large bowl, or the bowl of a stand mixer, beat the cream cheese (or labneh) briefly until smooth, then beat in the sugar, salt, orange zest and vanilla extract, followed by the flour. Beat in the crème fraîche or soured cream, then finally beat in the eggs, one at a time, until you have a smooth mixture.

Pour the mixture carefully into the lined tin and place in the oven. Bake in the oven for 35–40 minutes until the cheesecake is puffed up and almost burnt around the edges. It should wobble a little when you shake the tin. Take it out of the oven and leave to cool in the tin (it will sink elegantly!).

You can eat this while still just warm, or at room temperature, or let it cool completely and refrigerate it. When you're ready to serve, carefully pull the paper away from the sides. Serve in small slices, with crushed berries or fruit compote if you like.

285

Pannacotta with fresh berries

A wobbly, creamy pannacotta is always a treat. For many years now at River Cottage, we have been making this lighter version, with yoghurt as well as cream, and just enough sugar to sweeten it lightly. Macerated strawberries and raspberries are a blissful fruity finish, but all sorts of fruity combinations and compotes work well.

MAKES 6

Leaf or powdered gelatine (or vegetarian gelatine), ideally organic, to set 300ml liquid (usually about 2 leaves or 1 tsp powdered, see method)

100ml whole milk

250ml double cream

1 vanilla pod, split and seeds scraped

40g caster sugar

150ml natural full-fat yoghurt

BERRIES

100g strawberries, hulled

100g raspberries

A scant tbsp caster sugar, or a trickle of honey

A squeeze of lemon juice

Have ready 6 dariole moulds or ramekins, or one larger mould or dish (about 600ml capacity).

Follow the pack instructions to calculate how much gelatine, leaf or powdered, you need to set 300ml liquid (you will have more mixture than this but because it contains yoghurt and isn't entirely liquid, you don't need as much gelatine to get a nice, tender set). If using leaf gelatine, pour some cold water into a shallow dish, add the leaves and leave for a few minutes until soft and floppy.

Combine the milk and cream in a saucepan and add the vanilla pod and seeds. Add the sugar and bring gently to a simmer, then turn off the heat. Leave for a moment to settle.

If you're using gelatine leaves, gently lift them out of their dish, squeeze out any excess water, then stir them into the hot milk and cream mix until completely dissolved. (If using powdered gelatine, sprinkle it over the hot milk and cream and stir gently but thoroughly until dissolved.) If it's reluctant to dissolve, you can gently reheat as you stir, but don't let it boil.

Leave the mixture to cool for a good few minutes until tepid, then take out the vanilla pod and gently stir in the yoghurt. Pour the mixture into the darioles or ramekins, or the larger mould, and place in the fridge for at least 4 hours, or overnight, to set.

Prepare the fruit up to 2 hours before serving. Slice the strawberries into a bowl. Add the raspberries and sugar or honey and lemon juice and stir together, squishing a few raspberries to release some juice. Leave to macerate somewhere cool for an hour or so, stirring once or twice. (The fruit is nicer to eat if it's not fridge-cold.)

To unmould the pannacotta(s), dip the mould(s) in hand-hot water for a few seconds, invert onto your chosen plate, and give a little shake. It should drop obligingly onto the plate. (If reluctant, try slightly hotter water and a slightly longer dip.) Spoon some macerated berries beside the pannacotta(s) and serve.

286

Hot chocolate pudding

This quick (and utterly delicious!) chocolate pud, which I've been making for years to delight my family, occupies a space somewhere between a brownie, a soufflé and a cake. I think you'll agree that's not a bad place to be. It can be whipped up easily (and on demand!) from store-cupboard ingredients. Briefly baked until set on the outside but still gooey in the middle, it is excellent served with some fruit to cut the richness. It's gluten-free too.

SERVES 4

100g dark chocolate, broken into pieces

100g butter, cut into pieces, plus extra to grease the dish

3 medium eggs

50g soft light brown sugar

1 tsp vanilla extract

75g ground almonds

A pinch of salt

TO SERVE

Raspberries or other berries, or plum compote (see page 21)

Yoghurt or cream (optional)

Put the chocolate and butter into a saucepan and melt gently over a very low heat, watching all the time and stirring often so that the chocolate doesn't get too hot. Set aside to cool a little.

Preheat the oven to 190°C/170°C Fan/Gas 5 and butter a small oven dish.

In a large bowl, or the bowl of a stand mixer, whisk the eggs, brown sugar and vanilla extract together until pale, thick and mousse-like. Using a stand mixer or hand-held electric whisk on full speed, this should only take a few minutes, but whisking by hand with a rotary or balloon whisk will take a lot longer! The mix should be significantly paler, thicker and increased in volume.

Turn the mixer down to a low speed and, with the motor running, slowly pour in the tepid melted chocolate and butter mixture (or whisk it gently by hand). Use a rubber spatula to scrape the last drops of chocolate into the mix, and then to fold the mixture fully together.

Combine the ground almonds and salt. Add to the chocolate mixture and fold in carefully, using the spatula.

Turn the mixture into the prepared oven dish and shake the dish a little to spread it out. Bake in the oven for 12–15 minutes until the pudding is set on top and firm at the edges, but still wobbly and gooey in the middle.

Serve straight away, with fresh raspberries or plum compote, and a spoonful of yoghurt or a trickle of cream if you like.

Sticky, rooty, fruity pudding

This is a heavenly pud, very much in the prime comfort zone of a classic sticky toffee pudding: hot, fluffy and sweet (but not sickly). The grated parsnip brings a pleasing carrot cake texture (indeed you can use carrots), and the creamy date sauce is a revelation.

SERVES 8

2–3 fairly ripe pears or eating apples (about 250g prepared weight)

125g butter, softened, plus a knob for the fruit

75g soft dark brown or dark muscovado sugar

125g fine plain wholemeal flour

125g rye flour (or use another 125g fine plain wholemeal)

2 tsp baking powder

½ tsp bicarbonate of soda

A pinch of salt

3 medium eggs

50ml warm milk

1 medium parsnip or carrot (about 150g), scrubbed or peeled and grated

150g raisins or unsulphured dried apricots, chopped

DATE SAUCE

250g pitted dates, roughly chopped

A pinch of salt

Juice of 1 small lemon

100ml double cream

Start by making the date sauce: put the dates, salt and lemon juice into a blender, pour in 250ml boiling water and blitz until as smooth as possible. Add the cream and blitz again briefly to combine into a sweet, thick, creamy sauce. Set aside.

Preheat the oven to 180°C/160°C Fan/Gas 4. Line a round baking dish or springform cake tin, around 23cm in diameter, with baking paper. Peel the pears or apples, quarter and core them; if they are large and very round, cut each quarter in half again.

Melt the knob of butter in a non-stick frying pan over a medium heat. Add the pear or apple wedges and fry for about 5 minutes until lightly caramelised. Now add about one-third of the date sauce and let it bubble down until reduced in volume by about one-third. Arrange the sticky, saucy pears or apples over the base of the prepared dish.

291

Put the butter and brown sugar into a large bowl or the bowl of a stand mixer. Using an electric hand mixer or the stand mixer, beat together until light and creamy. In another bowl, combine the flours, baking powder, bicarbonate of soda and salt. Add one egg to the creamed mixture, along with a spoonful of the flour mix, and beat together. Repeat to incorporate the other eggs.

Tip the remaining flour into the mixture, with the milk, and use a large spoon to fold it in lightly but thoroughly. Now fold in the grated parsnip or carrot and the dried fruit.

Spread the mixture over the sticky pears or apples in the prepared dish. Bake in the oven for 35–40 minutes or until risen and firm, and a skewer pressed into the centre comes out clean.

When the pudding is cooked, heat the remaining date sauce gently just until steaming. Turn the pudding out onto a platter so the sticky pears are on top. Serve in slices or squares, piping hot, with the date sauce poured on top.

Baked apples

It's easy to forget that simple old-fashioned puds can be good and comforting just as they are. A baked apple ticks all the comfort boxes: hot, sweet and buttery. Eating apples are best for baking; they are smaller so you get more filling to flesh, and sweeter so you need less sugar! A splash of apple juice added to the baking tin helps form a buttery syrup to go over the apples as you serve them. Cold cream is good to serve with, but my lighter custard (page 275) is arguably even better.

SERVES 6

6 medium eating apples
(about 125g each)

60g butter, softened

30g soft light brown sugar

Finely grated zest of 1 orange
or lemon

30g dried cranberries
(unsweetened), or other
dried fruit

½ tsp ground mixed spice
(optional)

About 200ml cloudy apple
juice (i.e. not from
concentrate)

Custard (page 275), to serve
(optional)

Preheat the oven to 180°C/160°C Fan/Gas 4. Have ready a small baking tin or dish in which the apples will fit quite snugly.

Using an apple corer, remove the core from each apple. Now use a small, sharp knife to score a line through the skin around the 'equator' of each apple so that the flesh can expand in the oven without the skin bursting.

In a small bowl, mash together the softened butter, brown sugar, citrus zest, dried fruit and mixed spice, if using. Pack this buttery 'stuffing' into the apple cavities. Sit the apples in the baking tin or dish and pour enough apple juice around them to cover the base by 3–4mm.

Bake in the oven for 30–40 minutes, or until the apples are soft when you press a skewer into the middle. The time can vary a bit depending on the variety, and some will become more fluffy than others, but as long as the apple is tender, you are good to go.

Serve straight away with a little of the buttery syrup in the dish spooned over the top of each apple. I like to have a jug of my lighter custard on the table too.

Lemon and raisin sponge pudding

Is it a steamed lemon pudding? Is it a spotted dick? I'd say it's both.
A lemony dick no less... Crank up the comfort factor on a chilly evening
or indulgent weekend lunchtime with this hot, light and fruity pud.

SERVES 6–8

150g butter, softened, plus extra to grease the basin

100g raisins

150g fine plain wholemeal flour

2 level tsp baking powder

A pinch of salt

75g golden caster sugar

Finely grated zest of 2 lemons and juice of 1 lemon

3 medium eggs

LEMONY TOPPING

Juice of 1 lemon (use the other zested lemon, see above)

2 tbsp soft dark brown sugar

TO SERVE

Cream, yoghurt, crème fraîche or custard (page 275)

Butter an 850ml pudding basin.

For the lemony topping, in a small bowl stir together the lemon juice and brown sugar until well blended (don't worry if the sugar doesn't fully dissolve). Tip this mixture into the buttered basin.

Toss the raisins with 1 tbsp of the flour and set aside (the flour coating helps to stop the raisins sinking as the pudding cooks). Combine the remaining flour with the baking powder and salt.

Put the butter, sugar and lemon zest into a large bowl or the bowl of a stand mixer. Using an electric hand mixer or the stand mixer, beat together until light and fluffy. Add one egg, with a spoonful of the flour mix, and beat in. Repeat to incorporate the other two eggs.

Tip the remaining flour into the mixture and use a large spoon to fold it in lightly but thoroughly, then fold in the lemon juice. Finally, lightly fold in the floured raisins.

Spoon the mixture carefully into the pudding basin (the lemony topping at the bottom will rise up the sides; don't worry about this). Cover the basin with a pleated sheet of foil or a pleated double layer of baking paper; secure with string under the rim.

Put a small plate or trivet in the base of a large, deep saucepan and stand the pudding on it. Pour in enough boiling water to come halfway up the sides of the basin. Cover the pan with a tight-fitting lid and place over a low to medium heat to bring the water to a simmer. Steam the pudding like this for 2 hours, topping up the boiling water a couple of times as it cooks.

Lift the pudding basin out of the pan and remove the foil or baking paper. Loosen the sides of the pudding with the tip of a knife, then invert the pudding onto a plate.

Serve the pudding in slices, with a trickle of cream, a spoonful of yoghurt or crème fraîche, or my lighter custard.

Plum cobbler

Bubbling fruity juices and a crisp-but-tender scone topping make this homely pud an absolute winner. You can, of course, use the cobbler topping with a different fruit base – try some of the fruity ideas described in the crumble recipe on page 270.

SERVES 8

1.5kg plums (or greengages), halved or quartered, depending on size, and stoned

2 whole star anise or 1 cinnamon stick (optional)

3–4 tbsp honey (or use soft light brown sugar if you prefer)

COBBLER TOPPING

125g fine plain wholemeal flour

2 tsp baking powder

50g cold butter, diced

50g soft light brown sugar or golden caster sugar

75g ground almonds

1 medium egg

100ml milk

Flaked almonds, to finish (optional)

TO SERVE

Cream, yoghurt, crème fraîche or custard (page 275)

Preheat the oven to 190°C/170°C Fan/Gas 5.

Put the halved or quartered plums in an oven dish, about 2-litre capacity. Tuck in the star anise or cinnamon, if using. Trickle over 3 tbsp honey (or scatter over 3 tbsp sugar). Place in the oven and roast for around 30 minutes until the plums are soft and juicy. Stir gently to mingle the juices. Taste and stir in a little more honey or sugar only if you think it needs it.

To make the topping, combine the flour and baking powder in a large bowl or a food processor. Add the butter and rub it into the flour either using your fingers, or by pulsing the processor. Tip out of the processor, if using, into a bowl.

Stir the sugar and ground almonds into the rubbed-in mixture. In a jug, beat the egg and milk thoroughly together then pour this into the dry mix and combine lightly with a fork or spoon to make a sticky dough. Don't over-mix or your cobbles may be a bit heavy!

Use a tablespoon or an ice-cream scoop to scoop up 'cobbles' of dough (ideally eight, but don't worry if it's fewer) and drop them, one at a time, on top of the plums. Sprinkle with flaked almonds if using.

Bake in the oven for 30 minutes or until the cobbles are risen and golden and a skewer poked into the middle of one cobble comes out clean.

Serve your plum cobbler hot with cream, yoghurt, crème fraîche or my lighter custard.

Stovetop spelt pudding

If you like rice pudding I'm sure you will love this variation, made with plump grains of pearled spelt or barley. The grains swell and soften in the milk but have a nuttier flavour and nubblier texture than pudding rice (as well as more fibre!), making a lovely creamy-but-textured pudding.

SERVES 4–5

150g pearled spelt or barley

700ml whole milk

30g golden caster or soft light brown sugar

½ vanilla pod, or 1 tsp vanilla paste or extract (optional)

A few gratings of nutmeg (optional)

TO SERVE

Plum compote (page 21) or other fruit compote, or fresh berries

Yoghurt (optional)

A little honey (optional)

Put the spelt or barley in a fairly deep saucepan, cover with the milk and leave to soak in the fridge or a cool place for about 1 hour to start the softening process.

Add the sugar to the pan, and the vanilla, if using. Put the pan over a medium-high heat and bring to a simmer, stirring often. Cover the pan and turn the heat right down low. Simmer very gently for around 45 minutes, taking off the lid and stirring every 5–10 minutes (you may find the milk bubbles up a bit, which is why a deep pan is helpful!).

The pudding is ready when the grains are plump and tender and the milk reduced to a creamy silky coating for the grains. Grate a little fresh nutmeg over the pudding if you like, then take the pan off the heat and leave to stand for 10 minutes before serving. It will gradually thicken up as it cools.

I like this hot with a spoonful of chilled fruit compote, but it's also good cold (when it's firmer but still tender), again with a compote or crushed fresh berries, a spoonful of yoghurt and a trickle of honey if you like. If you want to reheat the pudding, stir in a little more milk as you do so.

299

VARIATION

Vegan spelt pudding: Replace the milk with a plant-based milk, such as oat or almond.

Vg

Pear and almond tart

This is a beautiful tart, with a delicate, fragrant frangipane filling and lots of fresh pears, which contribute plenty of natural sweetness. For a quicker version, you can bake the filling and pears in a lightly buttered ceramic dish, rather than the pastry case.

MAKES 10–12 SLICES

1 quantity sweet half-wholemeal shortcrust pastry (page 143)

About 500g ripe or nearly-ripe pears (3–4 fairly large ones)

25g flaked almonds

ALMOND FILLING

100g butter, softened

75g soft light brown sugar

A few drops of almond extract (optional)

100g ground almonds

20g fine plain wholemeal flour

2 medium eggs

TO SERVE (OPTIONAL)

Yoghurt or half-fat crème fraîche

Preheat the oven to 180°C/160°C Fan/Gas 4. Roll out the pastry thinly on a floured surface and use to line a 24cm loose-based tart tin, leaving the excess overhanging the rim of the tart tin.

Stand the tin on a baking tray. Prick the pastry in a few places with a fork. Line the pastry with baking paper, then add a layer of baking beans and bake for 15 minutes. Remove the paper and beans and return the pastry case to the oven for 5–10 minutes or until it looks dry and is just starting to colour. Leave to cool a little, then trim off the overhanging pastry with a small sharp knife. (You can do all this up to 24 hours in advance.)

To make the almond filling, in a large bowl or the bowl of a stand mixer, beat together the butter, sugar and almond extract, if using, until light and creamy. In another bowl, combine the ground almonds and flour.

Add one egg to the creamed mixture, with a spoonful of the dry almond mix, and beat until well combined. Repeat to incorporate the other egg. Now fold in the remaining almond/flour mix, using a large metal spoon. Spoon into the pastry case and spread evenly.

Peel, quarter and core the pears. Arrange over the almond mix and press them in gently. Sprinkle the flaked almonds over the top. Return the tart to the oven, still at 180°C/160°C Fan/Gas 4, and bake for about 30 minutes until the almond filling is golden brown and just firm to the touch. Remove from the oven.

Leave the tart to cool partially or completely. Serve in slices, on its own or with yoghurt or half-fat crème fraîche.

VARIATIONS

Use whatever seasonal fruit you have to hand, in place of the pears. Halved fresh apricots, plums or greengages, or whole blueberries or cherries all work well. Or 5–8cm lengths of rhubarb (first lightly poached in a little orange juice and honey). In the winter, prunes or dried apricots, soaked in a little apple juice or cider brandy, make a sumptuous addition.

300

Teatime Treats

This chapter is all about baking, a branch of cookery that has gained huge popularity and momentum in recent years. That's brilliant, but also sometimes a little bit scary. I mean, I have a naturally sweet tooth. I love cakes, biscuits, pies and tarts as much as (and very often more than!) the next man. But some recipes doing the rounds these days have *hundreds* of grams of sugar in them.

And I must hold my hands up: there are some sweet treats in some of my earlier books that call for amounts of sugar that would now alarm me. But I'm not disowning them, I'm disarming them: when I go back to those recipes now, I adapt them in the way I've adapted the recipes you're about to see, dialling up the good, and dialling down the sweet.

Everything I said about puddings in the previous chapter is true here, too. Wholer baking is definitely not less delicious baking. I have had enormous fun tackling some of our all-time favourite cakes and bakes and working out ways to make them better for us without sacrificing their winning qualities. In fact, when I 'whole up' the flour element in a cake, from white to brown (or, more precisely, to what is often labelled 'fine plain wholemeal flour'), I almost invariably find them improved. Wholemeal flour has more flavour and a pleasing wheaty nuttiness. It can make some cakes a shade heavier, but only subtly so, and the taste gained outweighs (!) any marginal lightness lost.

I have also found that taking some of the sugar (about 25 per cent, for starters) out of conventional cake and sweet treat recipes quite often passes unnoticed. If it does garner comment, it is most often along the lines of, 'this is delicious, what's in it?' And when I mention what isn't in it, i.e. that I've actually made the bake in question with significantly less sugar, I often hear even avowedly sweet-toothed folk say they actually prefer it that way.

One of the things we are teaching ourselves when we bake like this is to get more pleasure from less sugar. In today's world, where highly refined carbohydrate is such a dominant element in our diets that it's difficult to avoid and often hard to resist, this is an important and empowering thing. Knowing that we have made a recipe better for our bodies should be a source of extra gratification too.

So, enjoy these cakes and cookies, scones and crumpets – not necessarily every day, but as special treats that bring you and those you love dependable pleasure, warm satisfaction and the very best kind of comfort.

Chocolate cake

Who doesn't like a slice of chocolate cake once in a while? This lovely wholemeal version can be put together easily for a teatime treat, or whipped up as a birthday cake. The chocolate icing is luscious too.

MAKES 12 SLICES

50g cocoa powder

100ml hot coffee (or hot water)

150g fine plain wholemeal flour

100g ground almonds or hazelnuts

2 tsp baking powder

4 medium eggs

100ml whole milk

2 tsp vanilla extract

200g butter, softened, plus extra to grease the tin(s)

150g golden caster or light soft brown sugar (or a mixture)

FILLING AND TOPPING

200g dark chocolate, broken into pieces

75g unsalted butter, softened

50g light soft brown sugar or honey

Preheat the oven to 180°C/160°C Fan/Gas 4. Butter two 20cm sandwich tins, or one 23cm round cake tin and line the base(s) with baking paper.

In a small bowl, mix the cocoa and hot coffee or water together to make a thick, smooth paste.

Put the flour, ground almonds or hazelnuts and baking powder into a bowl and whisk to combine.

In a jug, beat together the eggs, milk and vanilla extract.

Put the softened butter and sugar into a large bowl or the bowl of a stand mixer and beat together until light and fluffy. Add the cocoa paste and beat until smoothly combined.

Add a splash of the egg mixture and a good spoonful of the flour and mix in. Repeat this until all the egg mix and flour are incorporated. Divide the mixture evenly between the sandwich tins or spoon it all into the larger tin and gently smooth the top.

Transfer to the oven and bake until firm to the touch and a skewer inserted into the middle comes out clean; allow 30–35 minutes for two sandwich cakes, 40–45 minutes for a larger cake.

Leave the cake(s) to cool in the tin for 10 minutes then carefully turn out and place on a wire rack to finish cooling.

When the cakes are completely cooled, make the filling/topping. Melt the chocolate in a heatproof bowl over a pan of barely simmering water (or melt it directly in a heavy-based pan over a very low heat, watching the whole time). Leave to cool slightly. In a medium bowl, beat the butter with the sugar or honey until light and fluffy. Slowly trickle in the melted chocolate, beating all the time, until fully incorporated.

Use a little less than half of the chocolate mixture to sandwich the cakes together, and the rest to cover the top. You don't have to ice the sides, but do encourage the icing to creep over the edges. If you have baked a single, larger cake, just ice the top, generously.

Sesame banana bread

This quick and easy, vegan-friendly banana loaf is full of fibre and the tahini topping is a delight (a nut butter also works well). Just the thing for a packed lunch or an afternoon tea break.

MAKES 10 SLICES

3 very ripe medium-sized bananas (350–400g unpeeled weight)

75g tahini (or a nut butter)

100g soft light brown sugar

1 tbsp cider vinegar

175g fine plain wholemeal flour

1 tbsp ground flaxseed

2 tsp baking powder

1 tsp bicarbonate of soda

¼ tsp salt

75g raisins (optional)

SESAME TOPPING

30g tahini (or a nut butter)

20g soft light brown sugar

1–2 tsp vegetable oil (if needed)

2 tsp sesame seeds (or flaked almonds)

Preheat the oven to 180°C/160°C Fan/Gas 4 and line a 1kg loaf tin with baking paper. If you tear off a sheet of paper and scrunch it up, place it in the loaf tin then wedge a second loaf tin over the top to 'mould' the paper – this is really easy!

The simplest way to make this cake is in a mixer, or using a hand-held mixer in a large bowl, but you can do it all by hand. Drop the peeled bananas into the bowl. Beat with the mixer or mash with a fork to get a rough purée. Add the tahini (or nut butter) and beat to combine with the banana. Add the brown sugar and beat thoroughly, then incorporate the cider vinegar.

In another bowl, thoroughly mix the flour, flaxseed, baking powder, bicarbonate of soda and salt together, making sure there are no little white lumps of bicarb still visible. Stir the raisins into this dry mix, if using. Add to the banana mixture and beat to combine. Tip the mixture into the prepared tin.

For the topping, mix the tahini (or nut butter) and brown sugar together to make a thick paste. You can add 1–2 tsp oil if it's very stiff. Dot this topping over the top of the mixture in the loaf tin then sprinkle over the sesame seeds (or flaked almonds). Bake in the oven for 50–55 minutes, until a skewer pressed into the centre comes out clean.

Leave the banana loaf to cool completely in the tin before removing. Serve cut into thick slices.

308

Lemon drizzle cake

Zesty and sweet, light but satisfying, lemon drizzle cake has achieved iconic teatime status. This version has far less sugar than conventional recipes and it still upholds the standard effortlessly. Every time I put it on the table, it's gone within minutes.

MAKES 10 SLICES

125g unsalted butter, softened

75g golden caster sugar, plus 1 tbsp to finish

Finely grated zest and juice of 2 large lemons

100g fine plain wholemeal flour

2 tsp baking powder

100g ground almonds

25g poppy seeds (optional)

3 medium eggs

A splash of milk or water

Preheat the oven to 180°C/160°C Fan/Gas 4. Line a 1kg loaf tin with baking paper (see page 308 for an easy way to do this).

Put the butter, sugar and lemon zest into a large bowl or the bowl of a stand mixer. Using an electric hand mixer or the stand mixer, beat together until light and fluffy.

In a separate bowl, thoroughly combine the flour, baking powder, ground almonds and poppy seeds if using.

Add one egg to the beaten mixture, with a spoonful of the flour mix, and beat until combined. Repeat to incorporate the remaining eggs, one at a time, adding a spoonful of flour each time and scraping down the sides with a spatula now and then.

Tip the remaining flour into the mixture and use a large spoon to fold it in lightly but thoroughly. Fold in the juice of 1 lemon to loosen the mix a little, with an extra splash of milk or water if needed to bring the mixture to a good dropping consistency.

Tip the mixture into the prepared loaf tin and bake in the oven for 35–40 minutes until a skewer pressed into the centre of the cake comes out clean. Transfer the tin to a wire rack and make deep holes all over the surface of the cake with a skewer.

Combine the juice of the other lemon with the 1 tbsp sugar – don't worry if the sugar doesn't dissolve. Spoon this lemony, crunchy drizzle all over the warm cake in its tin. Leave to cool completely before removing from the tin and slicing.

VARIATION

St Clement's drizzle cake: Replace one of the lemons with an orange (the zest goes in the cake, with half the juice, the other half of the juice goes in the drizzle). While the cake is baking, slice all the peel and pith off 2 large or 3 medium oranges, then cut across into 5mm slices. Add to a bowl with any saved juice. Serve the cake still warm as a pudding, with a few sliced oranges and a spoonful of yoghurt on each plate.

Victoria sandwich with apricot filling

This is my 'new normal' every-occasion sponge cake. It is delicious – and no one has ever commented on it not being sweet enough! You can, if you like, follow the time-honoured tradition of weighing the 4 eggs for the cake then using exactly the same weight of butter and flour – but when it comes to the sugar, use only a little over half the weight!

The jammy, sweet apricot filling has bags of flavour but no added sugar – inviting you to be extra generous with it. The dried apricots do need a few hours' soaking time so, if you are in a hurry, you can replace it with a shop-bought fruit spread or reduced-sugar jam, or serve it with crushed fresh berries and just a little sugar (see the variation overleaf).

MAKES 10 SLICES

225g butter, softened, plus a little extra to grease the tins

125g golden caster sugar

1 tsp vanilla extract

225g fine plain wholemeal flour

2 tsp baking powder

A pinch of salt (if using unsalted butter)

4 medium eggs

A little milk or water

1 tsp icing sugar (optional)

APRICOT FILLING

200g unsulphured dried apricots, roughly chopped

Finely grated zest and juice of 2 oranges (150ml juice)

Finely grated zest and juice of ½ lemon

Start the apricot filling ahead of time, ideally the night before. Put the dried apricots into a bowl with all the citrus zest and juice. Leave to soak until the apricots have plumped up and absorbed nearly all the juice, probably at least 4 hours.

Using a hand-held stick blender, blitz the apricots to a chunky, jammy consistency. (If you don't have a hand blender, you can bash the fruit up with a pestle or the end of a rolling pin.) Refrigerate until needed.

Preheat the oven to 180°C/160°C Fan/Gas 4. Lightly butter two 20cm sandwich tins and line the bases with baking paper.

Put the butter, sugar and vanilla extract into a large bowl or the bowl of a stand mixer. Using an electric hand mixer or the stand mixer, beat together until light and fluffy.

In a second bowl, thoroughly combine the flour and baking powder, plus a pinch of salt if you've used unsalted butter.

Add one egg and a spoonful of the flour mix to the beaten mix and beat to combine. Repeat to incorporate the remaining eggs, adding a spoonful of flour each time and scraping down the sides with a spatula now and then.

Tip the remaining flour into the mixture and use a large spoon to fold it in lightly but thoroughly, adding a splash of milk or water if needed to loosen the batter a little.

Continued overleaf →

313

You're looking for a good 'dropping consistency' – the batter should fall easily off a spoon knocked on the side of the bowl.

Divide the mixture evenly between the two prepared sandwich tins and lightly smooth the tops. Transfer to the oven and bake for 25 minutes, until risen, golden and shrinking slightly from the sides of the tins. A skewer pressed into the centre of the cakes should come out clean.

Let the cakes cool in the tins for 5 minutes, then turn them out onto a wire rack and leave to cool completely.

When the cakes are cooled, place the one with the least perfect top upside down on a serving plate. Spoon the apricot filling thickly over the surface. (There will probably be some left over which you can serve on the side with the cake, or have for breakfast with muesli or yoghurt, or on your wholegrain toast.) Put the second cake on top, domed side upwards. Finish, if you like, with a sifted dusting of icing sugar.

You can serve this cake straight up for tea. It also makes a lovely pud – especially if you spoon over some of the extra filling, and a dollop of natural yoghurt, or half yoghurt, half whipped cream.

VARIATION

Fresh berry pudding cake: You can make a lovely summer pudding of this cake by serving it with macerated fresh strawberries and/or raspberries. Hull and thickly slice 200g strawberries and place in a bowl. Or roughly crush 200g raspberries in the bowl. Even better, use 100g of each. Add the juice of ½ lemon and 1 tbsp (15g) sugar and mix well. Leave to macerate for half an hour or so, then stir again, taste and add a squeeze more lemon or a pinch more sugar if needed. You can sandwich the two cakes together with a few spoonfuls of the fruit, and serve the rest on the side. Or simply put slices of the cakes into bowls and spoon over the berries and their juice. Whipped cream, or yoghurt, or a mix of the two, will be a lovely addition.

Carrot cake

This recipe slashes the typical sugar content of conventional carrot cakes by around 50 per cent and tastes all the better for it. The light but luscious topping is based on yoghurt, strained into thick labneh.

MAKES 10–12 SLICES

200g grated carrots

Finely grated zest of 1 large orange

100g raisins

175g fine plain wholemeal flour

75g desiccated coconut

½ tsp bicarbonate of soda

1 tsp ground mixed spice

1 tsp ground cinnamon

A generous grating of nutmeg

A good pinch of salt

3 medium eggs

75g soft light brown sugar

1 tbsp honey

150ml vegetable oil

LABNEH TOPPING

475g natural full-fat yoghurt

A pinch of salt

50g butter, softened

50g icing sugar

Finely grated zest of 1 orange

TO FINISH (OPTIONAL)

Any of the following:

Edible flowers, such as borage, nasturtium or marigold

Walnuts or pecans (chopped or halves)

To start the labneh, line a sieve or colander with a clean wet tea towel and place over a large measuring jug if you have one, or a bowl. Stir a pinch of salt into the yoghurt and then pour it all into the lined sieve. The thin pale whey will start to drip through the tea towel into the bowl. Leave in a cool place for this process to continue while you make the cake.

Preheat the oven to 180°C/160°C Fan/Gas 4. Line a 20cm round springform tin with baking paper.

Combine the grated carrots, orange zest and raisins in a bowl and set aside. In another bowl, thoroughly mix the flour, coconut, bicarbonate of soda, spices and salt together; set aside.

Put the eggs, brown sugar, honey and oil into a large bowl or the bowl of a stand mixer. Whisk vigorously for a few minutes, using an electric hand whisk or the whisk attachment on the mixer, until emulsified and foamy.

Tip in the flour mixture and stir in lightly. Add the grated carrot mix and stir until well combined. Tip the mixture into the tin and smooth out.

Bake in the oven for 45–50 minutes until the cake is risen and golden and a skewer pressed into the centre comes out clean. Leave to cool in the tin for 15 minutes, then remove and place on a wire rack. Leave to cool completely.

Meanwhile, finish the topping. Strain out at least a third of the liquid from the yoghurt, and up to half (175–225ml). To get more whey out, lift the corners of the tea towel and twist and squeeze.

In a separate bowl, beat together the butter, icing sugar and orange zest until light and fluffy, then beat in the labneh.

Once the cake is completely cooled, spread the labneh topping thickly over the top. Decorate with edible flowers or nuts if you like. Because of the fresh labneh topping and lower sugar content, this cake is best kept in a cool place, or the fridge, if you're not having it straight away. Eat within 48 hours.

(The new) brownies

Brownies mean different things to different people, and those who make them usually have a recipe they swear by. One thing most recipes have in common is far more sugar than is necessary. That shed-load of sugar is a short cut to the fudginess we expect from a classic brownie, but it's not the only way to get there. This carefully concocted recipe has only about 50 per cent of the sugar you'll find in a 'normal' brownie, but it goes big on good-quality dark chocolate and uses grated apple, as well as ground almonds or hazelnuts, for a rich, tender texture. Whatever your go-to brownie recipe is now, I'm betting this one will win you over. *Pictured overleaf*

MAKES 16–20

175g unsalted butter, roughly chopped

300g dark chocolate (around 70% cocoa solids), roughly chopped

3 medium eggs

125g soft light brown sugar

2 tsp vanilla extract

75g fine plain wholemeal flour or wholegrain spelt flour

75g ground almonds or hazelnuts

A pinch of salt

2 medium eating apples

Preheat the oven to 180°C/160°C Fan/Gas 4. Line a baking tin about 20 x 25cm with baking paper.

Very gently melt the butter and 200g of the chocolate together in a pan over a low heat, watching and stirring regularly; don't let the mixture get too hot or the chocolate can go grainy. Take the pan off the heat as soon as, or even just before, everything is completely melted. Set aside to cool a little while you prepare the other ingredients.

Whisk the eggs, brown sugar and vanilla extract together in a jug or bowl until smoothly combined.

Combine the flour, ground almonds or hazelnuts and salt in another bowl.

Peel the apples and grate them coarsely onto a board or into a third bowl. You can leave the peel on, but I'd recommend picking out any big bits of skin.

Pour the whisked egg mixture into the tepid melted chocolate and stir until the mixture thickens. Stir in the apple, then tip in the flour mix and stir in lightly. Finally, fold in the remaining 100g chopped chocolate.

Tip the mixture into the prepared tin and spread it out so it's fairly even. Bake in the oven for 30–35 minutes until set on top, and a skewer pressed into the middle comes out clean. Set aside to cool completely, or at least mostly.

Cut into slices to serve. You can eat the brownies warm or at room temperature, or chill them in the fridge to become firm and fudgy.

318

VARIATIONS

Fruit and nut brownies: Fold 100g dried cherries, cranberries or raisins and 100g roughly chopped pecans, walnuts, almonds or hazelnuts into the mixture at the end in place of the final 100g chopped chocolate.

Beetroot brownies: Replace the apple with 200g cooked, cooled, coarsely grated beetroot.

Raspberry brownies: Reduce the apple to 100g and fold about 100g fresh or frozen raspberries into the batter at the same time. Spread the batter in the tin and press an extra 50g raspberries into the surface of the brownie before baking.

Gluten-free brownies: You can replace the flour with 75g gluten-free plain flour for a GF brownie.

Vegan brownies: Soak 3 tbsp ground flaxseed in 8 tbsp warm water for half an hour and use this to replace the eggs. Replace the butter with 140g coconut oil.

Vg

Fruity tea loaf

This gorgeous slab of fruity goodness is based on a recipe from *The River Cottage Baby and Toddler Cookbook*, by my key collaborator, the brilliant Nikki Duffy. The cake is vegan and completely free of refined sugar, yet delightfully juicy, sweet and delicious. Please try it even if you think you don't like fruit cakes!

MAKES 10 SLICES

150g dried cranberries (ideally unsweetened)

150g unsulphured dried apricots, roughly chopped

275g sultanas or raisins

300ml hot, strong tea (made with 2 tea bags)

225g fine plain wholemeal flour

50g ground almonds

2 tsp baking powder

2 tsp ground mixed spice

About 60g walnut halves or roughly chopped walnuts (optional)

Mix the dried cranberries, dried apricots and sultanas or raisins together in a large bowl. Squeeze out and discard the tea bags then pour the hot tea over the dried fruit and stir well. Leave for at least 30 minutes (an hour if you can spare it), stirring a few times, so the fruit starts to soak up the liquid.

Preheat the oven to 170°C/150°C Fan/Gas 3. Line a 1kg loaf tin with baking paper (see page 308 for an easy way to do this).

Thoroughly combine the flour, ground almonds, baking powder and mixed spice. Tip this dry mix into the bowl of soaking fruit and stir until thoroughly combined.

Spoon the mixture into the prepared tin, press it down and spread evenly. If you are using walnuts, press them lightly over the surface of the cake.

Bake for 50–55 minutes, until the cake is risen, golden brown and a skewer pressed into the centre comes out clean.

Leave the cake to cool completely in the tin before removing and slicing. It will keep well in an airtight container for several days.

VARIATIONS

You can, of course, mix and match the dried fruit here, depending on what you have available – roughly chopped dates or figs are both good, for example, as are dried apples and pears, chopped into small pieces. Flaked almonds or roughly chopped hazelnuts can replace the walnuts on top.

Browned butter wholemeal shortbread

Browning butter is a slightly cheffy but very simple trick, used in both sweet and savoury dishes, that deepens the buttery flavour giving you a 'less is more' richness. It works brilliantly in this lovely wholemeal shortbread, but you can certainly use ordinary (non-browned) butter if you prefer.

The finished shortbread is crumbly and quite fragile, but no less delicious for that. It's a fine teatime treat and also a great contrasting accompaniment to fruit fools and ices.

MAKES 8 SLICES

100g unsalted butter, softened

30g caster sugar or soft light brown sugar

150g fine plain wholemeal flour

A pinch of salt

324

To prepare the browned butter, if using, put the butter in a wide pan (ideally one with a light-coloured base, so you can see the colour of the butter change). Melt the butter over a low heat then increase the heat a little so it starts to bubble. Let it cook for about 5 minutes – it will bubble and spit at first as the water in the butter cooks off, then you will see particles start to brown (these are milk solids), followed by a deepening of the colour of the liquid butter.

When it smells sweet and toasty, the butter solids are brown (not black) and the liquid butter is a rich golden colour, take it off the heat and tip into a large bowl. Leave to cool at room temperature and re-set, so it is no longer melted, but soft and easy to beat.

Preheat the oven to 160°C/140°C Fan/Gas 3. Add the sugar to the butter (browned or not) and beat together thoroughly. Combine the flour and salt, add to the butter mix and keep beating until you have a mass of crumbs. Use your hands to knead and pack the dough into a lump (it's a very crumbly dough).

Lift the dough onto a piece of baking paper and either press flat with your hands, or use a rolling pin, to shape it into a rough circle, 7–8mm thick. Push in the edges a little to make sure they are even, not frayed, and the dough is nicely compacted. Use a sharp knife to cut the dough halfway through into 4 quarters, then into 8 equal triangles.

Lift the wholemeal shortbread on its baking paper onto a baking tray and place in the oven. Bake for about 25 minutes until it is just starting to colour at the edges. Remove from the oven and leave to cool completely. When cool, carefully break the shortbread into the 8 pre-cut triangles.

Millionaire's shortbread

I've never really enjoyed conventional millionaire's shortbread: it's just too sweet and cloying. This, however, is a different story. Based on a layer of browned butter shortbread, it includes a sticky date 'caramel' and a thin layer of dark chocolate, which cracks enticingly when cut into. The whole thing is just the right depth to feel like a treat – but not so deep and sugary as to leave you feeling queasy.

MAKES 12 PIECES

1 quantity wholemeal shortbread dough (page 324, made with browned butter or standard butter)

250g pitted dates, roughly chopped

A good pinch of salt

50g butter, diced

100g dark chocolate, broken into pieces

Preheat the oven to 160°C/140°C Fan/Gas 3. Line a small baking tin, about 16 x 24cm, with baking paper.

Once you've made the shortbread dough, tip it into the prepared tin (no need to form it into a ball) and use your hands to press it out into a fairly even layer. It doesn't need to be perfect, but do make sure the base is completely covered. Bake for about 25 minutes, until just starting to colour. Leave to cool completely.

Meanwhile, put the roughly chopped dates into a blender with the salt and butter. Pour on 100ml boiling water and blitz to a thick 'caramel'. This will probably take a few goes, as you may need to stop and scrape down the sides once or twice, but you should end up with a thick, rich purée that holds its own shape.

When the shortbread base is completely cool, spread the date caramel evenly over the surface. Melt the chocolate in a heatproof bowl over a pan of barely simmering water (or melt it directly in a heavy-based pan over a very low heat, watching the whole time). Pour the melted chocolate all over the caramel and use the back of a spoon to spread it evenly.

Put the caramel-and-chocolate-topped shortbread into the fridge to chill until the chocolate is completely set.

To serve, use the baking paper to lift the shortbread out of the tin and then cut it into pieces. Don't worry about cracking chocolate and oozing caramel. It's part of the fun.

Wholemeal hot cross buns

What could be nicer at Easter (or any other time), than a warm-from-the-oven, generously fruited, lightly spiced bun, with a hint of citrus zest? The fruit lends natural sweetness so little extra sugar is needed.

MAKES 12 SMALL OR
8 LARGE BUNS

250g wholemeal bread flour, or spelt flour

250g strong white bread flour, plus extra for the crosses

7g sachet (or 2 tsp) fast-action dried yeast

35g golden caster sugar

200g raisins

Finely grated zest of 1 orange

Finely grated zest of 1 lemon

1–2 tsp ground mixed spice, to taste

1 tsp fine salt

200ml tepid milk

50g unsalted butter, melted and slightly cooled

2 medium eggs

Vegetable oil, for oiling

TO FINISH

75g plain white flour, for the crosses

2–3 tbsp jam or marmalade, sieved, to glaze (optional)

In a large bowl, mix the flours, yeast, sugar, raisins, citrus zests, spice and salt together. In a jug, combine the tepid milk and melted butter and beat in the eggs. Pour into the dry ingredients and mix to a rough dough. Turn out onto a lightly oiled work surface and knead for about 5 minutes until the dough is fairly smooth.

Put the dough into a lightly oiled bowl, cover with a cloth and leave in a warm place to rise for 1½–2 hours or until roughly doubled in size. Line a baking tray with baking paper.

Tip the dough out onto a lightly oiled surface. Cut into 8–12 equal pieces. Shape each into a neat round bun, flatten slightly with the palm of your hand and place on the prepared tray. Cover with a cloth again and leave to prove for a further 45 minutes.

Preheat the oven to 220°C/200°C Fan/Gas 7.

For the crosses, mix the flour with about 50ml water to make a dough, roll out to a 2–3mm thickness and cut into strips. Brush the risen buns lightly with milk before placing the strips on them to form crosses. Trim as necessary and brush with milk.

Bake the buns for about 20 minutes, until risen and golden brown. Transfer to a wire rack to cool. If you'd like a sticky glaze, gently heat some sieved jam or marmalade, stirring, to loosen it, then brush over the warm buns with a pastry brush.

You can either eat the buns while still warm from the oven, split and buttered, or leave them until cool, split and lightly toast them before buttering. They are best eaten within 48 hours of baking.

VARIATION

Sourdough hot cross buns: Use 150g active starter instead of the yeast. Stir it into the warm milk, butter and egg, then mix with all the other ingredients, adding a little more flour if the dough is very loose, or a little more milk if it is tight. Knead as above. Leave the dough to rise for 4–6 hours until increased in volume. Shape the buns as above and leave to prove for 2 hours before applying the crosses and baking.

Wholer crumpets

On a winter's afternoon hot crumpets, topped with a smear of salty butter and perhaps a trickle of honey, are about as comforting as it gets. This half-wholegrain recipe is more wholesome and delicious than any shop-bought crumpets. You do need one bit of kit: crumpet rings, ideally non-stick, to hold the loose batter in shape while it cooks and sets. The standard size is 8.5–9cm diameter and that's what this recipe calls for.

While scrumptious fresh from the pan, the crumpets can be kept for a couple of days in a cool bread bin or sealed container in the fridge and then toasted to revive.

MAKES ABOUT 15

150g strong wholemeal bread flour

150g strong white bread flour

7g sachet (or 1 tsp) easy-blend dried yeast

300ml milk (dairy or plant-based)

2 tsp cider vinegar

¾ level tsp fine salt

½ tsp bicarbonate of soda

Vegetable oil, to cook

Butter and jam or fruit compote, honey or maple syrup, to serve

Mix the flours and yeast together in a large bowl. Combine the milk and 200ml water in a saucepan and heat gently until tepid (no hotter). Pour the warm liquid into the flour mix and whisk to a smooth batter. Whisk in the cider vinegar. Cover the batter and leave to stand in a fairly warm place for about 2 hours, until really bubbly.

When you are ready to cook the crumpets, set the oven to a low heat (around 80°C or, if using gas, as low as it will go). Sprinkle the salt and bicarbonate of soda over the bubbly surface of the crumpet batter and whisk them in.

Have a little dish of oil and a pastry brush at the ready. Heat a large heavy-based frying pan or griddle over a medium heat and brush a little oil over the base. Use the brush to liberally oil the inside of four 8.5–9cm diameter non-stick crumpet rings.

First, cook one tester crumpet: put one crumpet ring in the pan and use a small ladle or mini measuring jug to pour in about 50ml batter. The crumpet ring should be barely half-full. Let the batter cook, slowly bubbling and rising, until the crumpet is full of holes, nearly all 'set' and there's only a little uncooked batter still visible in the middle of the top. This will take at least 6–8 minutes – but watch your crumpet rather than the clock! Keep an eye on the heat of the pan – it should be moderate to keep the crumpet cooking, but not so hot that the base burns.

When the crumpet is nearly completely set, you should be able to use tongs to lift the crumpet ring off. Then use a spatula to

Continued overleaf →

331

gently flip the crumpet over. If the ring won't come off easily, flip the whole thing over and gently press the crumpet down to release it, so its uncooked surface is in contact with the pan. You can then lift off the ring. Cook for another couple of minutes, until the top is coloured a light golden brown. Transfer the cooked crumpet to a dish and place in the warm oven.

This test run will tell you if your batter is the right consistency: if the batter runs out from under the ring, it is too runny; if no holes appear in the crumpet, it is too thick. Add a little more flour or water to the batter accordingly, if need be.

Cook the rest of the batter in the same way, re-oiling the rings and the pan in between each batch. You should be able to get all 4 crumpet rings going at the same time if your pan is big enough.

Serve the freshly cooked crumpets straight away with butter and jam or fruit compote, honey, maple syrup or whatever else takes your fancy. They will be just as delicious the next day, reheated in the toaster.

VARIATIONS

Rye crumpets: You can add some rye flour to this batter if you like – swap in 75g dark rye flour for half of the wholemeal.

Seedy crumpets: Soak a handful of seeds (sunflower, pumpkin, barley or spelt) in a bowl of water in the fridge overnight, before adding them to the batter.

Sourdough crumpets: Take about 2 tbsp active sourdough starter and add 200g bread flour (half white/half wholemeal) then mix in enough water to let it down to a loose batter consistency – about 250ml. Leave the batter in a warm place for several hours or overnight, until bubbling and frothing. Then whisk in 1 tsp each of salt and bicarbonate of soda. Make the crumpets as above. If you have plenty of live, bubbly starter, you can actually make crumpets with it as is, instead of discarding it. Leave just enough starter for your next loaf...

Gluten-free crumpets: Swap in gluten-free bread flours (white and brown) for the standard flours used in the recipe and make sure your yeast and bicarbonate of soda are gluten-free too. You may need to cook your pancakes for a little longer because gluten-free batter takes a bit more time to 'set'.

Oaty dunking cookies

This is such a simple and rewarding little recipe – just right for when you get a hankering for something sweet to dip into a cup of tea. I've deliberately kept this batch small – so you don't have a tinful of cookies sitting around! But you can easily double up the quantities if you'd like to make more. Below are some lovely variations to this simple recipe.

MAKES ABOUT 8

125g butter

50g soft light brown sugar

125g fine plain wholemeal flour

75g porridge oats

A pinch of salt

Preheat the oven to 180°C/160°C Fan/Gas 4. Line a baking tray with baking paper.

Put the butter and brown sugar into a small saucepan over a low heat to melt the butter gently, stirring often. Take off the heat.

Mix the flour, oats and salt and stir into the melted mixture. Take dessertspoonfuls of the mix and place in piles on the baking sheet, then use the back of the spoon to flatten each pile into a rough circle, no more than about 1cm deep.

Bake in the oven for 10–12 minutes, until the cookies are turning golden at the edges. They'll still be soft at this point: leave to cool completely and crisp up before removing from the tray. Store in an airtight container for up to a week.

Serve with a mug of tea, coffee or hot chocolate (page 48), for dunking your cookies.

VARIATIONS

Fruity oat cookies: After mixing in the oats and flour, stir in the grated zest of an orange or lemon, or both, and mix in about 30g raisins or dried cranberries, or chopped dried apples.

Chocolate chip cookies: Fold about 50g roughly chopped chocolate into the finished cookie dough.

Chai masala cookies: Crush the seeds from 6–8 cardamom pods (or use ½ tsp ground cardamom). Add to the melted mixture with ½ tsp each of ground ginger and cinnamon before adding the flour etc.

Fruit scones

The perfect teatime treat, these half-wholemeal scones are sweetened with minimal sugar, dried fruit and a grated apple. The tiny sprinkle of sugar on top is a surprisingly treaty finish, though it's optional. Don't be alarmed by the very hot oven – it's needed to get the scones rising, and they don't stay in for long.

MAKES 6–8

125g plain flour, plus extra to dust

125g fine plain wholemeal flour

2 tsp baking powder

1 tsp bicarbonate of soda

½ tsp salt

25g golden caster or soft light brown sugar

50g cold unsalted butter, diced

100g raisins or sultanas, or dried apricots, prunes or dried apple, roughly chopped

1 medium eating apple, grated

1 medium egg

About 100ml milk

Demerara or caster sugar, to finish (optional)

Preheat the oven to 220°C/200°C Fan/Gas 7 and line a baking tray with baking paper, or flour it generously.

In a large bowl or a food processor, combine the flours, baking powder, bicarbonate of soda, salt and sugar. Add the butter and rub it in with your fingers, or by pulsing the food processor, until the mixture looks like very fine crumbs. Transfer the mixture to a bowl if you started in the processor.

Add the dried fruit and the grated apple to the mixture and stir well to combine.

Beat the egg in a small measuring jug, then add enough milk to make up to 150ml. Gradually trickle the liquid into the fruity mixture, stirring until you have a slightly sticky dough, without overworking it.

Tip the dough out onto a floured board and, with floured hands, pat it into a small cake, about 15cm in diameter and 4–5cm deep. Sprinkle a little more flour over the surface and cut the dough into 6–8 wedges.

Use a floured knife to transfer the scones to the prepared baking tray and scatter a pinch of demerara or caster sugar on top of each one, if you like. Bake in the oven for 20 minutes until roughly doubled in size and golden brown.

Leave the scones to cool a little, or completely, before eating.

337

VARIATION

If you don't happen to have an apple to hand, you can simply leave it out. Enriched with dried fruit, the scones will still be deliciously fruity.

Ingredients

Much of the goodness in these comforting recipes (and not a little of the comfort, come to that) depends on choosing good ingredients. Here are some thoughts and tips on ingredients you'll be using quite a lot.

AVOCADOS

Avocados are full of monounsaturated oils and vitamins and and a good source of fibre, with a unique, buttery-but-firm texture. But there are huge environmental and social problems with their production. Such is Western demand that vast plantations have been created in Mexico and South American countries, often on recently deforested land. This impacts on food security for local people. And in some of these places the production of avocados is linked to drug cartels. Fairtrade avocados exist but are currently not available in the UK. I don't think we should boycott avocados, but we should rethink our consumption. To quote Patrick Holden of the Sustainable Food Trust, 'Avocado isn't a problem in itself, it's the fact it's become a staple when it should be a luxury.' I think it's better to spend more on organic avocados (which are never grown on recently deforested land) and have them less often.

CHOCOLATE/CACAO

Chocolate is derived from a plant – the pods of the cacao tree – so the less that's been done to it, the more whole it remains. Ultra-processed, super-sweetened milk chocolate is about as far from whole as possible. I'm keen to intercept this ingredient a little closer to source. Raw (which means fermented but unroasted) cacao is sold either as 'nibs' or powder – bitter but delicious. A little further along the continuum are the raw, often vegan, chocolate bars sweetened with various types of sugar – they taste a little different to 'normal' chocolate but you can melt them and cook with them. At the more traditional end of the spectrum are chocolate bars made with roasted cocoa – I go for organic dark chocolate with at least 70% cocoa solids and as little sugar as possible (check the label because some brands of dark chocolate contain almost as much sugar as milk chocolate).

CREAM

Using cream, single or double – as an ingredient and to pour on dishes – adds treaty luxury and indulgent comfort. I also suggest organic half-fat crème fraîche in several recipes – it has 14–17% fat rather than the 30–40% of standard crème fraîche and the 46–50% of double cream. The brand I go for is Yeo Valley Organic; many other brands of reduced-fat crème fraîche employ stabilisers and thickeners such as pectin and starch. Yeo Valley only use a combination of bacterial cultures, time and temperature to create thickness naturally. Soured cream, which has a similar fat content to half-fat crème fraîche, is a good alternative.

DRIED FRUIT

Invaluable as a source of sweetness, fibre and texture, I use a lot of dried fruit. It's relatively high in sugars but they are part of the whole fruit – bound up with all the other goodness you'd get from the fresh version. I am rarely without raisins and unsulphured dried apricots, and prunes, cranberries and dates also make appearances on my shelves. I buy them from my local health food shop because I know I can get an organic product with little added except perhaps sunflower oil, which stops dried fruit sticking together. I try to avoid brands with added sugar (although with berries, that isn't always easy) and those treated with sulphur dioxide, which halts fermentation and preserves an unnaturally bright colour.

EGGS

All the eggs used in this book are medium. Please also choose free-range or organic, which have better welfare standards for laying hens. And if home-laid is an option that's open to you, it's probably the best choice of all.

FISH

There aren't many things that ebb and flow like the global fish situation – it can be confusing. But there are a few signposts to help you with your sustainable fish shopping. Firstly, aim not to eat the same type of fish all the time – a multi-species approach is inherently more sustainable. Second, get acqauinted with the Marine Conservation Society's Good Fish Guide (mcsuk.org/goodfishguide) which is an excellent way to navigate through stormy waters.

FLOUR

Wholemeal flour used to be a pretty coarse and heavy affair but it's now easy to find finer, plain wholemeal flours. These have around 10g fibre per 100g, compared to around 3g in a plain white flour. My go-to brand is Doves Farm, whose fine plain wholemeal flour is a staple in my cupboard. There are other brands, often labelled slightly differently: look for terms like light wholemeal plain, plain wholemeal baking flour etc. The key thing is that these are all plain flours, intended for baking cakes, biscuits and crumbles, not for bread – wholemeal bread flour is higher in gluten and is usually labelled 'strong'.

KRAUT/KIMCHI

Home-fermented veg is a revelation. Inexpensive and simple to make, it's bursting with good bacteria, and of course delicious (our River Cottage Handbook on Fermentation, by Rachel de Thample, is a fantastic resource). It has a tanginess and a savoury, umami quality that make it a superb substitute for everything from ketchup to cheese. If you prefer to buy your kraut or kimchi, you'll be spoilt for choice. Just make sure the brand you choose is fresh and unpasteurised ('live').

MEAT

Livestock farming is not new, but industrialised farming is. I have long rejected it and I am a determined advocate of diets that include much less meat and much better meat. I'm fortunate enough to be able to raise some meat at home, but also I look for meat that is free-range at least, if not organic. I'm lucky enough to have a local butcher (Anton's in Colyton) who sources his meat from nearby farms and always has free-range pork and chickens in stock. If you don't want to eat meat or dairy products, you'll find plenty of recipes for you here. But I believe grazing animals in a planned, intelligent way can actually be part of good land-management. Managed grazing is a fascinating subject. Look up Regenerationinternational.org and read the article on Regenerative Grazing – Increased production, biodiversity resilience, profits and a climate change solution, to learn more.

339

NUTS

Bashed or chopped, nuts are simply brilliant as a topping, blitzed up they thicken a soup really beautifully, and ground, they make a great baking ingredient. Replacing some of the flour in a cake or scone recipe with ground almonds or hazelnuts means extra protein, good fibre and a little natural sweetness. This can help us to feel more satisfied, as well as making for a lovely, tender texture.

OATS

Rolled oats make excellent, fast-cooking porridge but are also very useful in crumble toppings and breads, biscuits and flapjacks. They are rich in a form of soluble fibre called beta glucan and have been shown to help lower 'bad' cholesterol. 'Naked' oats are sold whole: they look very much like whole spelt and can be used in the same way, taking about 40 minutes to cook.

OILS AND BUTTER

My usual options for everyday frying and roasting are olive oil (not extra virgin) and generic 'vegetable oil' – which is usually refined rapeseed oil. I don't favour polyunsaturated fats such as sunflower oil for frying because there is evidence that when heated to high temperatures they can form toxic substances called aldehydes. There's no deep-frying in this book, but for recipes that require shallow-frying in a moderate amount of oil, I would use vegetable oil. For dressings and finishing a dish, extra virgin olive and rapeseed oils are always good, and I use cold-pressed seed and nut oils in a few recipes too, because they are so rich in healthy fats and antioxidants.

I use a lot less butter than I used to but I still add it to my food in moderate amounts. The flavour and richness it brings makes good ingredients taste even better. (A little melted butter on our greens helps us eat more of them, and that's a good thing!) I choose organic butter to support high-welfare, non-intensive dairy farming where untreated grass is a key part of the cows' diet. I often suggest coconut oil in place of butter to make recipes suitable for vegans.

PASTA AND NOODLES

You won't find any white pasta used in this book – I like a wholewheat or a whole spelt option instead. Switching from 'white to brown' takes a little getting used to. But make the effort to convert yourself and your family and I think you'll agree it wins on texture and flavour, as well as goodness and fibre (which means you can generally feel satisfied with less of it). You can also get wholegrain noodles based on whole wheat, brown rice or buckwheat, or even veg like edamame beans. If you're looking for a gluten-free option, check the ingredients, as some still contain wheat.

PULSES

I am never far away from a pulse-based meal, and my favourites are little Puy lentils, nutty chickpeas and fat creamy butter beans. Cannellini beans, kidney beans, black beans, red lentils, yellow split peas... they all get a look in. I usually cook lentils from dried but for beans I'm much more likely to open a tin, as dried ones need long soaking and simmering. It's also exciting to know that more and more pulses are now being grown in British soils, from carlin peas to fava beans (see hodmedods.co.uk). I have no hesitation in swapping one pulse for another in a recipe, depending on what I have to hand.

SPELT/BARLEY GRAIN

Whole spelt grain and 'pot' barley are sold completely 'whole', with only the outer husk removed. They can also be bought 'pearled', with the outer casing polished off, rendering them a little more tender and quicker to cook. All of them make lovely, tasty ingredients. Both spelt and barley grow well in Britain (though check

the label to see if they actually have been). In recipes, spelt and barley grain are interchangeable, the only real difference being in cooking time: spelt is usually done in 20–25 minutes, where barley can take up to 40 minutes or longer.

SUGAR AND HONEY

Reducing sugar quantities was one of my guiding principles as I developed the recipes in this book. Most cakes and biscuits can be made with a significantly reduced amount of sugar, without anyone really noticing, and that's before you start adding other sweet ingredients like fruit.

When I do want sugar in a recipe, I usually choose a soft light brown sugar. It has a good flavour from the residual molasses, which also gives it a rich brown colour, and it's relatively unrefined. What this choice doesn't signal is that brown sugars are somehow 'better for you'. They are still sugar, with the same amount of calories as white sugar, still to be kept in moderation.

I also use honey in some recipes. It should be used judiciously, but I love the fragrant diversity of it, especially the raw, local honeys that can be found in farm shops and roadside stalls. Honey tastes a bit sweeter than sugar too, so you get a bit more bang for your buck. You can always switch back from honey to sugar to make a recipe vegan.

YOGHURT AND LABNEH

I prefer natural, plain 'whole' yoghurt to anything with reduced fat. It rarely has more than 5% fat (Greek-style yoghurt can have a bit more). I always buy organic yoghurt, partly for welfare reasons (organic cows have a better life), but also because I have seen just how much chemical fertiliser goes on non-organic grazing fields. It is also full of friendly bacteria. I use yoghurt in countless ways: with breakfast, on puddings and cakes, as an ingredient in quick breads and often as labneh – a Middle Eastern-style strained yoghurt cheese, very similar to cream cheese, but less rich. Making your own labneh is simple: add a little salt to natural yoghurt, stir it in then let the whey drip out through muslin or a tea towel – the full method is on page 316.

Index

345

347

Acknowledgements

This book has been made by a brilliant team with whom I'm lucky enough to have been working for over a decade (in some cases, nearer two).

The hugest of thanks to my co-creator and long-time collaborator Nikki Duffy, who guides and steers me, and our recipes, from inception to fruition to print. Without her, no book.

My heartfelt thanks to Simon Wheeler, my photographic partner from the very first *River Cottage Cookbook*, who unfailingly finds the essence of my recipes, and in this case the heart-warming spirit of these favourite family dishes. Complementing his style perfectly and capturing the easy comfort of our kitchen at home are the beautiful drawings of Lucinda Rogers. It's been a pleasure to have her with us and watch her work. And thanks to Lawrence Morton, our wonderful designer, for such beautifully arranged pages. His deft touch and all-seeing eye make a complicated task look effortless.

And then there is Gill Meller, an extraordinary chef, teacher and author who found time in his schedule to come and cook, style and coordinate our hectic shoot days. His intuitive cooking brain and calm hands are visible (to me at least!) in so many of our pictures. He was assisted by talented River Cottage chefs Rosanna Unwin and Steven Kiernan (kindly released from their kitchen duties by our brilliant RC head chef Gelf Alderson), who both brought their own considerable skills to bear. And it was great to have Rex Johnson back with us again for the final marathon shoot day.

The recipes themselves were carefully tested in a domestic kitchen by Sarah Turner and Elizabeth Ribeiro. Their painstakingly detailed reports and excellent suggestions have been vital in helping us create and curate this collection. Thank you so much, Sarah and Lizzy.

Thanks to our endlessly patient project editor Janet Illsley, who steered the raw text onto the page word by carefully checked word, and seamlessly stitched it to fit. And to Sally Somers who went through the text with an eagle eye, hunting down those tiny discrepancies and putting them right.

Thank you totally Jess Upton, my PA and tireless right-hand woman. Your role as coordinator, scheduler and all-round safety net has been completely essential, as it always is.

Thanks to Antony Topping, my agent and first sounding board, who backed this book from the beginning, and helped guide it all the way down the long and sometimes winding road to print. And to his Greene and Heaton colleagues too, especially Holly Faulks, Jane Petrie and Carol Heaton.

My thanks to Rowan Yapp and Kitty Stogdon at Bloomsbury, who have supported us every step of the way with positivity, enthusiasm and expert judgement, and to Laura Brodie, our production controller, who polished every page as it went through the presses. And thank you to Ellen Williams for making sure this book finds itself on the desks of all the right people!

And finally my love and thanks always to Marie, Chloe, Oscar, Freddie and Louisa, whose ever-present love and comfort suffuses not only all these recipes, but also the many delicious things you have cooked for the family table.

BLOOMSBURY PUBLISHING
Bloomsbury Publishing Plc
50 Bedford Square, London, WC1B 3DP, UK
29 Earlsfort Terrace, Dublin 2, Ireland

BLOOMSBURY, BLOOMSBURY PUBLISHING and the Diana logo are
trademarks of Bloomsbury Publishing Plc

First published in Great Britain 2022
Text © Hugh Fearnley-Whittingstall, 2022
Photographs © Simon Wheeler, 2022
Except those on pages 17 and 189 © Hugh Fearnley-Whittingstall, 2022
Illustrations © Lucinda Rogers, 2022

A catalogue record for this book is available from the British Library

Library of Congress Cataloguing-in-Publication data has been applied for

ISBN: HB: 978-1-5266-3895-3; eBook: 978-1-5266-3896-0

2 4 6 8 10 9 7 5 3

Project Editor: Janet Illsley
Interior Design: Lawrence Morton
Photographer: Simon Wheeler
Food Stylist: Gill Meller
Illustrator: Lucinda Rogers
Indexer: Hilary Bird
Cover Design: Peter Moffat

Printed and bound in Germany by Mohn Media

FSC
www.fsc.org

MIX
Paper from
responsible sources
FSC® C011124

To find out more about our authors and books visit www.bloomsbury.com
and sign up for our newsletters